D0554250

KAFKA'S RHETORIC

KAFKA'S RHETORIC

The Passion of Reading

CLAYTON KOELB

Cornell University Press

ITHACA AND LONDON

First published 1989 by Cornell University Press.

International Standard Book Number 0-8014-2244-2
Library of Congress Catalog Card Number 88-43261

Printed in the United States of America

*Librarians: Library of Congress cataloging information
appears on the last page of the book.*

*The paper in this book is acid-free and meets the guidelines for
permanence and durability of the Committee on Production Guidelines
for Book Longevity of the Council on Library Resources.*

To Jan Edward Brooks Koelb

CONTENTS

PREFACE

This book has followed a long and circuitous path to its present state. It probably would have seen print much sooner if the theoretical introduction had not grown beyond all bounds and threatened to overwhelm the entire project. Finally, I realized that I had to write another book first, an independent theoretical study, before I could start the work on Kafka. The other book, *Inventions of Reading*, still represents in a certain sense the introduction to *Kafka's Rhetoric*.

Inasmuch as it would be unreasonable to expect readers of this book to read the other one first, I have summarized below in Chapter 1 the principal theoretical points of *Inventions of Reading* and have even reprinted a few paragraphs that deal explicitly with Kafka. Readers of the earlier book may therefore find the opening pages of this one more than slightly familiar, and I can only hope that they will understand my reason for repeating myself. Because *Kafka's Rhetoric* is addressed to a group by and large different from the intended readers of the previous volume, probably very few people will notice the overlap, and they are likely to be already unusually well disposed to my work. I extend to them my gratitude in advance.

I must also alert the reader to a feature of this book that may seem peculiar in view of the history of Kafka scholarship. Books devoted principally to the analysis of Kafka's fiction, as this one is, normally expend major portions of the text discussing the novel fragments *The Missing Person (Amerika)*, *The Trial*, and *The Castle*. The present book does not do so. Although I do treat aspects of these three texts at various points, they receive relatively less attention than do much shorter writings.

There are several reasons for my unorthodox distribution of critical scrutiny. The first and by far most important is, of course, that my topic is not "Everything There Is to Know about Kafka" or even "A Study of Kafka's Fiction" but indeed Kafka's *rhetoric*. As it happens, material pertinent to this topic is not proportional to the length of the work containing it, and therefore occasionally a very short story (such as "The Silence of the Sirens") offers roughly as much insight into Kafka's rhetorical construction as a very long one (such as *The Castle*). Sometimes the shortest texts of all, whether stories or letters or diary entries, provide the richest material, and the length of my analysis reflects this richness.

A second reason is that Kafka's novel fragments present philological problems that enormously complicate the process of interpreting them as artistic wholes. Kafka abandoned all of them before completion, leaving two (*The Missing Person* and *The Castle*) with no ending and the other (*The Trial*) without clearly indicating how the material should be arranged. These difficulties have not deterred scholars in the past, nor should they now, but they have caused me to think twice before attempting the kind of full-scale interpretation I offer for, say, "In the Penal Colony." Now that the texts of *Der Verschollene* and *Das Schloß* are available in a reliable critical edition, some of my hesitation has been eliminated, but I still feel a certain reluctance.

My third and most personal justification for privileging the shorter texts is that I believe Kafka displays in them his greatest strengths as a writer. In the short form he found his true calling, as he seems to have realized himself when he said, regarding the composition of "The Judgment," completed in one sitting, "only in this way can writing be done" (*DI1* 276). The novel fragments are great unfinished edifices, whereas the miniature parables such as "Give It Up!" and "On Parables" are polished little gems. The stories of intermediate length, such as "The Metamorphosis," "In the Penal Colony," and "A Country Doctor," are some of the finest that the German language has to offer and indeed some of the best in the whole European tradition. As a novelist Kafka cannot fairly be compared even to contemporaries such as Mann and Musil, but as a writer of short stories he stands comparison with anyone who has ever attempted to write in the genre.

My final preliminary duty is to recite my critical genealogy, so that the reader will know what sort of book to expect. I was trained, like

most members of my generation, in New Critical "close reading," and
in a fundamental sense I have never strayed far from that training. It
will be clear, however, that more recent developments in literary theory have profoundly influenced the sort of close reading in which I
engage. I have learned much from the deconstructive practice of Paul
de Man and from Jacques Derrida's analysis of the major tropes of the
Western philosophical tradition. I will not be surprised if many readers find this book basically poststructuralist in approach. But I have
also learned from sources unconnected to poststructuralism, from J.
L. Austin's version of speech-act theory, from semiotics, and of course
from classical rhetoric. I might add that my attempts to understand
Kafka, which began when I was an undergraduate barely able to
decipher German, considerably predate my knowledge of literary
theory. I must entertain the possibility that my interest in Kafka had a
decisive influence on the theoretical position I have subsequently
taken.

I am grateful to the Department of Germanic Languages and Liter-
atures at the University of Chicago for the flexibility in scheduling
courses, meetings, lectures, and other daily obligations that gave me
the time to write. The Kafka Society of America offered me a welcome opportunity to present some of the material published here in
the form of talks at its annual meetings, and I profited from the
responses I received. Other material in the book found its first public
exposure in lectures at Purdue University, New York University, the
American Semiotic Society, the Midwest Modern Language Association, and the University of Chicago. I am grateful to members of my
audiences for their useful comments and criticisms.

Parts of the following chapters have appeared before, in substantially different form: Chapter 1, in *PMLA* 98 (1983), in *Modern Fiction
Studies* 33 (1987, copyright © by Purdue Research Foundation, West
Lafayette, Indiana 47907, reprinted with permission), and in *Inventions of Reading: Rhetoric and the Literary Imagination* by Clayton Koelb
(copyright © 1988 by Cornell University, and used by permission of
the publisher, Cornell University Press); Chapter 3, in *PMLA* 98
(1983); Chapter 4, in *The German Quarterly* 55 (1982) and in *Kafka and
the Contemporary Critical Performance*, ed. Alan Udoff (copyright ©
1987 by Indiana University Press, reprinted with permission); Chapter 6, in the *Journal of the Kafka Society of America* 8, nos. 1/2 (1984) and in
The Comparative Perspective on Literature: Approaches to Theory and Prac-

tice, ed. Clayton Koelb and Susan Noakes (copyright © 1988 by Cornell University and used by permission of the publisher, Cornell University Press); Chapter 7, in *Semiotics 1984,* ed. John Deely (copyright © 1985 by the University Press of America); and Chapter 8 in *The Journal of the Kafka Society of America* 10, nos 1/2 (1988). I thank the editors and publishers of these publications for permission to use this material.

I am pleased to acknowledge permission to quote short passages from the following works by Franz Kafka granted by Schocken Books (the copyright holder except as noted), published by Pantheon Books, a Division of Random House, Inc.: *Franz Kafka: The Complete Stories,* ed. Nahum N. Glatzer (copyright © 1971); *Franz Kafka: Sämtliche Erzählungen,* ed. Paul Raabe (copyright © 1954); *Amerika,* trans. Willa and Edwin Muir (copyright © 1946 by New Directions Publishing Corporation); *Briefe an Felice,* ed. Erich Heller and Jürgen Born (copyright © 1967); *Beschreibung eines Kampfes: Die zwei Fassungen,* ed. Max Brod and Ludwig Dietz (copyright © 1969 by S. Fischer Verlag); *Briefe an Milena,* ed. Willy Haas (copyright © 1952); *Briefe 1902–1924,* ed. Max Brod (copyright © 1958); *The Castle,* trans. Willa and Edwin Muir (copyright © 1958 by Alfred A. Knopf, Inc.); *The Diaries of Franz Kafka 1910–1913,* ed. Max Brod, trans. Joseph Kresh (copyright © 1948); *The Diaries of Franz Kafka 1914–1923,* ed. Max Brod, trans. Martin Greenberg with Hannah Arendt (copyright © 1949); *Hochzeitsvorbereitungen auf dem Lande und andere Prosa aus dem Nachlaß* (copyright © 1953); *Letters to Felice,* ed. Erich Heller and Jürgen Born, trans. James Stern and Elizabeth Duckworth (copyright © 1973); *Letters to Friends, Family, and Editors,* trans. Richard and Clara Winston (copyright © 1977); *Letter to His Father/Brief an den Vater,* trans. Ernst Kaiser and Eithne Wilkins (copyright © 1966); *Letters to Milena,* ed. Willy Haas, trans. Tania and James Stern (copyright © 1953); *Die Romane* (copyright © 1935, 1946, 1963); *Tagebücher 1910–1923,* ed. Max Brod (copyright © 1951); *The Trial,* trans. Willa and Edwin Muir (copyright © 1964 by Alfred A. Knopf, Inc.); *Wedding Preparations in the Country and Other Posthumous Prose Writings,* notes by Max Brod, trans. Ernst Kaiser and Eithne Wilkins (copyright © 1953).

I also thank Oxford University Press for permission to reprint passages from *The Divine Comedy of Dante Alighieri,* translated by J. D. Sinclair; and the University Press of Virginia for permission to quote material from *The Works of Stephen Crane,* edited by Fredson Bowers, vols 2 and 10. An excerpt from *Homer, The Odyssey,* trans. by Robert Fitzgerald (copyright © 1961 by Robert Fitzgerald) is reprinted by permission of Doubleday, a division of Bantam, Doubleday, Dell Publishing Group, Inc.; and a poem from *The Fables of La Fontaine*, trans. Marianne Moore (copyright © 1952, 1953, 1954, © 1964 by Marianne Moore, copyright renewed © 1980, 1981, 1982 by The Estate of Marianne Moore. All rights reserved) is reprinted by permission of Viking Penguin, Inc.

Stanley Corngold's support, advice, and encouragement have been especially important to me in seeing this project through to completion. The intellectual debt I owe him is clearly evident throughout the book, and especially in the first chapter, but no number of footnotes or bibliographic citations can fully acknowledge it. I owe a special debt of thanks to the scores of students at three different universities who have participated in the seminars on Kafka I have offered over the past fifteen years. To say that I learned from them at least as much as they from me is a tired cliché, but in the rhetorical spirit of this enterprise, I offer it up once again.

My son, Jan, to whom the book is dedicated, perhaps suffered more than anyone else while the work was going on, obliged as he was to play by himself while his father labored in his study (as, for example, I do now). I thank him for his patience. Bernhard Kendler and Kay Scheuer, along with the rest of the staff at Cornell University Press, have once again displayed their good judgment and goodwill in the often frustrating process of seeing the manuscript through editing and production. Two anonymous readers for the Press deserve thanks for numerous suggestions directed toward improving the book.

I can say little here about my debt to Susan Noakes. She remains for me the resource sine qua non.

CLAYTON KOELB

Chicago, Illinois

ABBREVIATIONS

AM   *Amerika.* Translated by Willa Muir and Edwin Muir. New York: Schocken, 1962.

BF   *Briefe an Felice.* Edited by Erich Heller and Jürgen Born. Frankfurt: Fischer, 1967.

BK   *Beschreibung eines Kampfes: Die zwei Fassungen.* Edited by Max Brod and Ludwig Dietz. Frankfurt: Fischer, 1969.

BM   *Briefe an Milena.* Edited by Willy Haas. Frankfurt: Fischer, 1966.

BR   *Briefe, 1902–1924.* Edited by Max Brod. New York: Schocken, 1958.

CA   *The Castle.* Translated by Willa Muir and Edwin Muir. New York: Modern Library, 1969.

CS   *The Complete Stories.* Edited by Nahum N. Glatzer. New York: Schocken, 1971.

CT   *Franz Kafka (1883–1983): His Craft and Thought.* Edited by Roman Struc and J. C. Yardley. Waterloo, Ont.: Wilfrid Laurier University Press, 1986.

DI1   *The Diaries of Franz Kafka, 1910–1913.* Edited by Max Brod. Translated by Joseph Kresh. New York: Schocken, 1948.

DI2   *The Diaries of Franz Kafka, 1914–1923.* Edited by Max Brod. Translated by Martin Greenberg with Hannah Arendt. New York: Schocken, 1949.

DJK   *Der junge Kafka.* Edited by Gerhard Kurz. Frankfurt: Suhrkamp, 1984.

DVLG   *Deutsche Vierteljahresschrift für Literaturwissenschaft und Geistesgeschichte*

HO   *Hochzeitsvorbereitungen auf dem Lande und andere Prosa aus dem Nachlaß.* New York: Schocken, 1953.

JKSA   *Journal of the Kafka Society of America*

LB   *Letters to Felice*. Edited by Erich Heller and Jürgen Born. Translated by James Stern and Elizabeth Duckworth. New York: Schocken, 1973.

LE   *Letters to Friends, Family, and Editors*. Translated by Richard Winston and Clara Winston. New York: Schocken, 1977.

LF   *Letter to His Father/Brief an den Vater*. Translated by Ernst Kaiser and Eithne Wilkins. New York: Schocken, 1966.

LM   *Letters to Milena*. Edited by Willy Haas. Translated by Tania Stern and James Stern. New York: Schocken, 1962.

NKSA   *Newsletter of the Kafka Society of America*

RBC   Stephen Crane. *The Red Badge of Courage*. Vol. 2 in *The Works of Stephen Crane*. Edited by Fredson Bowers. Charlottesville: University Press of Virginia, 1975.

RO   *Die Romane*. Frankfurt: Fischer, 1966.

SE   *Sämtliche Erzählungen*. Edited by Paul Raabe. Frankfurt: Fischer, 1970.

TB   *Tagebücher 1910–1923*. Edited by Max Brod. Frankfurt: Fischer, 1951.

TP   *Franz Kafka: Themen und Probleme*. Edited by Claude David. Göttingen: Vandenhoeck & Ruprecht, 1980.

TR   *The Trial*. Translated by Willa Muir and Edwin Muir. New York: Modern Library, 1964.

W&D   Jacques Derrida. *Writing and Difference*. Translated by Alan Bass. Chicago: University of Chicago Press, 1978.

WP   *Wedding Preparations in the Country and Other Posthumous Prose Writings*. Notes by Max Brod. Translated by Ernst Kaiser and Eithne Wilkins. London: Secker & Warburg, 1954.

Chapter 1

RHETORIC, READING,
AND WRITING

My interest in Kafka always leads me back to questions of
rhetoric because I cannot rid myself of a certain naive curiosity. I still
wonder when I read a Kafka story, "Whatever made him think of
that?" I see this question as involving not origins or sources but an
investigation into rhetoric. After all, much of Kafka's writing has its
basis in his "reading," that is, in his attempt to understand the language of others. By "reading" I mean not the deciphering of marks on
paper but rather the process of trying to understand a particular
discourse as fully as possible, as if one were certain that all its elements
were saturated with meaning. Kafka's writing—"writing" in the sense
of "composing discourse intended to be read," whether on paper or
not—so frequently derives from the careful consideration of other
texts that we may regard language itself as the material (the classical
rhetorician's *res*) upon which his invention works. We may properly
describe his work, following Stanley Corngold's lead, as the product
of a "linguistic imagination."[1]

But what exactly is a "linguistic imagination," and how does it work?
A hint as to the direction that one might take in trying to answer this
question comes from a quarter seemingly far removed from anything
related to Kafka, from a notebook entry made by Samuel Taylor

---

1. "Kafka's *Die Verwandlung*: Metamorphosis of the Metaphor," *Mosaic* 3 (Summer 1970), 106.

Coleridge. The note reads: "Examine minutely the nature, cause, birth & growth of the *verbal* Imagination of which Barrow is almost the Ideal/."[2] There is no record that Coleridge ever actually followed up on this note, and possibly he did not even think about it any further after the idea first came to him. The plan certainly sounds ambitious: the "minute" examination of the "nature, cause, birth & growth" of anything is a formidable task. Its object, the "verbal imagination" (with the word "verbal" underlined for emphasis) comes tantalizingly close to Corngold's "linguistic imagination" and seems worth pursuing, but Coleridge has provided very little to help us. What could he mean here? Reference to his later development of a theory of imagination will not assist us much, because evidently the important issue for him was the underlined element, the *verbal* aspect of the notion. He seems to have wanted to investigate less the imagination, or a certain aspect of it, than the imaginative aspects of verbal behavior.

A suggestion in the entry can conceivably help us determine what Coleridge might have been talking about. He cites Barrow as "almost the Ideal" of his concept; he means Isaac Barrow, a seventeenth-century scholar and divine whose principal legacy was a set of sermons that remained quite popular long after his death and was several times reprinted. Such a new edition of Barrow's sermons had entered the possession of Coleridge, who obviously read them with great pleasure and attention. Now largely neglected, Barrow's works clearly had a substantial impact on Coleridge at one point in his life and were somehow decisive in the creation of this inchoate concept of the verbal imagination. We have reason to hope, then, that a look at Barrow's sermons will clarify Coleridge's aims.

Examination of the sermons is indeed helpful. Sermon XIII, a discourse based on the text from James 3:2, "If any man offend not in word, he is a perfect man," contains some very pertinent material. Barrow's topic is precisely the verbal behavior that apparently interested Coleridge, and he argues that the scriptural sentence from *James* implies that speech is centrally important in all human affairs:

> The extent of speech must needs be vast, since it is nearly commensurate to thought itself, which it ever closely traceth, widely ranging through all the immense variety of objects; so that men almost as often

2. *The Notebooks of Samuel Taylor Coleridge*, ed. Kathleen Coburn (New York: Routledge, 1957), I, #1275.

speak incogitantly, as they think silently. Speech is indeed the rudder of human affairs, the spring that setteth the wheels of action on going; the hands work, the feet walk, all the members and all the senses act by its direction and impulse; yea, most thoughts are begotten, and most affections stirred up hereby; it is itself most of our employment, and what we do beside it, is however guided and moved by it.[3]

These opinions, and especially the one maintaining that "most thoughts are begotten" by language, would surely have caught Coleridge's attention for at least two reasons.

First, they take a direction quite different from that of Coleridge's own thinking, which inclined to the traditional view that language represents or reflects thought and is therefore secondary to it rather than being its progenitor. Barrow's insistence on the primacy of speech over "most," if not all, thinking must have fascinated Coleridge by seeming alien. The notion might have suggested to him the existence of a way of thinking, a form of imagination, distinctly different from his own. A second reason for the special interest of these lines is the accuracy with which they reflect Barrow's own practice as a writer. Barrow takes the traditional practice of basing a sermon on a text from scripture to an extreme of thoroughness hardly equaled before or since. Barrow's thinking can profitably be understood as directly engendered by the language of the texts he reads, for he attends minutely to matters of semantics, grammar, and syntax as the fundamental framework around which he organizes his sermons. Barrow follows the logic of divine authorship with ruthless zeal, finding in every analyzable element of the scriptural text a fully functioning signifier operating under divine intention. In Sermon XLIV, for example, he discovers multiple meanings in the phrase "with all diligence," from Proverbs 4:23, "according to the various use or force" of a particular Hebrew particle. He develops three of these significations at length and concludes that the passage must be "understood according to any of those senses, or according to all of them conjointly."[4]

Coleridge, then, apparently intended the phrase "verbal imagination" to denote a process in which complex discourses are generated from close attention to all the possible meanings of other (usually more compact) linguistic structures. Coleridge suggests that we re-

3. *The Works of Isaac Barrow, D.D.*, 3 vols. (New York: John C. Riker, 1846), I, 142.
4. Barrow, I, 480–481.

gard the endless readability of texts such as the passages from the
Bible upon which Barrow descants as a resource from which inventive
readers can construct works of their own imagination. The verbal
imagination is characterized essentially less by its production of verbal
artifacts—if this were central all writers would possess it—than by its
use of verbal material as the res upon which to practice *inventio*. For
such a verbal imagination, the reading ("construction") of apparently
simple texts, such as commonplace rhetorical expressions and images,
makes possible the writing ("construction") of complex narratives.
The activity of the verbal imagination may therefore be regarded as
"rhetorical construction."

Let me introduce a concrete example of such rhetorical construction here, a passage from one of the best-known fictions in our canon:

> Nel mezzo del cammin di nostra vita
>   mi ritrovai per una selva oscura
>   chè la diritta via era smarrita. [vv. 1–3]
>
> In the middle of the journey of our life I came to
> myself within a dark wood where the straight way was
> lost.[5]

Dante's pilgrim has a problem that is simply presented but complex in
its implications: he has lost his way. The text exploits the fact that we
can understand the lost "way" either as something everyday and relatively trivial (the path through the forest) or as something of profound importance (the route to salvation). Dante introduces his story
of the way by mentioning what at first seems to be an actual road in
the middle of which the pilgrim is standing. But because *cammino* can
mean both "road, pathway" and the "journey" one makes along such a
road, it acts as a hinge upon which the frame allegory turns. After
thinking that the pilgrim is standing in a road, the reader is forced by
"di nostra vita" to reread *cammino* not only as a journey but as a
figurative journey. "The journey of our life" must be a lifetime, and
being in the middle of it would mean that the pilgrim is middle-aged.
The opening line perhaps says nothing, then, about where the pilgrim is physically, but instead it tells us his temporal location. Perhaps

---

5. I quote Dante from *The Divine Comedy of Dante Alighieri: Inferno*, ed. with
trans. and commentary by John D. Sinclair (New York: Oxford University Press,
1961). Line numbers refer to the Italian text of this edition, which has the English
on facing pages.

we should read it as "At age thirty-five . . ." Many Dante scholars, such as John D. Sinclair,[6] tell us to read it in this fashion, and the idea seems perfectly reasonable. But when we reach the next line, we are forced to reevaluate our confident figurative reading: "I found myself in a dark forest" returns us to the physical plane and urges us to take *cammino* once more as a literal road or journey. Of course we also have the option of deciding that none of the language should be taken literally, that these lines are really a figurative way of describing what we today would call a midlife crisis: "At age thirty-five I found myself depressed and confused to such an extent that I no longer knew how to lead my life." But if Dante were making only this point, it seems doubtful that we would still be interested in his poem nearly seven hundred years after its composition. In fact the literal level of the narrative is compelling and consistent in its own right and will not easily be effaced by the allegory. At no point in these lines—or in the whole poem—does the reader lose the sense that the pilgrim is journeying through various vividly described locations.

Dante's poem thus begins by means of "rhetoric" as I will use that term. He forces a confrontation between the literal and figurative meanings of the word *cammino* without taking sides as to which is the "correct" reading. He works by means of rhetorical *construction* in that he builds his discourse by construing other discourse. We find an even more subtle form of rhetorical construction at work in the second line, where Dante uses the preposition *per* to mean "within." This is not the most common significance of the word; it usually means "through," or "by," or "by means of." We read it as "within" here because the immediate context (the road, the dark wood) seems to require us to do so. In the context of the *Commedia* as a whole, however, it is entirely justifiable to understand the phrase to mean that the pilgrim "found himself" (in the sense of "became himself again") *by means of* his experience in the dark wood. In this interpretation, the third line would undergo a reevaluation as well. The loss of the "straight way" would not be an absolute loss but a temporary and ultimately felicitous obstacle. The direct path is replaced by an indirect one that is perhaps in the long run better for the pilgrim anyway, for by following it he is able to achieve his vision of the cosmic order and his place in it. Dante's use of *per* rather than *in* to indicate the relation of the "selva oscura" to the process of *ritrovarsi* proleptically

6. *The Divine Comedy of Dante Alighieri*, p. 28, n. 1.

indicates the movement of recovery and redemption begun in the depths of the forest's obscurity. The act of "finding" oneself begins in the very moment when one realizes that one is lost, and Dante makes this point dramatically here in the sequence of his discourse by letting the word *ritrovai* appear *before* the word *smaritta* ("lost").

The use of this *per* in two very different senses helps establish a characteristic and significant paradox of *The Divine Comedy*. The rhetorical reading is not a decorative device that adds something to a text capable of functioning nearly as well without it; it helps rather to found a notion that is constitutive of the fiction. We may therefore properly regard it as an example of a mode of imaginative rhetoric that makes stories from figures. In a manner essentially similar to the rhetorical mode that I have elsewhere termed "logomimesis,"[7] Dante's metaphor generates a story. Language like "Du bist ein Ungeziefer" ("You're a louse") offers rich possibilities for logomimesis, because when it is read literally, it presents a surprising implicit proposition: a person might be a bug. Such a proposition is capable of being acted out and elaborated in a narrative, as Kafka does in "The Metamorphosis." Likewise, there is the germ of a story in Dante's "per una selva oscura," even though no proposition is implied by it. The rhetoricity of Dante's second line (when it is understood in the context of the poem as a whole) generates a narrative impulse from the confrontation that it stages between two apparently incompatible possibilities. Either the dark wood is the cause of the pilgrim's losing himself, or it is the agency responsible for starting him on the way to finding himself. The narrative situation derives from language here just as surely as in examples of logomimesis, even though in this case there is no process of imitation.

Dante's opening sentence is a piece of rhetorical construction twice over. It calls upon us to construe it both as the literal description of a man losing his way in the woods and as the figurative depiction of depression and confusion in the middle years of life. At the same time, the sentence announcing that the pilgrim is "lost" (whether literally or figuratively) may also be read as a reassuring declaration that the action begun here is essentially one of "finding," of returning to oneself or to the correct path. The *Commedia* as a whole demands to be read in this way, the way that sophisticated theologians of Dante's time read the Bible, with a mind open to all the various interpretive

7. See Clayton Koelb, *The Incredulous Reader: Reading and the Function of Disbelief* (Ithaca: Cornell University Press, 1984), esp. pp. 41–42.

conventions under which it may be construed.[8] Boccaccio, himself an adept practitioner of rhetorical construction, argued vigorously that secular poems like Dante's should be read in this way.[9] Although Boccaccio in the concluding books of his *Genealogy of the Pagan Gods* saw his task as principally to insist that the literal level should not be taken at face value in a poem such as *The Divine Comedy*, we more frequently need to remind ourselves that figurative meanings do not always suppress or erase literal ones, that learned constructions do not necessarily replace or disqualify commonplace ones. The opening lines of the *Commedia* show Dante insisting that we allow his pilgrim to be *both* lost in the obscurity that surrounds him *and* able to find himself because of his experience in that obscurity. The story he tells is inscribed in the space between these two possibilities.

We may now read alongside Dante's opening lines another story of a man who has lost his way, Kafka's miniature parable "Give It Up!" ("Gibs Auf!"):

> It was very early in the morning, the streets clean and deserted, I was on my way to the station. As I compared the tower clock with my watch I realized that it was much later than I had thought and that I had to hurry; the shock of this discovery made me feel uncertain of the way, I wasn't very well acquainted with the town as yet; fortunately, there was a policeman at hand, I ran to him and breathlessly asked him the way. He smiled and said: "You asking me the way?" "Yes," I said, "since I can't find it myself." "Give it up! Give it up!" said he, and turned with a sudden jerk, like someone who wants to be alone with his laughter.[10]

The effectiveness of this tale depends upon rhetoric, that is, upon the readability of the phrase "breathlessly asked him the way" ("fragte

8. A contemporary Dantist who practices and argues for this kind of reading is Susan Noakes. See her "Dino Compagni and the Vow in San Giovanni: *Inferno* xix, 16–21," *Dante Studies* 86 (1968), 41–63; and "The Double Misreading of Paolo and Francesca," *Philological Quarterly* (1983), 221–239.

9. Book 14, chap. 10, of *The Genealogy of the Pagan Gods* contains an explicit reference to Dante.

10. *CS*, 456; *SE*, 358: "Es war sehr früh am Morgen, die Straßen rein und leer, ich ging zum Bahnhof. Als ich eine Turmuhr mit meiner Uhr verglich, sah ich, daß es schon viel später war, als ich geglaubt hatte, ich mußte mich sehr beeilen, der Schrecken über diese Entdeckung ließ mich im Weg unsicher werden, ich kannte mich in dieser Stadt nicht sehr gut aus, glücklicherweise war ein Schutzmann in der Nähe, ich lief zu ihm und fragte atemlos nach dem Weg. Er lächelte und sagte: 'Von mir willst du den Weg erfahren?' 'Ja,' sagte ich, 'da ich ihn selbst nicht finden kann.' 'Gibs auf, gibs auf,' sagte er und wandte sich mit einem großen Schwunge ab, so wie Leute, die mit ihrem Lachen allein sein wollen."

atemlos nach dem Weg") and on the potential, here realized, for enormous differences among possible readings. The crucial narrative moment takes place when the policeman understands the narrator's request in a way that diverges radically from the way the reader is likely to have understood it. This difference in understanding is possible because the requirements governing the structure of reported speech acts are quite different from those governing the acts themselves. The phenomenon is the same in German, in English, and in many other languages. We can be far less specific in the report of an act of requesting, promising, warning, or whatever than we would have to be in the performance itself; that is, we may say things like "He promised her something" or "He asked for directions," though obviously we may not say—to any real effect—"I hereby promise you something" or ask someone to give us directions without specifying where it is we want to go. We would not, unless we were seeking religious instruction, say to someone, "Please, sir, kindly tell me the way." Such an utterance would seem foolish and indeed incomprehensible. We might very well say, "Please tell me the way to the station," and later say, "I asked him the way"; in a report a reference to an unspecified object is both possible and occasionally necessary.

Kafka's story cleverly exploits the gap between a speech act and the report of a speech act by moving from narration to dialogue just as the policeman replies to the narrator's request. When the narrator reports that he went up to the policeman and "breathlessly asked him the way," we suppose that he said to the policeman something like, "Please tell me the way to the station," but the policeman responds as if the man had said, "Please tell me the way." Of course, we do not suppose that the man would have actually posed such an inappropriate question, but the form of the *report* authorizes the reading. The policeman is in fact replying, not to any actual illocutionary act of asking we can imagine the narrator performing, but to the form of the report. If the dialogue had begun earlier, with the request itself, the story would have lost its point completely: the policeman's reply would no longer be appropriate. "You asking me the way?" and so on is not a reasonable reply to "Sir, please tell me the way to the station." The policeman's response is justified only as a reading, not of the man's actual request, but of his narration of it. There is a temporal gap between the narration and the policeman's quoted utterance, a gap that the narrative procedure carefully ignores. The narrative at one moment assumes (like all narratives) the priority of the events reported but then reports an event that presupposes the story, so that we are led back in an infinite regression of describing text and described action.

It turns out, then, that one of the characters in the story is also a reader of it, and he reads the narrative in a way that diverges widely from the way we do—but not, we must admit, in a way that is unjustified. We assume, because of the context, that the narrator's words "asked him the way" are a report of something like "Please tell me the way to the station." But the policeman could be right: the same words could be a report of the vague but philosophically provocative request, "Please tell me the way." Although we do not suppose that the narrator would have been so distracted that he would actually have framed his request in this way, it is a perfectly valid reading of the report. The phrase "breathlessly asked him the way" becomes the hinge on which a trivial, everyday matter assumes portentous significance. In the policeman's reading, the narrator has not simply forgotten how to get to the station; he has lost his way in life, and the loss is not remediable by a hasty question asked of a patrolman on the street.

As presented in Kafka's parable, the phrase "asked him the way" represents an interpretive crux, a moment of undecidability with which we have become familiar as "aporia." The aporia in question is not a feature of Kafka's text that we have discovered by our reading but rather a feature of the text that Kafka read in order to write his story. And far from being something that Kafka's text reveals about the crucial phrase, it is something that the text presupposes in order to do its work. My reading of Kafka's story is therefore not a deconstruction of that story, nor is it equivalent to the discovery that Kafka deconstructed the phrase "asked him the way." For this reason I prefer to consider Kafka's text more a construction of rhetoric than a deconstruction because I see the story as structured by an act of construing. Such construction presupposes deconstruction in that it attends to fictions that are based on exploiting the narrative possibilities of language that is in a way *already* deconstructed. In Kafka's story, for example, the action performed by the narrative is clearly not the deconstruction of the text it reads: the story not only indicates the existence of the interpretive crux but exploits the dramatic possibilities created when the two incompatible readings are played off each other.

This book will ordinarily use the term "rhetoric" to refer to such language, that is, to language understood as readable under more than one interpretive convention, as well as to the activity of "reading" and "writing" such language. "Rhetoricity" will refer to a discourse's openness to radically divergent interpretations. As Paul de Man observed, rhetoric "allows for two incompatible, mutually self-destructive points of view," as for example in the so-called rhetorical question, where "a perfectly clear syntactical paradigm (the question) engenders a sentence that has at least two meanings, of which the one asserts and the other denies its own illocutionary mode."[11] Kafka uses as the impetus for his narrative the aporetic moment in which one cannot decide whether to read "asked him the way" as "asked him the way to the station" or "asked him the way to lead one's life."

I do not wish to exclude from my usage more traditional meanings of the term "rhetoric," such as "discourse intended to persuade" or even "figurative language," and at times I will call attention to features of a text that are rhetorical in those senses. As a general rule, however, I will intend "rhetoric" to have this special sense. It is in any case not a radical departure in the usage of the term: it is merely a more inclusive way of identifying a feature of discourse especially visible in figurative language. It is intentionally broad; it is inclusive enough to potentially refer to all possible utterances—but only in very particular circumstances. The rhetoricity of any individual piece of discourse is not a quality that resides somehow in the nature of the discourse; rather, it derives from the circumstances of usage.

Rhetoricity is a quality that may be more or less prominent in a given text, and it is not everywhere equally important in Kafka's writing. We can distinguish degrees of rhetoricity in the following example (which I have constructed ad hoc): "Hector and Achilles battle on the plain before Troy. Achilles' sword is swift, and his lance drips with blood. But Hector is a lion. All give way before him." All of the sentences in this discourse are open to interpretation, but we can easily distinguish degrees of openness, which we can test in the simplest manner by taking the individual sentences out of context. "Hector and Achilles battle on the plain before Troy" presents only minor problems and relatively narrow openings for deconstruction, even if we do not know the context. We might read "Troy" as a person rather than a place, for example, though the phrase "on the plain" discourages such a reading; but a radically divergent interpretation—for

---

11. Paul de Man, *Allegories of Reading: Figural Language in Rousseau, Nietzsche, Rilke, and Proust* (New Haven: Yale University Press, 1979), 131, 10.

instance, that Achilles and Hector are making love—is not easily accomplished. The next sentence is more rhetorical. It is easier to read this language in contrary ways: Achilles' lance might drip with blood because it is bleeding from many blows sustained in defeat, in a figure of so-called pathetic fallacy. Such a reading directly opposes the possibly more orthodox interpretation, and though it is not exactly called for by the locutionary form of the discourse, it is entirely plausible. When we reach "Hector is a lion," however, we have rhetoricity in its most highly developed form. In the absence of an explanatory context we will be unable to determine whether we are being told something about a lion named Hector (to wit, that he is a lion) or a person named Hector who has certain leonine characteristics. One of Kafka's most typical gestures is to remove just enough context from such potentially rhetorical discourse so that its rhetoricity emerges.

The locutionary form of an utterance in conjunction with contextual clues affects the degree of its rhetoricity. But although every text must allow itself to be read in contrary ways, no text can *require* us to read it so. Texts can only encourage or discourage acts of rhetorical construction: they cannot, as texts, demand or preclude it absolutely. In other words, rhetoricity always exists as a potential to be tapped by an act of reading. Narrative texts that are developed out of rhetorical reading show us in a concrete way the results of realizing the rhetorical potential of other texts. In fact, rhetorical potential can be realized only by such means, that is, by producing supplementary texts. This is one of the familiar lessons of poststructuralist theory: no text can ever fully exhaust its own meaning. Rhetorical constructions, by offering themselves as supplements exploring the rhetoricity of other texts, make a poetic use of rhetoric beyond self-deconstruction. They *make* something out of it; they construct out of construing.

The act of rhetorical reading performs two important functions in Kafka's writing. In addition to acting as a generative stimulus or mode of invention, it forms the essential connection between the experience of his fiction's readers and a kind of narrative material that appears to depart from experience altogether. We may not believe that a man can be suddenly transformed into a verminous insect, but we know that language regularly proposes such an equivalence in such commonplace tropes as "You're a louse." We do not expect ever to encounter in real life a coal bucket that will carry a person about like a magic carpet, but we have all used hyperbolic tropes exactly analogous to the phrase "My bucket is so light I can ride on it," from which

Kafka generates his little story "The Bucket Rider." The widely recognized aptness of Kafka's fantasic images derives as much from this anchor in the everyday world of language as from his supposed allegorization of bureaucracy-ridden modern man.

The generative function of figuration has long been recognized by sensitive readers of Kafka's fictions. Günther Anders was probably the first to note the role played by everyday tropes and other linguistic commonplaces in the development of some of the stories. Anders points to the metaphor of "reading with one's wounds" as an example of Kafka's procedure: "Language says, 'to feel it with your own body' when it wants to express the reality of experience. This is the basis of Kafka's 'In the Penal Colony,' in which the criminal's punishment is not communicated to him by word of mouth, but is scratched into his body with a needle."[12] Heinz Politzer takes up this line of inquiry as well, identifying another trope as a possible starting point for the tale:

> A popular German adage says: "He who refuses to hear must feel," feel the pain of punishment. Moreover, there exists an etymological connection between "hearing," "listening," and "obeying" (*hören, horchen*, and *gehorchen*) so that Kafka could rely on his German readers to understand instinctively the meaning of his machine: he who disobeyed was bound to feel the consequences on his body. Translating a proverb into an image, Kafka followed an old convention related to the technique of the fable.[13]

More recently, Ruth V. Gross has demonstrated the extensive role of topoi, particularly proverbs, in "A Common Confusion," arguing for the primacy of language over all other elements of the story: "The proverb seems to contain the weight of human experience in the form of a commonplace: it resides in the language at that level. Kafka . . . has created a one-page wordplay with 'Eine alltägliche Verwirrung,' and it is precisely a play on Kafkan language—*gemeine Sprache*."[14]

The direction initiated by Anders has also been taken by two other important contemporary Kafka scholars, Walter Sokel and Stanley Corngold. In Corngold's seminal essay on "The Metamorphosis," en-

12. Günther Anders, *Kafka—Pro und Contra* (Munich: C. H. Beck, 1951), 41. The translation is Stanley Corngold's ("Metamorphosis of the Metaphor," 93).
13. Heinz Politzer, *Franz Kafka: Parable and Paradox* (Ithaca: Cornell University Press, 1962), 99–100.
14. Ruth V. Gross, "Rich Text/Poor Text: A Kafkan Confusion," *PMLA* 95, 2 (1980), 180.

titled "Metamorphosis of the Metaphor," the exact nature of the issue at stake becomes particularly clear. Corngold's title derives from a passage in Sokel's *Franz Kafka* in which an interesting refinement of Anders's observation takes place:

> German usage applies the term *Ungeziefer* (vermin) to persons considered low and contemptible, even as our usage of "cockroach" describes a person deemed a spineless and miserable character. The traveling salesman Gregor Samsa, in Kafka's *The Metamorphosis*, is "like a cockroach" because of his spineless and abject behavior and parasitic wishes. However, Kafka drops the "like" and has the metaphor become reality when Gregor Samsa wakes up finding himself turned into a giant vermin. With this metamorphosis, Kafka reverses the original act of metamorphosis carried out by thought when it forms metaphor; for metaphor is always "metamorphosis." Kafka transforms metaphor back into his fictional reality, and this counter-metamorphosis becomes the starting point of his tale.[15]

If the act of figuration can be understood as the transformation of the literal (facts) into the figurative (pure language), Kafka's procedure may be seen as the opposite, the "literalization" of tropes. The first metamorphosis, according to Sokel, transforms the observation that a person is spineless into a trope that changes him into an *Ungeziefer*. The second, counter-metamorphosis is Kafka's authorial act of making the facts of his story conform to the gesture of the trope: the hero actually becomes a verminous insect.

Corngold agrees with this analysis up to a point. The problem arises, he suggests, when we try to envision the "literalization" of a metaphor. The essential point for Corngold is precisely that Gregor is never fully transformed into an insect *and never could be* if there is to be a story. If the vehicle were really to efface the tenor totally,[16] as Sokel seems to claim it does, then it could no longer function as a vehicle. We would see only an insect and no longer Gregor Samsa in the shape of an insect. "Anders is not correct to suggest that in *The Metamorphosis* literalization of the metaphor is actually accomplished; for then we should have not an indefinite monster but simply a bug."[17] Sokel's suggestion of counter-metamorphosis fits the situat-

15. Walter Sokel, *Franz Kafka* (New York: Columbia University Press, 1966), 5.
16. "Tenor" and "vehicle" are terms used by I. A. Richards to refer to the signified and signifier, respectively, of a metaphor (I. A. Richards, *The Philosophy of Rhetoric* [New York: Oxford University Press, 1936], p. 96).
17. Stanley Corngold, "Metamorphosis of the Metaphor," 98.

tion better, though perhaps not in just the way Sokel intended. For Corngold, the metamorphosis of metaphor is not the act that "becomes the starting point" of the fiction but the process going on in the course of the story: "Indeed the progressive deterioration of Gregor's body suggests ongoing metamorphosis, the *process* of literalization and not its end-state."[18] The tale becomes an allegory, as well as an artifact, of linguistic distortion expressing Kafka's deep skepticism about metaphorical discourse:

> As the story of a metamorphosed metaphor, *The Metamorphosis* is not just one among Kafka's stories but an exemplary Kafkan story; the title reflects the generative principle of Kafka's fiction—a metamorphosis of the function of language. In organizing itself around a distortion of ordinary language, *The Metamorphosis* projects into its center a sign which absorbs its own significance (as Gregor's opaque body occludes his awareness of self), and thus aims in an opposite direction from the art of the symbol; for there, in the words of Merleau-Ponty, the sign is "devoured" by its signification.[19]

Where the tradition calls for the tenor to efface the vehicle, the signified to render the signifier transparent, Kafka forces us to consider the possibility that just the opposite might happen, that the insect vehicle might slowly and painfully efface the human tenor.

The argument of Corngold's "Metamorphosis of the Metaphor" focuses attention on the problem of metaphor in order to suggest the relation of Kafka's narrative art to his distrust of figuration and to stress the self-destructive nature of his form of writing. Corngold has continued in this direction in his more recent work, for example in "The Author Survives on the Margin of His Breaks," where shifts in narrative perspective are seen as a gesture undermining the basis of the stories in which they occur.[20] My interest, as will be evident, takes a different tack. Although I do not by any means deny that Kafka's use of figuration results in fictions that often undermine themselves, sometimes in a dramatic fashion (for example, "The Bridge"),[21] I

18. Ibid.
19. Ibid., 103.
20. Stanley Corngold, "The Author Survives on the Margin of His Breaks: Kafka's Narrative Perspective," in Corngold, *The Fate of the Self: German Writers and French Theory* (New York: Columbia University Press, 1986).
21. Ruth V. Gross discusses this story in detail in "Fallen Bridge, Fallen Woman, Fallen Text," *Literary Review* 26 (Summer 1981), 577–587. See also Clayton Koelb, "The Turn of the Trope: Kafka's 'Die Brücke,'" *Modern Austrian Literature* 22 (1989), forthcoming.

remain fascinated by the implications of Corngold's perceptive remarks about metaphor for an investigation of Kafka's mode of literary invention. The problematic of "literal" and "figurative" operates both to create and to subvert Kafka's fictional structures, and I want to pay special attention to the creative side.

By reminding us of the essential duplicity of metaphor, Corngold helps remind us also of the duplicity of all discourse readable as rhetoric. Because tropes are "turned" (or, as Corngold says, "distorted") language and do not necessarily mean what they say, they are always readable in two ways, especially if they are placed in an unfamiliar context. "You're a louse" will mean one thing when addressed to a person and quite another when addressed to the insect infesting that person's coat. As Paul de Man observed, there is no reliable way to determine which of these readings is correct in the absence of what he calls "an extra-textual intention."[22] Although this statement is clearly true of tropes, it also applies to many other forms of discourse. In fact, any text or utterance that can be understood under more than one interpretive convention is subject to the same indeterminacy. Just as no linguistic test that we can perform will tell us whether the louse in question is actual or figurative, there is no way to tell whether "How can we know the dancer from the dance?" is a genuine or rhetorical question or whether "You're under arrest" performs an act of arresting or merely reports the effect of such an act. All such language is potentially rhetorical. Even the name "Kafka" is readable as rhetoric, as I will explain below, because there are circumstances in which we cannot tell whether it is the name of a person or a word for a species of carrion-eating vermin.

The discovery of this rhetoricity is a moment of negativity to which Corngold has properly directed our attention. Because the two readings potentially available for a rhetorical utterance are mutually incompatible, the reader may well experience rhetorical discourse as self-destructive. If we cannot decide whether "How can we know the dancer from the dance?" is a request for information about a difference assumed to exist or a denial that such a difference exists, the interpretive effort may seem self-annihilating. In his fiction, however, Kafka shows that this negative moment may be a productive one as well. *Before* Gregor's insect body overwhelms and occludes his human psyche, there exists a fictional situation in which both (apparently conflicting) readings of "Du bist ein Ungeziefer" are actualized. In the

22. *Allegories of Reading*, 10.

context of the story's opening, one may read this trope either literally or figuratively and be correct in each case. The story makes good—at least temporarily—on both interpretations.

Such an act of poetic invention is founded upon "reading" in the sense indicated earlier—not the decipherment of a written text but rather the specific act of interpreting a particular discourse, whether written or not. Kafka's mode of reading was of a refined type that probed an utterance past the point necessary for practical under-standing. He was what we might call a rhetorical reader in that he was particularly sensitive to the rhetorical potential of language. It was not enough for him to know what a given discourse intended to say in a given context: he was (as a writer) more often concerned with mean-ings that such a discourse would have if its context-determined inten-tion were ignored. Kafka knew very well what was ordinarily intended by the trope "Du bist ein Ungeziefer" when it was addressed to partic-ular persons, but by ignoring that intention he found in it the possibil-ity for a story. The possibility that signifiers might detach themselves from their immediate contextual limits was apparently part of Kafka's earliest experiences. He claims in the "Letter to His Father" that Herr-mann never abused him verbally but that direct abuse was not neces-sary: "You had so many other methods, and besides, in talk at home and particularly at business the words of abuse went flying around me in such swarms, as they were flung at other people's heads, that as a little boy I was sometimes almost stunned and had no reason not to apply them to myself, too."[23] Kafka's image makes these "words of abuse" into independent creatures, birds or insects that fly about the room and land on anyone in the way. They are no longer connected to any specific intention, and they have no particular target. They circle in the air ("flogen . . . rings um mich") like vultures or crows. They are, in this case quite literally, free-floating signifiers. Herr-mann Kafka may have spawned them, but they are no longer answer-able to his wishes and no longer necessarily mean what he supposed them to mean.

The world is full of pieces of language flying about, and their existence could be, at such times as the one just described, a terrible problem. It could also be a great opportunity, however, and Kafka

23. *LF* 34–35: "Du hattest so viele andere Mittel, auch flogen im Gespräch zu Hause und besonders im Geschäft die Schimpfwörter rings um mich in solchen Mengen auf andere nieder, daß ich als kleiner Junge manchmal davon fast be-täubt war und keinen Grund hatte, sie nicht auch auf mich zu beziehen."

seized upon it (or it seized upon him) as the means to initiate an authorial practice. Writing for Kafka is an activity that almost always arises from an experience of reading, from a confrontation with another text. Very often these other texts are the commonplaces of our tradition.[24] Sometimes we cannot be sure exactly what the precise form of the text being read might be, as in the case of "In the Penal Colony." Other evidence, however, leaves no doubt that reading is centrally involved. My goal is to investigate Kafka's understanding of the reading process, the way in which he thematizes the problematic of reading, and above all his writing as it emerges from his passion of reading.

24. I will discuss in detail Kafka's use of classic texts such as *Don Quixote*, the *Odyssey*, and the Bible in later chapters.

Chapter 2

THE RHETORICAL "KAFKA"

Kafka reports that his parents gave him the Hebrew name of Amschel, "like my mother's maternal grandfather, whom my mother, who was six years old when he died, can remember as a very pious and learned man with a long, white beard."[1] The honor thus done to the Löwy side of the family must have pleased Julie and her relatives greatly, because the firstborn Kafka son would thus carry in his Hebrew name the tradition of the highly literate old family. But the Kafkas, lacking such a distinguished family history, could still feel that honor was being done to them as well in this ritual of naming; for although it was actually derived from the name "Anselm," "Amschel" was regularly associated with the word *Amsel* (blackbird),[2] an acceptable translation of the Czech *kavka*. Herrmann Kafka used a depiction of a blackbird in his business advertising,[3] and such depictions had

1. *DI1* 197; *TB* 212: "Ich heiße hebräisch Amschel, wie der Großvater meiner Mutter von der Mutterseite, der als ein sehr frommer und gelehrter Mann mit langem weißem Bart meiner Mutter erinnerlich ist, die sechs Jahre alt war, als er starb."

2. S.v. *Amschel* in Benzion C. Kaganoff, *A Dictionary of Jewish Names and Their History* (New York: Schocken, 1977). See also Pavel Trost, "Der Name Kafka," *Beiträge zur Namenforschung* 94 (1983), 184–204.

3. Klaus Wagenbach, *Franz Kafka: Eine Biographie seiner Jugend* (Bern: Francke, 1958), gives the most complete account available of Kakfa's youth. In *Franz Kafka in Selbstzeugnissen und Bilddokumenten* (Hamburg: Rowohlt, 1964), 17, Wagenbach reproduces the business logo used by Herrmann Kafka.

commonly been used to signify persons called "Amschel" for genera-
tions. To call this young Kafka "Amschel" was on the one hand to
recall his Löwy heritage of learning and piety and on the other to
hammer home once again that this "Kafka" was a kavka. In the gesture of whispering "Löwy," the infant's Hebrew name shouted "Kafka" even louder than before.

Here began the future writer's first lessons in rhetoric. The name
bore concealed in its few syllables an abundance—an overabun-
dance—of meanings not all of which sat comfortably with the others.
The lesson must have been repeated on numerous occasions throughout Franz's childhood, as he was unnecessarily reminded over and
over again that he bore the name of a comical and not altogether
respectable bird. One wonders how often the Czech-speaking children with whom he played cawed at him in mockery. Considering
how frequently the syllable "ka" (as in the German pronunciation of
the letter "K") appears in Kafka's fiction, it was evidently often
enough. The boy could never forget for long that this word, which
should have been in a certain sense uniquely personal, something that
referred only to himself and to members of his family, could be at any
moment snatched up as it were by some disgraceful jackdaw. Even his
parents, in naming him Amschel, seemed to be making the same
point: "You are a 'crow,' and don't you forget it." Perhaps he wished
at times that he could have been a Löwy like his mother, so that he
could have roared back at his tormentors like a real *Löwe* (lion). But
even then the basic situation would have been unchanged: the lion
may be a more noble beast than the blackbird, but it is still a beast.
Which was he, he must have wondered to himself, a person or an
animal? Perhaps, in some deeper, unseen, and magical fashion, he
was both. Perhaps the outer form of a human being harbored a miserable, carrion-eating vermin. Chance, language, and the boy's parents
conspired to make the possiblity seem all too plausible.

There resides already in the very name "Franz (Amschel) Kafka" an
enormous narrative potential. The fact that words like "Kafka" and
"Amschel" (not to mention "Frank," his usual nickname) can be understood in two radically different ways establishes a tension of same-
ness and difference that teases the imagination. It does so all the more
when it is proposed (by a pure linguistic coincidence) that the tension
exists within the confines of a single self. Of course one has the option
of ignoring the matter: it is, after all, only an accident of language.
But someone as sensitive to verbal structures as Franz Kafka could not

ignore it. A man who could claim, or who could even pretend to claim, that he consisted of nothing but literature, as Kafka once did in a letter to Felice Bauer,[4] would not be able to resist the possibility of reading his own name. Indeed the confluence of self and literature exists nowhere more dramatically than in a name like "Amschel Kafka" read as rhetoric. Because it invites autonomasia (the trope by which a proper noun is used with its common-noun significance), such a name provides a powerful stimulus toward a recognition of the rhetorical possibilities in other language as well.

A fragment from the fifth octavo notebook displays in a nutshell the possibilities and problems that Kafka found in the rhetorical reading of his own name:

> You raven, I said, you old bird of ill-omen, what are you always doing on my path? Wherever I go, you perch there, ruffling up your scanty plumage. Nuisance!
>
> Yes, it said, and paced up and down before me with its head lowered, like a schoolmaster talking to the class, that is true; it is becoming almost distressing even to me.[5]

The opening apostrophe, "Du Rabe" ("You raven"), is without question an address to the self,[6] at the very least to that part of the self which is represented by the name "Amschel Kafka," which helps to explain why the narrating voice regularly finds the raven wherever he goes. The morpheme *Rabe* is presented twice, first by itself but then as part of the compound *Unglücksrabe*, translated as "bird of ill omen." Kafka's formulation is more ambiguous and also richer: by address-

---

4. *BF* 444; *LB* 304: "I have no literary interests, but am made of literature, I am nothing else, and cannot be anything else."

5. *WP* 126; *HO* 132: "Du Rabe, sagte ich, du alter Unglücksrabe, was tust du immerfort auf meinem Weg. Wohin ich gehe, sitzst du und sträubst die paar Federn. Lästig! Ja, sagte er und ging mit gesenktem Kopf vor mir auf und ab wie ein Lehrer beim Vortrag, es ist richtig; es ist mir selbst schon fast unbehaglich."

6. "'I am a quite impossible bird,' said Franz Kafka. 'I am a jackdaw—a *kavka*. . . . I hop about bewildered among my fellow men. They regard me with deep suspicion. And indeed I am a dangerous bird, a thief, a jackdaw" (Gustav Janouch, *Conversations with Kafka*, trans. Goronwy Rees [New York: New Directions, 1971], 16–17). Though some doubt is cast on the reliability of Janouch's recollections in Eduard Goldstücker, "Kafkas Eckermann? Gustav Janouchs 'Gespräche mit Kafka,'" *TP* 238–255, I remain persuaded that Janouch's volume presents material that is basically accurate.

ing a "raven of misfortune" he can imply both that the bird brings misfortune on others and that it is itself unhappy. The term *Unglücksrabe* thus serves as a rhetorical hinge that moves on the one hand to the "old" tradition about ravens, presenting them as a generalized emblem of misfortune, and on the other toward the characterization of his own personal situation.

But the recognition that the raven is essentially congruent with the narrating self does not fully answer the question of what the bird is "always doing" on the writer's path. The next sentence suggests that the raven is more than the writer's shadow or alter ego, for it does not simply appear: it "sits" and "ruffles its few feathers." In a sense, this expansion of the trope is to be expected; from time to time we do see birds ruffling their feathers. But the German phrase "sträubst die paar Federn" will not sit still for such a straightforward reading. The words *sträuben* and *Feder* form a familiar combination in a commonplace expression that is inevitably recalled by the German-speaking reader: "Die Feder sträubt sich" ("the pen refuses to write"). This bird possesses a few feathers, which are at the same time a few pens, and it may or may not encourage writing with them. In any case, its feather-ruffling, pen-brandishing behavior is burdensome to the writer, who labels it a "nuisance" (lästig).

The raven then goes on to act out its congruence with the narrator by mirroring his opinion. What is burdensome to the writer is becoming "almost distressing" ("fast unbehaglich") to the old crow as well. But the bird does not simply express agreement: it does so while taking on the features of an orator, a teacher in the act of presenting a formal discourse (Vortrag). Decked out thus, with the Feder and his Vortrag, the old crow seems a highly rhetorical sort of bird. By pacing back and forth, he even acts out the paronomastic significance of his name: he engages in *rabantern,* that is, moving about restlessly.

In this passage Kafka shows himself highly aware of the fact that in addressing himself as a "raven" he is engaging the rhetorical aspect of himself. The possibility that "Kafka" will turn into a *Rabe* is the possibility for the deployment of pens and of formal discourses, that is, the possibility of literature. He is also aware that this rhetorical character is a regular feature of his literary activity: it is "always on my path." There is no escaping from the old bird, even though its presence is at least as much a burden as it is an enabling condition. The bird is a problem for both the writer and his writing, though neither could exist without it. The figure expresses an ambivalence typical of what I call "the passion of reading."[7]

One of Kafka's earliest surviving literary efforts, the fragment called "Wedding Preparations in the Country" ("Hochzeitsvorbereitungen auf dem Lande"), shows the young writer playing with some literary ideas linked to the rhetoric of his name. The hero of the narrative is called Raban, a gesture that in a way merely repeats the action performed by Julie and Herrmann in calling their son Amschel. It is another Teutonic translation of *kavka*, based this time on the word *Rabe* (crow) rather than on *Amsel* (blackbird). The very translatability of the name, however, depends on and reminds us of its identity with a common noun signifying a particular nonhuman creature. If "Kafka" can be transformed into "Amschel" or "Raban," the "Raban" in turn can be transformed by autonomasia into *Rabe*, something no longer the name of a man but an actual animal. The logic of this rhetoric is carried out in Raban's fantasy of remaining at home in his bed in the form of a giant insect: "As I lie in bed I assume the shape of a big beetle, a stag beetle or a cockchafer, I think . . . . yes. Then I would pretend it was a matter of hibernating, and I would press my little legs to my bulging belly."[8] The insect is only a slight displacement of the crow: both are flying creatures often regarded as pests.

No reader of these pages will fail to recognize the next step in the semantic chain: the creature that Raban only dreams of being makes its famous appearance again in "The Metamorphosis," but this time it is not a fantasy in the hero's mind. The union of person and verminous animal proposed by the name Amschel Kafka is carried out with severe logic. The name Kafka is present not merely in the slightly deformed orthographic image presented by Gregor's surname "Samsa" but more significantly in the stuff of the narrative itself.

Autonomasia plays an important role as a rhetorical beginning for many of Kafka's stories. One in which it is most readily visible is "Jackals and Arabs," in which the main characters are a European

---

7. Ambivalence is a well-recognized feature of Kafka's writing. See, for example, Hermann Pongs, "Ambivalenze in moderner Dichtung," in Adolf Haslinger, ed., *Sprachkunst als Weltgestaltung* (Salzburg: Pustet, 1966), 191–228.

8. *CS* 45; *SE* 236: "Ich habe, wie ich im Bett liege, die Gestalt eines großen Käfers, eines Hirschkäfers oder eines Maikäfers, glaube ich . . . ja. Ich stelle es dann so an, als handle es sich um einen Winterschlaf, und ich preße meine Beinchen an meinen gebauchten Unterleib."

traveler, an Arab caravan leader, and a group of jackals.[9] One would have to say that the jackals are the protagonists: they receive the bulk of the attention, and their spokesman, an elder jackal, speaks a substantial portion of the tale's discourse. I propose that only the son of Herrmann Kafka and Julie Löwy could have written this story, because the jackals are the rhetorical extension of a reading of the family names. Jackals are carrion eaters, like crows, but they are also in a certain sense lions. The German word *Schakal* is virtually identical to the Hebrew word used in the Bible to mean "lion." The jackal represents a semantic union of the kavka and the Löwe as Franz represents a biological union of a Kafka with a Löwy. A number of the story's features confirm the idea that the jackals represent certain attitudes and problems of their creator. Most prominent among these is their deep and urgent desire for cleanliness: "Cleanliness, nothing but cleanliness is what we want."[10] Kafka's lifelong interest in what we would today call "health foods," with vegetarianism and nudism, stemmed from a preoccupation with personal cleanliness that bordered on fanaticism.[11] The paradox that a man with such a profound hatred for anything unclean should bear the name of a carrion eater was not lost on Kafka's verbal imagination. This very story tries to explore the paradox in an imaginative narrative that posits a way in which carrion eating can be understood as the result of a desire to keep the world clean. For the jackals, disgust is caused by living things, particularly the living flesh of the Arabs:

> "You misunderstand us," said he [the oldest jackal], "a human failing which persists apparently even in the far North. We're not proposing to kill them. All the water in the Nile couldn't cleanse us of that. Why, the mere sight of their living flesh makes us turn tail and flee into the cleaner air, into the desert, which for that very reason is our home."
> And all the jackals around, including many newcomers from farther away, dropped their muzzles between their forelegs and wiped them with their paws; it was as if they were trying to conceal a disgust so overpowering that I felt like leaping over their heads to get away.[12]

9. William C. Rubinstein, "Kafka's 'Jackals and Arabs,'" *Monatshefte* 59 (1967), 13–18, offers another approach to this story.

10. *CS* 409; *SE* 134: "Reinheit, nichts als Reinheit wollen wir."

11. Wagenbach, *Selbstzeugnisse*, 82, cites Kafka's "suicidal battle for *cleanliness*" (emphasis in the original).

12. *CS* 409; *SE* 134: "'Du mißverstehst uns,' sagte er, 'nach Menschenart, die

The jackals cannot even stand to approach the Arabs near enough to kill them, and so they try to enlist the aid of the narrator, whom they entreat as if he were a deity: "and so, dear sir [or dear Lord], by means of your all-powerful hands slit their throats with these scissors!"[13] The dialogue is interupted by the arrival of the Arab leader, who orders the reeking carcass of a camel to be brought forth. The jackals are drawn to it as if "the stinking carrion bewitched them" (CS 410) and cannot stay away from it, even when the Arab lashes them with his whip.

The jackals bear a substantial similarity to another set of characters, the nomads of "An Old Manuscript" ("Ein altes Blatt").[14] Their eating habits are in a sense just the opposite of the jackals', but they are just as distressing, especially to a vegetarian: they eat great quantities of meat. Even their horses eat meat, and "often enough a horseman and his horse are lying side by side, both of them gnawing at the same joint, one at either end."[15] Worst of all, they do not share the jackals' fastidious avoidance of living flesh:

> Not long ago the butcher thought he might at least spare himself the trouble of slaughtering, and so one morning he brought along a live ox. But he will never dare to do that again. I lay for a whole hour flat on the floor at the back of my workshop with my head muffled in all the clothes and rugs and pillows I had simply to keep from hearing the bellowing of that ox, which the nomads were leaping on from all sides, tearing morsels out of its living flesh with their teeth.[16]

---

sich also auch im hohen Norden nicht verliert. Wir werden sie doch nicht töten. Soviel Wasser hätte der Nil nicht, um uns rein zu waschen. Wir laufen doch schon vor dem bloßen Anblick ihres lebenden Leibes weg, in reinere Luft, in die Wüste, die deshalb unsere Heimat ist.' Und alle Schakale ringsum, zu denen inzwischen noch viele von fernher gekommen waren, senkten die Köpfe zwischen die Vorderbeine und putzten sie mit den Pfoten; es war, als wollten sie einen Widerwillen verbergen, der so schrecklich war, daß ich am liebsten mit einem hohen Sprung aus ihrem Kreis entflohen wäre."

13. *CS* 410; *SE* 134: "Darum, o Herr, darum o teurer Herr, mit Hilfe deiner alles vermögenden Hände, mit Hilfe deiner alles vermögenden Hände [*sic*] schneide ihnen mit dieser Schere die Hälse durch!"

14. For more on these nomads, see Carol B. Bedwell, "The Force of Destruction in Kafka's 'Ein Altes Blatt,'" *Monatshefte* 58 (1966), 43–48.

15. *CS* 417; *SE* 130. "Oft liegt ein Reiter neben seinem Pferd und beide nähren sich vom gleichen Fleischstück, jeder bei einem Ende."

16. *CS* 417; *SE* 130–131: "Letzthin dachte der Fleischer, er könne sich wenigstens die Mühe des Schlachtens sparen, und brachte am Morgen einen

What kind of creatures are these? They are allegedly human beings, but they act more like ravening beasts. They are, of course, another narrative transformation of the problematic inherent in the rhetoric of Kafka's name: "They communicate with each other much as jackdaws do. A screeching of jackdaws is always in our ears."[17] Kafka uses the word *Dohle*, another permissible German equivalent of *kavka*. They act like jackdaws, too; they "grab at" things in a manner that cannot be described as "taking by force." They are a plague of sometimes horrifying pests.

At the core of the horror is the fact that these barbarous nomads somehow seem to have taken over the capital city, the center of the nation, virtually overnight: "In some way that is incomprehensible to me they have pushed right into the capital, although it is a long way from the frontier."[18] This beastly element is discovered in the very heart of the political and social organism, almost as if it had always been there but was just now suddenly recognized. It is analogous— and deliberately so—to the discovery of a beastliness within the self, a recognition that a terrible appetite lurks inside a refined and civilized exterior. Behind the narrator, appalled to find that this disgraceful foreign element now dwells virtually on the steps of the Imperial Palace, stands a consciousness equally appalled to learn that an element he had hoped was foreign to his character, an urge to indulge in unclean acts, resides within him. When he looks carefully, the writer discovers that there really is a kavka inside this Kafka.

These initial examples serve to show not only that autonomasia played a significant role in the development of some of Kafka's fictions but also that this form of rhetoricity leads quickly and almost inevitably to others as well. The fact that the name "Kafka" is readable under two radically different interpretive conventions opens the door to a variety of tropes. One of them, evident in both "Jackals and Arabs" and "An Old Manuscript," I have called "syllepsis," the figure

---

lebendigen Ochsen. Das darf er nicht mehr wiederholen. Ich lag wohl eine Stunde ganz hinten in meiner Werkstatt platt auf dem Boden und alle meine Kleider, Decken und Polster hatte ich über mir aufgehäuft, nur um das Gebrüll des Ochsens nicht zu hören, den von allen Seiten die Nomaden ansprangen, um mit den Zähnen Stücke aus seinem warmen Fleisch zu reißen."

17. *CS* 416; *SE* 130: "Unter einander verständigen sie sich ähnlich wie Dohlen. Immer wieder hört man diesen Schrei der Dohlen."

18. *CS* 416; *SE* 230: "Auf eine mir unbegreifliche Weise sind sie bis in die Hauptstadt gedrungen, die doch sehr weit von der Grenze entfernt ist."

that brings together into unity two things that we ordinarily regard as belonging apart. When Pope describes a certain superficial young lady as concerned lest she "stain her honour or a new brocade," the witty effect of the line results from the juxtaposition of the literal and figurative senses of "stain" as morally equivalent. For the lady in question, it is proposed, a spot upon her honor (that is, "reputation for sexual virtue") is of no greater or lesser consequence than a spot on her dress. The word "stain" acts as a meeting place for the two otherwise incommensurable acts of spilling food or wine on a garment and engaging in illicit amorous dalliance.[19] The word "Kafka" is capable of acting in exactly the same way; that is, Franz could have said to himself something like, "That disgusting creature perched on a decaying carcass and consuming it is a *kavka*, and so am I." There is not supposed to be this degree of kinship between a verminous creature proscribed by the Torah (compare Leviticus 11:15) and a nice Jewish boy. The very word of God commands that they be kept apart. But here they are, in the intimate embrace of a single word.

Both the meat-eating nomads and the talking jackals are developments of the syllepsis on Kafka's name. They bring together animal and human characteristics that we believe nature keeps rigorously separate. Animals do not speak, or if they do they merely imitate the outer form of human speech, like parrots. Kafka's jackals not only speak but also engage in a subtle discourse about matters of some intellectual complexity. They seem very human and indeed not at all unsympathetic. At the same time, however, the story dramatically reminds us that these are still jackals, still carrion-eating animals driven by dark urges that they are unable to control. The nomads of "An Old Manuscript" look like human beings and in many respects behave humanly as well. But they do not speak in a human tongue—from the narrator's point of view, at any rate—and their table manners will not bear serious inspection. In both cases a biological identification that ought to be easy is rendered impossible by the combination of animal and human traits presented. We are not dealing with conventional allegorical animals in "Jackals and Arabs." They do not, like La Fontaine's creations, represent some identifiable human characteristic imaged in a consequential manner. They speak like psychologically complex human beings but, in the presence of carrion, act like simple,

19. For more on this sort of syllepsis, see Clayton Koelb, *The Incredulous Reader* (Ithaca: Cornell University Press, 1984), 81–110.

instinct-driven beasts. The nomads, too, present an uncomfortable combination of human and animal, but the syllepsis is troubling for a different reason. Kafka's jackals are distressing because the human aspect of their behavior seems impossible: animals simply do not converse in perfect German in the world we inhabit. The nomads' behavior shocks us because it *is* possible. Human beings ought not to act in such a way, but they could.

Kafka's most successful syllepsis of animal and human is his most famous, the man/bug Gregor Samsa.[20] Stanley Corngold has shown that the metamorphosis reported at the opening of the narrative is not complete: Gregor has not been thoroughly transformed into a bug; there is still a recognizably human consciousness inside the insect's body.[21] Insects, we feel sure, do not worry about missing their trains or agonize over their family relationships, but Gregor does, even though he now looks exactly like a large beetle and has a repertory of insectlike behavior. Gregor is a narrative extension of the problematic of coexisting animal and human readings of the name "Kafka," reinforced by the many insulting tropes of the type "Du bist ein Ungeziefer" (that is, "You're a louse"). Because the kavka is, according to the law of the Old Testament and long-standing tradition, a verminous creature, an *Ungeziefer,* such tropes would have carried a particular sting for people named Kafka—or at least for those among them with a high level of sensitivity to language. It is no very great step (especially when one is a child) from the recognition that "I carry the name of vermin" to the fearful suspicion "I must therefore *be* in some way vermin." The circumstances of young Franz's life, especially his relationship with his father, could only make that step seem smaller and more inevitable. Powerful forces, both linguistic and otherwise, thrust young Amschel Kafka toward the unhappy but potent notion that he was what his name said he was. "The Metamorphosis" is the fictional expression of that notion. Many of his other stories exploit it as well.

The same rhetorical potential that generates sylleptic narratives can

20. Because "The Metamorphosis" is one of Kafka's most frequently discussed stories, I touch upon it here only as the occasion demands. For both a subtle reading of the story and an annotated bibliography of scholarship treating it, see Stanley Corngold, *The Commentators' Despair* (Port Washington, N.Y.: Kennikat Press, 1973).

21. Stanley Corngold, "Kafka's *Die Verwandlung*: Metamorphosis of the Metaphor," *Mosaic* 3 (Summer 1970), 91–106 (reprinted in *The Commentators' Despair*).

work in an analogous but opposite direction. Although one can understand the name "Kafka" as combining two things that ought to—and in the rest of the world do—remain apart, one could also regard the name as natural and its mutually incompatible readings as perverse. From this point of view, "Kafka" represents a single, unitary concept that is inappropriately divided up by reading it as person on the one hand and animal on the other. Such rhetorical division, which I have called "dialepsis," can be found wherever language presents entities as divided that we ordinarily suppose to be indivisible.[22] The following example comes from a well-known English nursery rhyme:

> Elizabeth, Libby, Betsy and Bess,
> They all went together to seek a bird's nest;
> They found a bird's nest with five eggs in,
> They all took one, and left four in.

The riddle is explained, of course, by the realization that Elizabeth, Libby, Betsy, and Bess are variant names of a single person. They "all went together" because they could not do otherwise, and when "all took one" egg out of the nest only one egg was taken. The rhyme makes a little paradoxical story from the purely linguistic division of a single self into four different names, all of which might (but in this case do not) refer to different persons. The creature named Kafka is similarly divisible by autonomasia into a person, the son of Herrmann and Julie, and a beast, the common jackdaw.

The divisibility of the self becomes another feature of Kafka's fictions. It is already prominently visible in his earliest surviving work, especially in Raban's fantasy of self-division, mentioned above.[23] Raban dreads making the necessary visit to his fiancee and her family, but he dreams of a way to solve the problem: "I don't even need to go to the country myself, it isn't necessary. I'll send my clothed body."[24] Significantly, not the clothed body but the spiritual self remains behind, transformed into a big beetle. The relation of body to spirit is just the opposite of that which we find in "The Metamorphosis," where Gregor's body took on the characteristics of an insect. Even

22. Dialepsis is discussed in detail in *The Incredulous Reader*, pp. 111–139.
23. Charles Bernheimer examines this self-division in his important essay "The Splitting of the 'I' and the Dilemma of Narration: Kafka's *Hochzeitsvorbereitungen auf dem Lande*," *CT*, 7–24 (German version in *DJK*).
24. *CS* 55, *SE* 235–6: "Ich brauche nicht einmal selbst aufs Land fahren, das ist nicht nötig. Ich schicke meinen angekleideten Körper."

more important for my purpose here is the fact that, while Gregor represents a syllepsis, an incredible union of man and beast, Raban's fantasy proposes a dialepsis, an incredible division of the self into two independent entities.

Raban is in fact from the first quite fascinated with the question of the divisibility of the self that language makes possible and with the advantages such a division brings with it. He is particularly concerned with the act of narration, as he imagines himself telling the tale of his troubles to a woman he sees in the street:

> One works so feverishly at the office that afterwards one is too tired even to enjoy one's holiday's properly. But even all that work does not give one a claim to be treated lovingly by everyone; on the contrary, one is alone, a total stranger and only the object of curiosity. And so long as you [*du*] say "one" [*man*] instead of "I" [*ich*], there's nothing in it and one can easily tell the story; but as soon as you admit to yourself that it is you yourself, you feel as though transfixed and horrified. . . . But if I myself distinguish between "one" and "I," how then dare I complain about the others?[25]

This passage abounds with rhetorical complexity generated from the proliferation of pronouns. Raban sees the act of distancing possible by replacing the very personal "I" by a neutral and general "one" as enabling discourse: it keeps the pain and horror far enough away so that one can go on talking. But that replacement is also an act of self-alienation that makes "one" a stranger not only to others but to one's self as well. How can he complain about others treating him like a stranger rather than "with love" when he is prepared to treat himself that way? To this degree Raban is explicitly conscious of the problematic involved. Implicit in his discourse, however, is a further complication: in order to talk about the relation of "one" to "I," Raban must pull yet another pronoun out of the hat, *du* ("you"). But this *du* is again just another way to refer to the self, something halfway between the complete identification of "I" and the third-person distance of

---

25. *CS* 53; *SE* 234: "Man arbeitet so übertrieben im Amt, daß man dann sogar zu müde ist, um seine Ferien gut zu genießen. Aber durch alle Arbeit erlangt man noch keinen Anspruch darauf, von allen mit Liebe behandelt zu werden, vielmehr ist man allein, gänzlich fremd und nur Gegenstand der Neugierde. Und solange du *man* sagst an Stelle von *ich*, ist es nichts und man kann diese Geschichte aufsagen, sobald du aber dir eingestehst, daß du selbst es bist, dann wirst du förmlich durchbohrt und bist entsetzt. . . . Wenn ich aber selbst unterscheide zwischen *man* und *ich*, wie darf ich mich dann über die andern beklagen."

"one." The German *du* works so well because it implies both otherness and intimacy: it is the second-person pronoun closer to *ich*, whereas *Sie* is closer to *man*. Though this use of *du* works very successfully to mediate between the extremes represented by *ich* and *man*, it divides the self yet again by introducing a new version of the speaking subject.

Raban's discovery that he is divisible into *ich*, *man*, and even *du* and that this linguistic self-alienation can work to his advantage sets the stage for his dream of physical self-alienation. The dialeptic fantasy of sending forth the clothed body while the true self remains at home in bed is a narrative elaboration of the scene of self-narration that has taken place already in Raban's imagination and is occurring in Kafka's own act of writing. The possibility of translating the Czech name "Kafka" into other languages, first realized by the "Hebrew" name Amschel, allows Kafka to split himself up into countless "clothed bodies" that can act out in narrative all the scenes in which Kafka would prefer not to participate himself. The "real" Franz Kafka remains at home, very near his bed, engaged quietly in his "nocturnal scribbling" ("nächtliches Gekritzel"), snug as a bug. Meanwhile, creatures named Raban or Gracchus or Samsa pace out their moments of pain in some distant literary space.

The price for this convenience, as Kafka knew, is self-alienation. One has to see one's self as a stranger and to experience a permanent sense of self-loss in order to be able to dispatch pieces of the self into the uncanny territory of literature. The self becomes in a sense indistinguishable from a stranger or perhaps a chance acquaintance—someone, at any rate, with whom one might come into conflict. The early fragment "Description of a Struggle" ("Beschreibung eines Kampfes") chronicles the adventures of a self divided into multiple, sometimes hostile, entities. The struggle to which the title alludes takes place within a single consciousness alienated from itself by, among other things, the act of writing. The title names with great precision the process taking place in the fiction: "Be-schreib-ung," the literal writing-into-being of a conflict. I will discuss this story in detail later;[26] for now I want only to advert to the connection between self-division and the process of writing made explicit in the name Kafka gave his text.

The act of writing inscribes a division discovered in an act of reading and is therefore a form of "construction," a structure made by

26. See Chapter 8.

construing.[27] The text upon which the process of construction is based may be any piece of discourse read as rhetoric, that is, any text understood as readable under more than one interpretive convention. I have taken as a heuristic model of such rhetorical discourse the name Amschel Kafka partly because it appears likely that the name served as such a model for the writer himself and also because the name is one of the most important points of contact between the structure of language and the structure of a human personality. Because as readers of Kafka we are concerned with Kafka's use of language, it is appropriate to begin with the one text in which we can be sure the writer had a profound and enduring interest. This statement does not mean, however, that the name Kafka explains the stories or even serves as their source. It serves for us, and I believe it did for him, as a kind of provocation: it urgently demands consideration as rhetoric and thereby promotes the consideration of rhetoricity in general. In the case of young Franz Kafka, a person with an extremely sensitive verbal imagination, the recognition of the rhetoricity of his own name could only have marshaled him the way that he was going.

The rhetorical multiplicity of meaning in the name Amschel Kafka can occur by means of a number of figurative turns, including both syllepsis and dialepsis, as well as autonomasia itself. Perhaps not surprisingly, other possibilities for figuration are suggested here as well. We might notice, for example, that the given name Amschel repeats the equation of personal name and common noun made by "Kafka," but it does so, as it were, in advance. It says what the surname is going to say before the surname has a chance to say it. If we understand "Kafka" to be the original text and "Amschel" the derivative one—a correct understanding in terms of the historical sequence of acts of naming—then "Amschel" is a classical prolepsis, an anticipatory imitation of a text to follow. Prolepsis is most commonly applied in argumentation, where an opponent's expected line of reasoning or objections to your line of reasoning are frequently cited in advance in order to refute them: "I know that my worthy opponent will say such-and-such, but he is wrong to do so because . . ." It is most often, then, a way of disarming an adversary's weapons before he or she has a chance to use them.

27. This concept of construction is explained in detail in Clayton Koelb, *Inventions of Reading: Rhetoric and the Literary Imagination* (Ithaca: Cornell University Press, 1988), chap. 1.

Not surprisingly, Kafka often exploits the rhetoric of prolepsis in his fiction, where it functions in a way slightly different from its forensic usage. A noteworthy example is the opening sentence of *The Trial* (*Der Prozeß*), in which the narrator announces in advance the principal event he is about to relate: "Someone must have traduced Joseph K., because without having done anything wrong he was arrested one fine morning."[28] Initially at least, we understand this passage less as prolepsis than as a kind of narrative prologue, an outline description of the events to be reported in detail later on. Only in retrospect (or on second reading) do we realize that this announcement in fact proleptically undercuts or contradicts the later narration. The sentence states unequivocally, for instance, that Josef K. was arrested, whereas the narrative proper does not allow us to draw that conclusion. As the story unfolds, it is never clear whether K. has been arrested or not, and this uncertainty is crucially important for the development of the plot. By stating with assurance that K. was arrested, the narrator proleptically contradicts the facts of his own story. He also undermines in advance the narrative perspective characteristic of the novel as a whole, for the opening sentence gives a powerful impression of an omniscient narrator who is sure of the facts of the case. Actually, as we come to learn, the narrative voice can never be understood as free of K.'s own perspective because of Kafka's use of the "erlebte Rede" technique.[29] But *this* voice cannot be that of K., because K. could not know of his arrest in advance; it must know things he does not. At the same time, however, what it "knows" appears to be false, a misinterpretation or at the very least an overhasty leap to a conclusion.

In a certain sense, the classical forensic purpose of prolepsis is served here: it undermines the credibility of a discourse to come. In this case, however, the discourse to come is not that of an opponent but that of the very same narrator. The weapons being disarmed here are the story's own weapons. The opening statement sets up by means of its prolepsis a situation of rhetorical undecidability. A sentence that resembles a straightforward announcement of facts discloses a radical denial of the basis of its own claim. On returning to it a second time

28. *TR* 3; *RO* 259: "Jemand mußte Josef K. verleumdet haben, denn ohne daß er etwas Böses getan hätte, wurde er eines Morgens verhaftet."

29. Dorrit Cohn, "Erlebte Rede im Ich-Roman," *Germanisch-Romanische Monatsschrift* 19 (1969), 305–313, was one of the first to demonstrate the importance of this device in Kafka's fiction.

the reader cannot suppress a suspicion that the whole statement might be ironic; the rest of the story, that is, impels us to suspect that this proposition means the opposite of what it says. The suspicion can never be confirmed, however. The statement's claim to narrative authority, given its leading position in the text, can never be definitively demolished.

Kafka's prolepsis usually works in this paradoxical and unsettling fashion. A statement whose meaning we have no reason to question is discovered to anticipate later discourse suggesting or requiring an entirely different interpretation. This use of prolepsis is a rhetorical construction, in the sense in which I have used the term, in that it not only produces a text readable in two conflicting ways but also actualizes both readings in the text. The temporal gap between a discourse and its proleptic anticipation becomes a semantic gap as well. That semantic space can become the scene of action for a story, which acts out the terms of the semantic conflict.

The fragment "Blumfeld, an Elderly Bachelor" ("Blumfeld, ein älterer Junggeselle") demonstrates the kind of narrative tension that Kafka generates from prolepsis. The first paragraph is proleptic in many of its details inasmuch as it consists mainly of Blumfeld's thoughts about what he is going to do. He thinks about putting on his dressing gown, lighting his pipe, reading his French magazine, drinking some kirsch, and going to bed. Later we observe him doing all these things in order—except drinking the kirsch, which the narrator tells us he forgot. These anticipatory musings also include his vague desire for company: "Some companion [*Begleiter*], someone to witness these activities, would have been very welcome to Blumfeld."[30] In the course of the story, this wish comes true and indeed much sooner than Blumfeld could have expected. There are two bouncing balls already waiting for him in his room, jumping up and down like the dog he daydreams about. These balls—which I will discuss again in another connection below—are in a certain way the "companions" that Blumfeld had been wishing for, but they turn out to be not at all "welcome" in his well-ordered life.[31] He expends considerable energy trying to subdue and eventually to eliminate them. Whether he suc-

30. *CS* 183; *SE* 264: "Irgendein Begleiter, irgendein Zuschauer für diese Tätigkeiten wäre Blumfeld sehr willkommen gewesen."

31. Ethan Goffman, "Blumfeld's Balls: Notes on a Situation in a Kafka Short Story," *Neue Germanistik* 4 (Fall 1985), 3–6, has commented on the odd importance of these objects.

ceeds or not is never revealed in the fragment Kafka left, but in a certain sense it does not matter. The balls, too, it turns out, were a kind of proleptic announcement of another problem Blumfeld has, namely his two "assistants"[32] in the factory where he works. These two companions are just as strange and just as much underfoot as the bouncing balls. In this case, however, Blumfeld has practically no hope of ridding himself of them because they were given to him at his own request. They are far worse than no help at all, and in terms of their usefulness at the office, they could hardly be described as "very welcome to Blumfeld."

We cannot, however, simply dismiss the earlier claim that Blumfeld really wants companionship. He just does not want the kind of companionship he gets. He appears to want a family, especially children, but he is at the same time terrified of actually having children about. Both the balls ("children's balls") and the assistants ("pale, weak children") are associated with children explicitly in the narrative. Blumfeld would probably like to be as prolifically fruitful as the field of flowers he carries in his name. But in fact he is an elderly bachelor for whom all companionship is a nuisance.

Prolepsis thus produces another multiplication of antithetical meanings from which a story can be developed. Syllepsis, dialepsis, and prolepsis are only some of the figures readable in the name Amschel Kafka upon which rhetorical construction can be based. An additional trope can be discovered there as well. We recall, for example, that the "Hebrew" name Amschel is etymologically a variant of Anselm but was regularly associated in popular use with Amsel. This association is a figurative one, suggested by the phonological similarity of the two words. The Amsel becomes a sign for Amschel by means of paronomasia; that is, because they sound almost, though not exactly, alike they may be substituted one for the other. Amschel produces the same meaning as Kafka but by different means. ("Kafka" is a graphic variant of *kavka* and not an etymologically distinct lexeme.) The schoolyard must have provided some unforgettable lessons in this form of rhetoric for the young Kafka: it would have been only incredible good fortune if Franz had not heard his name transformed by some taunting youngster into *Kacke*, "excrement." This kind of scatological wordplay has an irresistible and seemingly univer-

32. Kafka calls them *Praktikanten,* a title he himself held at the Workers Accident Insurance Company.

sal fascination. In any case, the principle of verbal transformation by means of paronomasia could not fail to make its presence felt in Kafka's early experiences. In a way, it fit together all too well with the results of other rhetorical strategies of which he had become aware. The kavka, the verminous winged creature, was just not very different from that other miserable creature, the *Mistkäfer* (dung beetle), which lived by ingesting excrement. The semantic level seemed to confirm the propriety of the equation of *kavka* and *Kacke*.

The generative power of paronomasia can be seen at work in many of Kafka's fictions. I will cite just one especially striking example here. Blumfeld begins, as mentioned above, by introducing the reader to the elderly bachelor's desire for some kind of "companion" (*Begleiter*) to share in his otherwise lonely life. His first thought is to acquire a dog: "These animals are gay and above all grateful and loyal; one of Blumfeld's colleagues has a dog of this kind; it follows no one but its master and when it hasn't seen him for a few moments it greets him at once with loud barkings."[33] Blumfeld returns to this thought again a bit later, the thought of a "companion, an animal to which he doesn't have to pay much attention, . . . but which nevertheless, when Blumfeld feels like it, is promptly at his disposal with its barking [*Bellen*], jumping [*Springen*], and licking of hands."[34] Just a few lines later, as if by magic, the very companions Blumfeld had wished for appear, but they are not exactly the animals he had imagined: "two small white celluloid balls with little blue stripes jumping up and down side by side on the parquet."[35] The imaginary dog is described by its Bellen, a trait that is almost instantly transformed by paronomasia into the *Bälle* Blumfeld finds in his room. The connection is reinforced by the context: where the dog was to greet him with "Bellen, Springen," and so on, Blumfeld discovers that "Zelluloidbälle springen" on his very doorstep. Later, they are described as "submissive companions" ("untergeordnete Begleiter")—exactly what he had hope his imagined pet

33. *CS* 183; *SE* 264–265: "Ein solches Tier ist lustig und vor allem dankbar und treu; ein Kollege von Blumfeld hat einen solchen Hund, er schließt sich niemandem an, außer seinem Herrn, und hat er ihn ein paar Augenblicke nicht gesehen, empfängt er ihn gleich mit großem Bellen."
34. *CS* 284; *SE* 266: "Blumfeld dagegen will nur einen Begleiter haben, ein Tier, um das er sich nicht viel kümmern muß, . . . das aber, wenn es Blumfeld danach verlangt, gleich mit Bellen, Springen, Händelecken zur Verfügung steht."
35. *CS* 185; *SE* 266: "Zwei kleine, weiße blaugestreifte Zelluloidbälle springen auf dem Parkett nebeneinander auf und ab."

would be. Unfortunately for Blumfeld, these supernatural companions prove to be more an unwelcome intrusion than a comfort to the elderly bachelor.

The story never explains where these peculiar balls come from or how they end up in Blumfeld's room, but it does give us enough information to determine how Kakfa came upon the idea of their appearance. The Bälle emerged from Bellen in just the same way that Amsel emerges from Amschel. The process of association of ideas by means of wordplay is so common that we do not often examine it closely. Substantial phonological similarity between otherwise unrelated words is an inevitable feature of language because every individual dialect uses only a severely restricted repertory of phonemes. Puns are exploited in every sort of discourse, from the jokes we hear in the street to the famous "quibbles" of Shakespeare. Kafka's use of paronomasia is special in that he uses it not to embellish his discourse but to generate it. Much of the narrative in "Blumfeld" concerns the doings of the two celluloid balls, their incessant jumping, their "sleeping" under his bed, and so on. This narrative exists, however, only because of the paronomasia *Bellen/Bälle*, a phonological similarity that suggests to Kafka's verbal imagination some kind of essential similarity. These Bälle do not become completely separated from the semantic field of canine matters surrounding Bellen in which they were first found. Kafka even goes out of his way to remind us of this point with a little paradoxical joke: Blumfeld, tired of the antics of the balls, wishes he had a dog to chase them, catch them, and destroy them: "Right now Blumfeld could have made good use of a dog, such a wild young animal would soon have dealt with these balls." ("Jetzt könnte Blumfeld einen Hund gut brauchen, so ein junges, wildes Tier würde mit den Bällen bald fertig werden.")[36] One could easily substitute *Bellen* for *Bällen* in this sentence, and in fact, given the subject matter, it is almost impossible not to do so. An additional joke is disclosed thereby, however, because a "wild young dog" who would easily "deal with the balls" ("mit den Bällen fertig werden") would not likely ever finish his barking ("mit dem Bellen fertig werden"). In any case, the joke confirms our sense that the two magical little balls really do belong in a central way to the canine world. It is no wonder that

36. *CS* 188; *SE* 269.

Kafka referred to this as a "dog story" in spite of the fact that no dogs actually appear in it.[37]

Kafka's imaginative writing shows itself to be intimately connected to a particular mode of reading. Kafka could not have written his story about Blumfeld without first reading the word *Bellen* as containing and in a certain sense uniting two otherwise unrelated and perhaps even opposed concepts. His story takes from the word's phonology, by means of the trope of paronomasia, a meaning that leads us to the world of lifeless objects. But from its "literal," untroped semantic context he takes such notions as "jumping" and "companionship"— traits we associate with living creatures. Kafka's fictional balls inhabit both realms: they are inanimate objects that behave like living creatures. The combination is striking in its paradox, but it is justified in a sense by its origin. Kafka did not make it up; he merely found it in the structure of ordinary German. But such an act of reading obviously requires a special point of view and a kind of double vision that lets the reader see the text as the repository of two (or more) fully functioning semantic systems. When Kafka reads *Bellen*, he does not understand it as signifying *either* "barking" *or* "balls" but as *both* at once. The fantasy presented in the narrative demonstrates how the two might go together.

Another trope, perhaps the most common of all, is suggested by the addition of "Amschel" to the already significant "Kafka." The doubling of the semantic field by the addition of the second ravenish word produces a certain excess that is comparable to the effect of everyday hyperbole. The piling up of signifiers with the same signified suggests that this Kafka is in fact more a kavka than any other, so much so in fact that he deserves the doubled appellation. The name could thus be read like the hyperbolic joke about New York, New York: "the town so nice they named it twice." The young Franz would easily see himself as the embodiment of such a hyperbole, except in his case the cultural connotations of the doubling are not "nice" at all. If a kavka is an unlucky bird, how much more so an Amschel Kafka?

We would expect, then, that Kafka would find it familiar and natural to read hyperbolic language in a way different from the rest of us,

---

37. See the entry on "Blumfeld" in Hartmut Binder, *Kafka Kommentar zu sämtlichen Erzählungen* (Munich: Winkler, 1975).

and indeed he does. Hyperbolic locutions that might seem relatively harmless to the ordinary listener are not so for Kafka. The most notorious example, perhaps, but still the most telling, is the one Franz reports in the *Letter to His Father*: "It was enough that I should take a little interest in a person . . . for you, without any consideration for my feelings or respect for my judgment, to move in with abuse, defamation, and denigration. Innocent, childlike people, such as, for instance, the Yiddish actor Löwy, had to pay for that. Without knowing him you compared him, in some dreadful way that I have now forgotten, to vermin."[38] Kafka may have forgotten the exact details, but he clearly remembered the figural description of someone close to himself as vermin (*Ungeziefer*), a hyperbole he was unable to dismiss. Because Kafka's friendship with Löwy took place in 1911–1912, the father's remark was most likely made not long before the time in late 1912 when the story of Gregor Samsa's metamorphosis into a gigantic vermin ("ein ungeheures Ungeziefer")[39] was written. The son's story makes good—or so he thought—on his name's hyperbolic attribution of ravenlike characteristics. The kavka is, after all, a kind of Ungeziefer.

One of Kafka's most successful recipes for fiction was to be the narrative interpretation of a hyperbolic trope. We can confidently assume that Kafka did just this with "The Metamorphosis," but we need make no assumptions at all in the case of "The Bucket Rider" ("Der Kübelreiter"). Kafka tells us outright. After introducing himself to us as one who is able to "ride off" on his empty coal bucket ("often I am upraised as high as the first storey of a house; never do I sink as low as the house doors"),[40] the narrator and hero sets forth the basis of the fiction: "'Coal dealer!' I cry in a voice burned hollow by the frost and muffled in the cloud made by my breath, 'please, coal dealer, give me a little coal. My bucket is so light that I can ride on it. Be

38. *LF* 24–25: "Es genügte, daß ich an einem Menschen ein wenig Interesse hatte . . . daß Du schon ohne jede Rücksicht auf mein Gefühl und ohne Achtung vor meinem Urteil mit Beschimpfung, Verleumdung, Entwürdigung dreinfuhrst. Unschuldige, kindliche Menschen wie zum Beispiel der jiddische Schauspieler Löwy mußten das büßen. Ohne ihn zu kennen, verglichst Du ihn in einer schrecklichen Weise, die ich schon vergessen habe, mit Ungeziefer."

39. *CS* 89; *SE* 56.

40. *CS* 413; *SE* 195: "Oft werde ich bis zur Höhe der ersten Stockwerke gehoben; niemals sinke ich bis zur Haustüre hinab."

kind. When I can I'll pay you.'"[41] Hyperbolic figures are transformed into the sober language of matters of fact: the cold so "burns" the narrator's voice that it is made hollow, and the cloud made by his condensing breath is so thick that he can hide in it. The bucket's balloonlike lightness exceeds the bounds of language and lifts the narrator off the ground. The bucket is so light, in fact, that at the end of the story, when the coal dealer has refused even a "shovelful of the worst coal," the narrator riding upon it is carried up even further "into the regions of the ice mountains," where he is "lost forever."[42] We must agree that this is a very light bucket indeed.

We must not be mistaken, however, and suppose that the story is simply an exaggerated tall tale of the Baron Münchhausen variety. This little tale is different and typical of Kafka in that the figurative import of the hyperbolic trope does not disappear behind the literal reading. "The Bucket Rider" results from a rhetorical reading of the hyperbole that understands both the literal *and* figurative meanings as functioning at the same time. The conclusion, with its implication of death by freezing, can be read as a figure for the real-world consequence of the narrator's plight. Of course it can also be taken literally as the final acting out of the literal reading of the bucket's exaggerated lightness, but it need not be. Both options always remain open in Kafka's practice of rhetorical reading.

41. *CS* 413; *SE* 195: "'Kohlenhändler!' rufe ich mit vor Kälte hohlgebrannter Stimme, in Rauchwolken des Atems gehüllt, 'bitte, Kohlenhändler, gib mir ein wenig Kohle. Mein Kübel ist schon so leer, daß ich auf ihm reiten kann. Sei so gut. Sobald ich kann, bezahle ich's.'"

42. *CS* 414; *SE* 196: "Und damit steige ich in die Regionen der Eisgebirge und verliere mich auf Nimmerwiedersehen."

Chapter 3

ACTS OF RHETORIC

If Kafka learned some modes of rhetorical reading by examining his own name, others must have come to his attention no later than the time of his legal studies. The law as a profession was never Kafka's calling; it was, at best, a way of earning a living on a schedule that would give him some hours to devote to literature. But despite his distaste for the day-to-day requirements of his legal or paralegal work at the insurance company,[1] Kafka maintained an abiding interest in matters associated with the law. An impressive number of his fictions, including the novel fragment *The Trial*, is centrally concerned with courts, lawyers, verdicts, law codes, contracts, and other matters of professional interest to attorneys. A hallmark of Kafka's special perspective on these matters is his interest in the status of performative language.

Many sorts of legal proceedings are acts or sequences of acts that take place in language itself. They are what J. L. Austin called "speech acts." Speech-act theory, founded by Austin (*How to Do Things with Words*) and elaborated by John R. Searle (*Speech Acts: An Essay in the Philosophy of Language*) and others, attempts to define and classify "performative" utterances—locutionary structures that in the very

---

1. This distaste seems to have faded with time. See Klaus Hermsdorf, "Arbeit und Amt als Erfahrung und Gestaltung," in Hermsdorf, ed., *Franz Kafka: Amtliche Schriften* (Berlin: Akademie, 1984), 9–87.

process of being spoken perform an action. Examples of such "illocutionary acts" are promising, swearing, warning, commanding, and questioning. In the original statement of the theory, Austin also considered the effects of utterances on the addressee, using the term "perlocution" for speech acts that, for example, amuse, convince, or insult. A speech act accomplished *in* saying something, then, is *illocutionary*, and one accomplished *by* saying something is *perlocutionary*. Obviously, the same locutionary structure can have both illocutionary force and perlocutionary effect, as when the illocutionary act of warning has the perlocutionary effect of frightening. Legal issues often turn about questions of illocutionary acts and perlocutionary effects. A contract is simply a formalized act of promising, which—under specified circumstances—has the effect of obligating the contracting parties in specified ways. The act of sentencing a person may have the effect of causing him or her to be executed. The effect of an indictment (the word itself declares its illocutionary force) is, ordinarily, to bring a person to trial. We could extend the list of examples at will.

Much of the law has to do with formalizing and codifying the circumstances in which certain illocutionary acts secure uptake (that is, do the things they say they are doing) and what sort of perlocutionary effects they should have. Lawyers are important figures for insurance companies—such as the Workers Accident Insurance Company that employed Kafka—because insurance is fundamentally a matter of a complex structure of promises formulated in contracts or statutes or some combination of the two. No lawyer can fail to become aware of the complex relation between illocutionary acts and their perlocutionary effects, even in the absence of a terminology such as Austin's to specify the relation. All lawyers, including Kafka, become aware early in their training of the complexities and uncertainties of performative discourse.

Most of the work done by philosophers and linguists has focused attention on the theory of illocutionary acts. Far less has been done with perlocutions. Students of both the law and literature, however, need to understand that the distinction between illocution and perlocution can become a matter of critical importance. At the heart of the matter is the fact that such a distinction is not always easy to make. Jerrold Sadock, one of the few speech-act theorists who have focused on the theory of perlocutions, notes that illocutions and perlocutions are similar in certain respects. The theory holds, for example, that "illocutionary acts are supposed to be capable of failing to be felicitous, to secure uptake, to take effect. In this respect, they are similar to perlocutionary effects." Furthermore, "the effect of both is posterior to the speech act."[2] The perlocution has its effect, the illocution secures uptake, *after* (usually immediately after) completion of the speech act. Such considerations lead Sadock to suggest, in fact, "that an illocutionary act is a special kind of perlocutionary act, with characteristics that distinguish it from all other kind of perlocutions."[3] For this reason, it is perfectly reasonable to make such statements as "by saying, 'I now pronounce you man and wife,' Reverend Kornblatt pronounced them man and wife," wherein the speaker asserts both (1) the successful uptake of the illocutionary act of "pronouncing" and (2) the perlocutionary effect of the minister's illocution. In essence both assertions are the same.

Because the "felicity" or "uptake" of an illocutionary act is indistinguishable from a perlocutionary effect, it is possible to perform an illocutionary act by means of a locutionary structure that simply asserts a perlocutionary effect. Indeed good grammar sometimes actually requires this to be done. As Sadock observes, current usage does not allow us to say "I fire you" but requires instead the apparent assertion "You're fired." No one would deny that the sentence "You're fired" is an illocutionary act. The assertion of perlocutionary effect, when uttered under the proper conditions by the appropriate speaker, has undeniable illocutionary force, as when the pope says, "You are excommunicated," or a police officer says, "You are under arrest." Under other conditions, however, these same locutionary structures may simply describe perlocutionary effects and possess no illocutionary force whatever. For example, the speaker who says, "I can't take you to mass with me, Martin; you're excommunicated," is asserting or reporting a perlocutionary effect but is certainly not performing the illocutionary act of excommunicating the hearer. Sadock, who has given careful attention to these distinctions, now believes that the speech-act status of such locutionary structures is genuinely ambiguous. He has sought purely linguistic (that is, grammatical or syntactic) methods of deciding which is to prevail but has found no reliable ones.

It is not difficult to see how such language could become just as rhetorical as the figurative language discussed in the last chapter.

2. Jerrold Sadock, *Toward a Linguistic Theory of Speech Acts* (New York: Academic, 1974), 152.
3. Ibid., 153.

Actually, one could justifiably argue that such expressions as "You're fired" and "You're under arrest" are themselves figurative usages; that is, they represent metonymic substitutions of the effect for the cause. When used with illocutionary intent, they "turn" their apparent non-performative structure to a performative end. They do not, in such cases, mean just what they say. In the absence of a clarifying context to establish a probable intention, there is no way to decide whether such an expression as "You're under arrest" performs the act of arresting or merely asserts, possibly incorrectly, that someone has previously performed an act of this kind. As an assertion, "You're under arrest" is true only if a felicitous illocutionary act of arresting has taken place earlier. If someone else has not placed you under arrest, I may not properly say "You're under arrest," unless I am arresting you now.

It follows that such utterances as "I believe you're under arrest" or "You're under arrest, I'm sure," which you would readily understand if you had been arrested earlier, would be highly perplexing in the mouth of an official with the power of arrest. If a police officer appears at the door and proclaims, "I think you're under arrest," when no authority has mentioned such a thing before, the statement must appear rhetorical; that is, it presents a locutionary form whose performative status cannot be determined. The officer is either arresting you (in which case the "I think" would undermine the intended act) or not (in which case the phrase "You're under arrest" would be false). Unless the officer or someone else supplies some kind of clarification, you will never know whether you have been arrested or not.

This very performative uncertainty Kafka exploits in the opening chapter of his novel fragment *The Trial*. In spite of the narrator's proleptic announcement of K.'s arrest in the first sentence of the book, it never becomes clear that any illocutionary act of arresting takes place anywhere in the story. Assuming for the moment that K.'s consciousness does not coincide with that of the narrator in the first sentence, the protagonist first hears of his arrest from one of the "warders" who appear in his room: "You may not go out," they tell him, "you're under arrest" ("Sie dürfen nicht weggehen, Sie sind ja verhaftet").[4] Why does the warder express himself in this way, with that important little particle *ja* in the midst of his discourse? Can we

4. *TR* 5–6; *RO* 260.

read this statement as performative? Not easily. To make an arrest, one would not normally say "Sie sind *ja* verhaftet"; one would simply say "Sie sind verhaftet" or perhaps, if one wanted to be particularly clear, "Sie sind hiermit verhaftet." Of course, if an arrest has already taken place, one might say "Sie sind ja verhaftet," but as far as the reader knows, none has. Is the warder placing K. under arrest? It is not clear that he has the authority to do so, and his *ja* suggests that he does not.

Curiously enough, this *ja* makes a certain kind of sense but only in terms of the logic of the structure of the narrative, not in terms of the logic of the narrated events. The reader (though not the characters) does indeed already know about an arrest, precisely because of the narrator's prolepsis in the opening sentence. In an uncanny way, this prolepsis appears suddenly displaced from the future into the past. The story actually begins by apparently assuming an event that has "happened" only in narrative anticipation. Because the storyteller declares at the outset that his story concerns a man who is arrested, the story of the arrest proceeds in a certain sense as if that declaration were the arrest itself. One could therefore legitimately claim that the answer to the question "Who arrests K.?" is "the narrator." But of course this explanation of the warder's *ja* ought not to have any relevance to the character Joseph K. There is no reason to believe that he has heard the proleptic narration of these events. From his point of view, the warder's statement should appear outrageous.

Kafka's tale takes a remarkable turn here because K. does not press the warder on the matter. We would expect a statement of such rhetorical complexity to elicit a request for clarification. Joseph K., however, either ignores or fails to recognize the rhetoricity of the warder's remark, thereby accepting the peculiar nature of his arrest and allowing the *Prozeß* to proceed. Even when K. has another opportunity, he fails to question the status of his arrest, though he vehemently questions other matters. He is prepared to doubt the official status of the "Inspector" and "warders" because they are not in uniform, but he apparently finds nothing objectionable in the Inspector's statement, "You're under arrest, that's correct, that's all I know."[5] Here again, the form of the utterance suggests that we are to understand it as a statement of perlocutionary effect: "that's right" and "that's all I know" attest to the truth of an assertion, not to the felicitous uptake of

5. *TR* 17; *RO* 268: "Sie sind verhaftet, das ist richtig, mehr weiß ich nicht."

an illocutionary act. The Inspector is therefore evidently assuming that K. is already under arrest. But the warder of course also apparently made the same assumption, and even the narrator did so in the opening sentence. Who has arrested K.?

We can readily understand why readers of *The Trial* feel the need to suppose a degree of complicity on K.'s part in his arrest, even to speak (as I do above) of his "accepting" it. Under other circumstances, such talk of acceptance would make little sense. The following description, for example, strikes us as odd: "The officers attempted to arrest the culprit, but he refused to accept it." It is odd because we hardly expect a person being arrested to participate willingly. Such an unwillingness can have no effect on the uptake of the illocutionary act; if it did, no one would ever successfully be arrested. Obviously, then, one may not decline to be arrested. One can, however, deny the assertion that one is under arrest, and that K. does not do so, except in the most perfunctory manner, is genuinely surprising. The closest he comes to questioning the fact of his arrest comes in his sarcastic response to the Inspector's comment questioning "what sense there would be" in K.'s telephoning a lawyer: "What sense would there be in telephoning a lawyer when I'm supposed to be under arrest?"[6] The phrase "wenn ich angeblich verhaftet bin" ("when I'm supposed to be under arrest") expresses doubt about the truth of the Inspector's announcement of his arrest but thereby also assumes that it is a perlocutionary report. Its ironic point might be that, if there is no point in calling a lawyer, K. could not really be under arrest. He does not press the point but rather lets it drop with a petulant declaration that he no longer wants to call his lawyer. The reader can only find this statement perplexing. Ulrich Füllerborn in fact calls it "astounding" that K. "accepts the arrest."[7] It is so because the rhetorical nature of the discourse announcing his arrest would allow K. to reject it, to say in effect, "No, you're mistaken, no one has arrested me." Instead he replies to the warder's ambiguous "Sie sind ja verhaftet" by observing, "So it seems" ("Es sieht so aus").[8]

With these words K. produces his own rhetorical text. The statement "Es sieht so aus" can be understood either to affirm or to deny a

6. *TR* 18; *RO* 268: "Welchen Sinn es hätte, an einen Staatsanwalt zu telephonieren, wenn ich angeblich verhaftet bin?"

7. Ulrich Füllerborn, "Der Einzelne und die 'geistige Welt': Zu Kafkas Romanen," *TP,* 92.

8. *TR* 6; *RO* 260.

state of affairs and provides no clue as to the alternative intended. K. could mean, "So it seems, so it must be so," or, with equal probability, "So it seems, but in reality it is otherwise." His response leaves the reader in doubt as to whether or not K. has really "accepted" the fact of his arrest, as does his later behavior. By affirming the appearance of his arrest, he both affirms and denies its reality. He does make clear, however, that he understands the warder's remark, not as an illocutionary act of arresting, but as the description of a perlocution-ary effect. "Es sieht so aus" makes no sense as a response to a perfor-mative. From the legal standpoint, though, it makes no difference what K.'s understanding is. If the proper authority speaks the words placing him under arrest, then he is arrested, whether he under-stands it or not.

Even when circumstances appear so clearly defined that there is no question about the perlocutionary effects of an utterance, or its per-formative status, questions can be introduced by the back door. Be-cause the felicity of an illocution depends absolutely on contextual factors, and because no secure limits can be set upon the context of any discourse, speech acts are always open to radical reinterpretation. As Derrida observes in his discussion of Austin and the problematic of performatives, there can be no such thing as a completely determin-able context:

> Every sign, linguistic or non-linguistic, spoken or written (in the current sense of this opposition), in a small or large unit, can be *cited*, put between quotation marks; in so doing it can break with every given context, engendering an infinity of new contexts in a manner which is absolutely illimitable. This does not imply that the mark is valid outside of a context, but on the contrary that there are only contexts without any center or absolute anchoring.[9]

The problem of citationality brings with it the perennial question of intention: "In order for a context to be exhaustively determinable, in the sense required by Austin, conscious intention would at the very least have to be totally present and immediately transparent to itself and to others, since it is a determining center of context."[10] These two issues can be seen to come together in the following account. An employer fires one of his employees one morning in a fit of rage.

9. Jacques Derrida, "Signature, Event, Context," *Glyph* 1, 185–186.
10. Ibid., 192.

Later in the day, as the employee is clearing out his desk to leave, his superior repents and says, "Listen, when I said 'You're fired,' I didn't mean it. I was just frustrated and angry." The employer's "You're fired," cited in this new context, is clearly not an illocutionary act of firing, and indeed its citation is undertaken in order to show that, even in its former context, it was none. The employer in effect proclaims that his "real" intention, at that time clear neither to his employee nor to himself, was simply to express anger and frustration. How could an illocutionary act secure uptake in the absence of a genuine intention to perform it? But what happens the next time this employer tells someone he or she is fired? His utterance will be read as rhetorical, no doubt, because no one will be sure whether or not he means what he says.

An example of such uncertainty, combined with an ambiguity of locutionary structure, occurs in the eighth chapter of *The Trial*, in which K. performs, or at least apparently performs, a simple but important illocutionary act. He fires his lawyer. But a seemingly straightforward operation becomes immediately complex and ambiguous:

> "Did you come here this evening for some specific reason?" "Yes," said K., shading the light of the candle a little with one hand so as to see the lawyer better. "I came to tell you that I dispense with your services as from today." "Do I understand you rightly?" asked the lawyer, half propping himself up on the bed with one hand on the pillows. "I expect so," said K., sitting bolt upright as if on guard. "Well, that's a plan we can at least discuss," said the lawyer after a pause. "It's no plan, it's a fact," said K. "Maybe," said the lawyer, "but we mustn't be in too much of a hurry." He used the word "we" as if he had no intention of letting K. detach himself.[11]

A long conversation follows in which they discuss the lawyer's handling of K.'s case. Finally it becomes clear that the lawyer has no inten-

---

11. *TR* 230–231; *RO* 409: "'Sie sind heute mit einer bestimmten Absicht zu mir gekommen?' 'Ja,' sagte K. und blendete mit der Hand ein wenig die Kerze ab, um den Advokaten besser zu sehen, 'ich wollte Ihnen sagen, daß ich Ihnen mit dem heutigen Tage meine Vertretung entziehe.' 'Verstehe ich Sie recht?' fragte der Advokat, erhob sich halb im Bett und stützte sich mit einer Hand auf die Kissen. 'Ich nehme es an,' sagte K., der straff aufgerichtet, wie auf der Lauer, dasaß. 'Nun, wir können ja auch diesen Plan besprechen,' sagte der Advokat nach einem Weilchen. 'Es ist kein Plan mehr,' sagte K. 'Mag sein,' sagte der Advokat, 'wir wollen aber trotzdem nichts übereilen.' Er gebrauchte das Wort 'wir,' als habe er nicht die Absicht, K. freizulassen."

tion of changing his strategy, which he is certain is the best, no matter
how impatient K. becomes. The lawyer suggests that K. sit by and
observe his conference with another accused, the tradesman Block:
"'With pleasure,' said K. . . . ; he was always ready to learn. As a
precaution, however, he asked once more: 'You realize that I am
dispensing with your services?' 'Yes,' said the lawyer, 'but you may
change your mind about it yet.'"[12] In spite of K.'s apparent resolve in
the matter, it is actually not clear whether or not he has dismissed the
lawyer. Neither we nor the lawyer himself has any way of knowing
whether K., in saying "daß ich Ihnen mit dem heutigen Tage meine
Vertretung entziehe," is performing (or trying to perform) the act of
firing him or whether he is merely describing a performative act he
intends. In English, we distinguish between an act completed in the
present moment ("I dispense with your services") and an act in progress ("I am dispensing"), whereas the German present tense admits of
no such distinction. K. could mean, "I wanted to tell you that I am
dispensing with your services (but I'm not sure I'll really do it)." The
same distinction can be made between "I wanted to tell you that I am
firing you (so that maybe you can talk me out of it)" and "I wanted to
tell you that you're fired (here and now)." An illocutionary act takes
place in the second statement but not in the first. Because we could
correctly understand K.'s sentence in either of these ways, its performative status becomes undecidable.

This is an excellent example of the problematic of citationality. K.'s
use of the introductory phrase "I wanted to tell you that" places the
rest of his sentence in unseen quotation marks. K. does not so much
say "I dispense with your services" as *quote himself* saying it, perhaps
now or perhaps sometime in the future. We are therefore not able to
make any certain judgment as to the statement's proper context. If
the proper context is the present moment, then we might safely assume that K. is performing an illocutionary act of firing. But if the
cited discourse actually belongs to a context yet to come, a context
with characteristics not yet specified, it cannot be understood as a
performative in the here and now. By citing his speech instead of
speaking it straight out, K. opens up endless possibilities for recontex-
tualization.

12. *TR* 336; *RO* 413: "'Gerne,' sagte K. . . . ; zu lernen war er immer bereit. Um
sich aber für jeden Fall zu sichern, fragte er noch: 'Sie haben aber zur Kenntnis
genommen, daß ich Ihnen meine Vertretung entziehe?' 'Ja,' sagte der Advokat,
'Sie können es aber heute noch rückgängig machen.'"

Kafka has introduced a further complication into this already complicated matter. Because the lawyer understands K. to be in a position to cancel or revoke ("rückgängig machen") his dismissal (assuming for the moment it really was a dismissal), and because it is by no means clear what action, if any, K. would have to take in order to effect such a cancellation, the status of the dismissal becomes even more uncertain. It is not simply that K. seems to want the lawyer to agree to the dismissal (as K. in a sense "agrees" to his arrest); it is rather that the lawyer understands the uptake of certain illocutionary acts to be conditional on the seriousness, over some period of time, of the speaker's intention. The example of the angry employer cited above demonstrates the possibility of cancellation to which a performative is subject when the speaker's intention is unclear or subject to vacillation. Another example appears in Kafka's own writing. Near the close of chapter 14 of *The Castle* (*Das Schloß*), Landsurveyor K. finds himself in a somewhat distracted state as he tries to disengage himself from the company of the sisters Olga and Amalia:

> A little relieved, K. spoke of Frieda . . . and in the haste of his narrative—for he wanted to go home at once—so far forgot himself when bidding them good-bye as to invite the sisters to pay him a call. He began to stammer in confusion, however, when Amalia, giving him no time to say another word, interposed with an acceptance of the invitation; then Olga was compelled to associate herself with it.[13]

Because the narrator tells us that K. "forgot himself," we know that he is not fully present to himself when he makes the invitation. Although he says it, he does not mean it. Still, both sisters accept the unintended invitation before he has a chance to correct himself. Even this acceptance, however, does not represent, much less guarantee, the felicitous uptake of K.'s inadvertent performance:

> But K., still harassed by the feeling that he ought to go at once, and becoming uneasy under Amalia's gaze, did not hesitate any longer to confess that the invitation had been quite unpremeditated and had

13. *CA* 221; *RO* 630–631: "Ein wenig gereizt dadurch, erzählte K. ausführlicher, als er sonst getan hätte, von Frieda . . . und vergaß sich in der Eile des Erzählens—er wollte ja gleich nach Hause gehen—derart, daß er in der Form eines Abschieds die Schwestern einlud, ihn einmal zu besuchen. Jetzt allerdings erschrak er und stockte, während Amalia sofort, ohne ihm noch zu einem Worte Zeit zu lassen, die Einladung anzunehmen erklärte; nun mußte sich auch Olga anschließen und tat es."

sprung merely from a personal impulse, but that unfortunately he could not confirm it, as there was a great hostility, to him quite incomprehensible, between Frieda and their family.[14]

Undeterred by the sisters' taking his words at face value, K. voids his apparent illocutionary act by refusing to confirm it (*aufrechterhalten*). This course of action is precisely analogous to the lawyer's apparent expectations from Joseph K.; that is, when it comes down to cases, the lawyer believes, K. will refuse to "maintain" or "preserve" the apparent intention of his discourse. Simple failure to preserve an intention is sufficient to retract an illocutionary force. Amalia plays this same game upon K. after his confession: "And now go away, go to your young woman, I can see you're in a hurry. You needn't be afraid that we'll come, I only said it at first for fun, out of mischief."[15] She thus claims that her act of acceptance was no more a genuine performative than K.'s act of invitation.

An important implication of these interchanges is that performance of a speech act can take place only when the speaker "preserves and maintains" (*aufrechterhalten*) his or her intention over a considerable period of time. Failure to do so cancels the illocutionary act. It is useful to note in this connection that an employer does not need to perform an additional speech act to cancel the apparent act of dismissal effectively. He may simply fail to follow up on the implications of his utterance—fail to stop paying salary, fail to speak of the matter again, and so forth. K.'s illocutionary act of dismissing the lawyer can therefore be valid only if K. follows up on its implications; if he does not, and the lawyer evidently thinks he will not, he will have in effect "revoked" it. Until it becomes clear whether or not such a revocation is to take place, the act of firing the lawyer remains in the same problematic rhetorical space as utterances like "Sie sind ja verhaftet."

The question of whether a character has been fired or not plays an

14. *CA* 221; *RO* 631: "K. aber, immerfort von Gedanken an die Notwendigkeit eiligen Abschieds bedrängt, und sich unruhig fühlend unter Amalias Blick, zögerte nicht, ohne weitere Verbrämung einzugestehen, daß die Einladung gänzlich unüberlegt und nur von seinem persönlichen Gefühl eingegeben gewesen sei, daß er sie aber leider nicht aufrechterhalten könne, da eine große, ihm allerdings ganz unverständliche Feindshaft zwischen Frieda und dem Barnabasschen Hause bestehe."

15. *CA* 221; *RO* 631: "Und nun geh, geh zu deiner Braut, ich sehe, wie du eilst. Fürchte auch nicht, daß wir kommen, ich sagte es gleich anfangs nur im Scherz, aus Bosheit."

important role in another of Kafka's fictions, his first effort at a novel, *The Missing Person* (*Der Verschollene*, published by Max Brod as *Amerika*). Karl Rossmann's traveling companion Robinson appears at the Hotel Occidental, where Karl is employed as an elevator operator, and interferes with Karl's work. While dealing with Robinson, Karl leaves his elevator for a time without asking anyone's permission, an infraction of the hotel's work rules. When his delinquency is discovered, Karl is warned by the Head Waiter that the consequences are severe: "You were absent from duty without leave. Do you know what that means? It means dismissal."[16] The Porter, who witnesses the Head Waiter's warning, assumes the worst: he hopes, he says, that Karl will act more respectfully toward porters in his "next job." This mention of a next job brings home to the boy the seriousness of the situation:

> Karl understood now that he had really lost his post, for the Head Waiter had already told him so and here was the Head Porter repeating it as an accomplished fact, and in the case of a lift-boy there was probably no need for the hotel management to confirm a dismissal. Yet it had happened with a rapidity he had not expected, for after all he had worked here for two months as well as he could, and certainly better than many of the other boys. But obviously such considerations were taken into account at the decisive moment in no part of the world, neither in Europe, nor in America; the verdict was determined by the first words that happened to fall from the judge's lips in an impulse of fury.[17]

But it is not exactly true that the Head Waiter had "already declared" the boy to be fired, although Karl is right enough in assuming that his fate is sealed. We can observe, however, how he weighs in his mind the question of the uptake of the Head Waiter's implied illocutionary

16. *AM* 173; *RO* 139: "Du hast deinen Posten ohne Erlaubnis verlassen. Weißt du, was das bedeutet? Das bedeutet Entlassung."

17. *AM* 176–177; *RO* 141: "Karl sah ein, daß er eigentlich seinen Posten schon verloren hatte, denn der Oberkellner hatte es bereits ausgesprochen, der Oberportier als fertige Tatsache wiederholt, und wegen eines Liftjungen dürfte die Bestätigung der Entlassung seitens der Hoteldirektion nicht nötig sein. Es war allerdings schneller gegangen, als er gedacht hatte, denn schließlich hatte er doch zwei Monate gedient, so gut er konnte, und gewiß besser als mancher andere Junge. Aber auf solche Dinge wird eben im entscheidenden Augenblick offenbar in keinem Weltteil, weder in Europa noch in Amerika, Rücksicht genommen, sondern es wird so entschieden, wie einem in der ersten Wut das Urteil aus dem Munde fährt."

act. Would he be considered actually and finally fired without the approval of the hotel management? Probably so, because Karl's position had been so menial. Would mitigating circumstances, such as his previous good service, be taken into account? Probably not; matters all over the world seem to be decided firmly and forever, in the very moment a "judgment" (or "sentence"—*Urteil*) escapes one's lips. The formal notice of his firing would have to be expected now as a certainty.

The formal notice comes soon enough. The Head Waiter does indeed perform the illocutionary act of firing Karl a bit later, though he does so in an almost offhand manner: "Well, Rossmann, . . . you are dismissed here and now."[18] The Waiter then tells him to take off his uniform, turn it in, and leave the hotel at once. In the course of trying to comply with these instructions, however, Karl finds himself thwarted by several circumstances. At one point he encounters again the Head Porter, who actually prevents Karl from leaving the hotel:

> "No, no, this way in," said the Head Porter, turning him round again.
> "But I've been thrown out," said Karl, meaning that nobody in the hotel had a right to give him orders now.
> "As long as I keep hold of you, you're not thrown out," said the porter, which was also true enough.[19]

Although this exchange might seem to reopen the question of whether or not Karl has been fired (*entlassen*), Karl does not take it so and with good reason. The Porter does not mean to deny that Karl has been fired by saying "you're not thrown out." The verb *entlassen* can mean "to set free" as well as "to fire," and the Porter only means to tell Karl that, as long as he is physically held in the Porter's grasp, he has not been set free.

But the porter's casual wordplay makes it possible to rethink the entire process of Karl's Entlassung. To what degree is the issue being set free from something awful rather than being dismissed from something desirable? Although Karl does not regard his leaving the hotel in this way, he very well might, especially if he were to take

18. *AM* 193–194; *RO* 156: "Also, Roßmann, . . . Sie sind auf der Stelle entlassen."

19. *AM* 195; *RO* 157. "'Nein, nein, hier geht man hinein,' sagte der Oberportier und drehte Karl um. 'Ich bin doch schon entlassen,' sagte Karl und meinte damit, daß ihm im Hotel niemand mehr zu befehlen habe. 'Solange ich dich halte, bist du nicht entlassen,' sagte der Oberportier, was allerdings auch richtig war."

seriously his own thoughts on the interpretation of all words: "He knew that all he could say would appear quite different to the others, and that whether a good or bad construction was to be put on his actions depended alone on the spirit in which he was judged."[20] At this point, Karl sees only how acts of interpretation could work to his disadvantage. The exchange with the Porter, however, hints at the possibility that a recuperative act of interpretation could transform his dismissal into his liberation. The rhetoricity of Entlassung allows it to be read either way.

It is perfectly correct, then, to regard Karl's "dismissal" as rhetorical though not quite in the same way that Joseph K.'s arrest is rhetorical. The uncertainty in this case does not concern whether or not an illocutionary act has taken place: there is no doubt that the Head Waiter performs an act of Entlassung. The uncertainty relates to the act's moral value. We cannot be sure whether Karl is being thrown out of a good situation or is being released from a bad one. The story, as it develops, seems to play out both versions. At first there is little doubt that the action is a dismissal and that Karl is losing something valuable. Karl tries very hard to keep his position by defending his actions to the Head Waiter and the Mangeress. When it is clear that the outcome will be his dismissal, he cannot imagine construing it as anything but a disaster. When Therese suggests to him that "everything has turned out well" for him, he is baffled:

> "Oh yes," said Karl, and he smiled at her, yet could not see why he should be glad because he had been dismissed as a thief. Therese's eyes shone with the purest joy, as if it were a matter of complete indifference to her whether Karl had committed a crime or not, whether he had been justly sentenced or not, if he were only permitted to escape, in shame or in honor.[21]

After he runs into the Porter and is detained, however, the issue of liberation becomes more and more prominent. The Porter seems

20. *AM* 188–189; *RO* 151: "Er wußte, daß alles, was er sagen konnte, hinterher ganz anders aussehen würde, als es gemeint war, und daß es nur der Art der Beurteilung überlassen bleibe, Gutes oder Böses vorzufinden."

21. *AM* 192–193; *RO* 155: "'O ja,' sagte Karl und lächelte ihr zu, wußte aber nicht, warum er darüber froh sein sollte, daß man ihn als einen Dieb wegschickte. Aus Theresens Augen strahlte die reinste Freude, als sei es ihr ganz gleichgültig, ob Karl etwas verbrochen hatte oder nicht, ob er gerecht beurteilt worden war oder nicht, wenn man ihn nur gerade entwischen ließ, in Schande oder in Ehren."

determined to prevent Karl from leaving, as if being kept in the hotel were a greater punishment than being sent away. "I myself have an obligation," he tells Karl, "to the hotel management to let no one out of the hotel who is in the slightest degree suspicious. And you are just the person who strikes my fancy as being a highly suspicious character."[22] Finally, while the Porter is searching the pockets of his coat, Karl slips out of the coat and manages to escape, in spite of the fact that the doorway is so full of hotel staff "that one might almost have thought that they wanted unobtrusively to make it impossible for anyone to get out."[23] His ultimate departure, then, is actually presented as a liberation. The Entlassung that at first seemed—and indeed was—a dismissal from pleasant security is transformed by a changed context into an escape from constricting confinement.

Because all rhetoric, including speech acts, is very sensitive to every element in the context, it should not be surprising that the performative status of an utterance can hinge upon tiny differences in that context. Performative status often depends, for example, on characteristics of the speaker that can be hard to determine, such as the state of the speaker's mind (because intention is so important), the speaker's social status, and the legitimacy of any claim to authority implied by the speech act. Without the authority to fire, the Head Waiter could not have dismissed Karl by uttering the phrase "Sie sind auf der Stelle entlassen"; the phrase would have had no illocutionary force whatever. But what is the illocutionary force of the Head Porter's telling Karl that he is *not* entlassen? Does this remark countermand the Head Waiter's action in any way, or is it just a malicious joke? It appears to be the latter, but can one be absolutely sure?

Rhetorical utterances whose performative status is undecidable have an important place in Kafka's fiction, and nowhere more prominently than in the narratives involving legal or quasilegal issues. In *The Trial*, K. discovers that the acquittal (*Freisprechung*) he is seeking from the court can be obtained but only in rhetorical form. The painter Titorelli explains that, through his connections, he could help

---

22. *AM* 200–201; *RO* 161: "Gegenüber diesen großen Ehren habe ich natürlich andererseits vor der Hoteldirektion die Verpflichtung, niemanden hinauszulassen, der nur im geringsten verdächtig ist. Gerade du aber kommst mir, weil es mir so beliebt, sogar stark verdächtig vor."

23. *AM* 203; *RO* 164: "Hotelangestellte gingen zwar im Torgang in solcher Anzahl kreuz und quer, daß man fast daran denken konnte, sie wollten in unauffälliger Weise den Ausgang unmöglich machen."

K. persuade various judges to subscribe to an affidavit attesting to K.'s innocence; the painter would then present the document to the judge conducting K.'s trial. Titorelli tells K.:

> "The judge is covered by the guarantee of the other judges subscribing to the affidavit, and so he can grant acquittal with an easy mind, and though some formalities will remain to be settled, he will undoubtedly grant the acquittal to please me and his other friends. Then you can walk out of the court a free man." "So then I'm free," said K., doubtfully. "Yes," said the painter, "but only ostensibly free, or more exactly, provisionally free. For the judges of the lowest grade, to whom my acquaintances belong, haven't the power to grant a final acquittal, that power is reserved for the highest Court of all, which is quite inaccessible to you, to me, and to all of us."[24]

The acquittal offered K., then, will not be final and certain (*endgültig*) but merely ostensible (*scheinbar*). The charge, under such circumstances, "is lifted from your shoulders for the time being, but it continues to hover above you and can, as soon as an order comes from on high, be laid upon you again."[25] Such an illocutionary act of "acquitting" has the same status as the act of "arresting" that opens the novel. "Scheinbare Freisprechung" is the appropriate counterpart of "scheinbare Verhaftung": "Sie sind ja verhaftet." "Es sieht so aus."

The rhetoricity of so much of the crucial legal discourse that is uttered or cited in *The Trial* generates a gap in which the story operates. The original impetus for the plot, its initial rhetorical moment, is a piece of discourse and its interpretation—K.'s "arrest" and his attitude toward it—the peculiar performative status of which generates a set of profound uncertainties. Quite analogous uncertainties continue to be generated thoughout the novel. Because this narration describes

24. *TR* 197; *RO* 386–387: "'Der Richter besitzt in der Bestätigung die Bürgschaft einer Anzahl von Richtern, kann Sie unbesorgt freisprechen und wird es, allerdings nach Durchführung verschiedener Formalitäten, mir und anderen Bekannten zu Gefallen zweifellos tun. Sie aber treten aus dem Gericht und sind frei.' 'Dann bin ich also frei,' sagte K. zögernd. 'Ja,' sagte der Maler, 'aber nur scheinbar frei oder, besser ausgedrückt, zeitweilig frei. Die untersten Richter nämlich, zu denen meine Bekannten gehören, haben nicht das Recht, endgültig freizusprechen, dieses Recht hat nur das oberste, für Sie, für mich und für uns alle ganz unerreichbare Gericht.'"

25. *TR* 197; *RO* 387: "Das heißt, wenn Sie auf diese Weise freigesprochen werden, sind Sie für den Augenblick der Anklage entzogen, aber sie schwebt auch weiterhin über Ihnen und kann, sobald nur der höhere Befehl kommt, sofort in Wirkung treten."

a legal proceeding—though a very peculiar one—the story continues
to turn upon performative utterances. Kafka the fiction writer exploits the experience of Kafka the attorney to make a story from the
possibility for conflicting readings inherent in rhetorical discourse.
The parable "Before the Law" ("Vor dem Gesetz"), the only piece of
this long fragment that Kafka deemed worthy of publication, emphasizes exactly this problem and can therefore properly be seen as a
kind of emblem for the novel as a whole. The discussion that follows
the chaplain's recitation of the parable leads to no interpretive certainty; on the contrary, it demonstrates with convincing thoroughness
the endless readability of such a text. Parables as a genre are rhetorical texts, as I will show in detail in Chapter 7. The story of *The Trial* is
like the dialogue between the chaplain and K., for it is generated from
an attempt to read rhetorical language. The story of Joseph K. exists
precisely in the space between conflicting readings of the same text,
between being arrested and not arrested, acquitted and not acquitted,
firing and not firing his lawyer, and so on. If ostensibly performative
utterances could be reliably understood, if we could always tell exactly
what their perlocutionary effects were, there could be no story like
The Trial.

There could be no story like *The Castle*, either. A legal or quasi-legal
issue stands at the heart of this narrative as well. In his lengthy quest
Landsurveyor K. seeks *Aufnahme*, admission to the Castle village and
the official Castle service. And here, as in Joseph K.'s arrest, the
illocutionary act that ought unambiguously to perform the legal
deed—accept the Landsurveyor—is presented in a rhetorical form.
The crucial statement comes in a letter from the official Klamm to the
newly arrived Landsurveyor. It begins: "My dear Sir, As you know,
you have been engaged for the Count's service."[26] The letter might be
understood as an illocutionary act of accepting K., but it might not. If
it had said, "You are hereby accepted" ("Sie sind hiermit aufgenommen"), there would have been no question. The locutionary form
presented in the novel, though, seems rather to report a perlocutionary effect of some earlier utterance that should have brought about
K.'s acceptance. It does not, however, clearly acknowledge a previous
official act, as it would if it said, "You are, as I told you" or "This is to
confirm that you are." It reports K.'s admission as something that he
already knows. But who admitted him?

26. *CA* 30; *RO* 500: "Sehr geehrter Herr! Sie sind, wie Sie wissen, in die herr-
schaftlichen Dienste aufgenommen."

K. reads the letter carefully, but because it is a letter and not a person, he cannot interrogate it to clarify its "contradictions" and ambiguities. Particularly struck by the phrase "wie Sie wissen," he ponders the relation between his admission and his personal efforts:

> Nor did the letter pass over the fact that if it should come to a struggle, K. had had the hardihood to make the first advances; it was very subtly indicated and only to be sensed by an uneasy conscience—an uneasy conscience, not a bad one. It lay in the three words "as you know," referring to his engagement in the Count's service. K. had reported his arrival, and only after that, as the letter pointed out, had he known that he was engaged.[27]

K.'s "uneasy conscience" prompts him to suspect that the letter is neither a document of admission nor an acknowledgment of any earlier admission but simply a delicate statement that K., by his act of reporting, had in effect admitted himself. It is by no means certain that Klamm would agree that the Castle had admitted K., by this letter or by any other act. The implication is that this act of admission needed Landsurveyor K.'s complicity as much as the arrest in *The Trial* needed Joseph K.'s. What is given by the phrase "you are . . . engaged" is taken away, in a very real sense, by the phrase "as you know," and the sentence as a whole becomes difficult, disquietingly complex—rhetorical.

Klamm's letter to K. is by no means his only rhetorical discourse in the novel. He and the other Castle officials are understood by the villagers as engaging regularly in this sort of thing. Take for example the landlady's account of the relationship Frieda once had with Klamm:

> It was Frieda's great distinction, a distinction I'll be proud of to my dying day, that he used at least to call out her name, and that she could speak to him whenever she liked and was permitted the freedom of the peephole, but even to her he never talked. And the fact that he called her name didn't mean necessarily what one might think, he simply mentioned the name Frieda—who can tell what he was thinking of? And that Frieda naturally came to him at once was her affair, and that

---

27. *CA* 33; *RO* 502: "Der Brief verschwieg ja auch nicht, daß K., wenn es zu Kämpfen kommen sollte, die Verwegenheit gehabt hatte, zu beginnen; es war mit Feinheit gesagt, und nur ein unruhiges Gewissen—ein unruhiges, kein schlechtes— konnte es merken, es waren die drei Worte 'wie Sie wissen' hinsichtlich seiner Aufnahme in den Dienst. K. hatte sich gemeldet, und seither wußte er, wie sich der Brief ausdrückte, daß er aufgenommen war."

she was admitted without let or hindrance was an act of grace on Klamm's part, but that he deliberately summoned her is more than one can maintain.[28]

The question of what Klamm was doing when he called out the name "Frieda" cannot, according to the landlady, be settled in the conventional manner. Ordinarily we assume that calling someone's name is the performance of an illocutionary act of summoning. We do not normally have to use an explicit performative such as "I hereby summon Frieda." The name alone is sufficient when it is called out. But is the utterance of a name always such an act of summoning? Not necessarily; one might just like the sound of the name and enjoy "mentioning" (in other words, citing) it as a form of recreation. In Kafka's original German, the landlady distinguishes between "Frieda rufen" and "den Namen 'Frieda' rufen," that is, between calling Frieda the person and calling out the name "Frieda." That the translator construes this as a distinction between "summoning" and "mentioning" is both appropriate and telling because it points up the crucial issue of the presence or absence of an intention to perform an illocutionary act. The landlady is careful to explain that the perlocutionary effect (Frieda's going to Klamm) is the same in both cases and cannot be understood as evidence regarding Klamm's intention. That intention is in fact absolutely unavailable for inspection, and the locutionary form of his utterance—the name Frieda and nothing more—provides insufficient grounds for reaching a decision. It is therefore impossible to tell whether he summoned Frieda, just as it is impossible to tell whether he accepted K.

The rhetoricity of Landsurveyor K.'s acceptance, like that of Joseph K.'s arrest, defines a gap that becomes the fictional space wherein both novels move. One character seeks to avoid and the other to embrace the consequences of illocutionary acts that have and have not

---

28. *CA* 64; *RO* 523–524: "Es war ja die große Auszeichnung Friedas, eine Auszeichnung, die mein Stolz sein wird bis an mein Ende, daß er wenigstens Friedas Namen zu rufen pflegte und daß sie zu ihm sprechen konnte nach Belieben und die Erlaubnis des Gucklochs bekam, gesprochen aber hat er auch mit ihr nicht. Und daß er Frieda manchmal rief, muß gar nicht die Bedeutung haben, die man dem gerne zusprechen möchte, er rief einfach den Namen 'Frieda'—wer kennt seine Absichten?—, daß Frieda natürlich eilends kam, war ihre Sache, und daß sie ohne Widerspruch zu ihm gelassen wurde, war Klamms Güte, aber daß er sie geradezu gerufen hätte, kann man nicht behaupten."

taken place. The space of these fictions is a place neither here nor there, an in-between world in which the protagonists seek to clarify the problem of the existential status (arrested or not arrested, that is, guilty or innocent; admitted or not admitted, that is, belonging or not belonging). It is not a "mere" rhetorical problem because the utterances involved are speech acts: they do things in the world or are supposed to do things. Whether one is arrested or not, admitted or not, is surely an issue arising out of language, but the anxiety produced thereby in Kafka's characters is by no means directed toward the linguistic issue. These characters are properly concerned about their place in the world. It is—or can quickly become—a matter of life and death.

Once again the courtroom provides perhaps the clearest example of the potentially deadly effects of language. Judges regularly engage in speech acts that can mean life or death for a convicted criminal: they sentence such criminals to prison and sometimes to death. Although the act of sentencing to death does not kill (it does exactly what it says: it "sentences"), it often enough has the perlocutionary effect of causing someone to be killed. If the authority or correctness of any part of the procedure leading to such an act of sentencing is legally questionable, however, the judge's illocutionary act may fail to secure uptake. In the United States, only the definitive failure of the appeals process at some high level of the judiciary can absolutely confirm such illocutionary acts and let them have their expected perlocutionary effects. Even then, though, even when there is no question that a genuine act of sentencing to death has duly taken place, something may intervene—a pardon from the governor, for example—to prevent actual execution. In other words, an illocutionary act of sentencing to death may secure uptake and yet fail to have the perlocutionary effect of causing death. To our sorrow, we can also think of examples in which no genuine illocutionary act of sentencing takes place but an execution happens anyway.

Kafka explored such performative ambiguity in his first major published work, "The Judgment" ("Das Urteil"). A crucial issue in this story is the performative status of an apparent act of sentencing to death. After a heated discussion between the protagonist, Georg Bendemann, and his father about whether to tell Georg's friend in Russia about his engagement, the father makes a remarkable announcement: "So now you know what else there was in the world besides yourself, till now you've known only about yourself. An innocent child, yes, that you were, truly, but still more truly have you been a devilish human being!—And therefore take note: I sentence you now to death by drowning."[29] Georg's response is as remarkable as the father's discourse: he runs from the house, feeling himself "driven" (*gejagt*) to the bridge, from which he drops quietly into the water to drown.

Although the father's words of "sentencing" seem to lead directly to Georg's self-execution, we still cannot say for certain that a genuine illocutionary act of sentencing to death has taken place. As we know, genuine acts of sentencing to death do ordinarily, but not always, lead to the death of the person so sentenced as an expectable perlocutionary effect. The father's words have also had such an effect on Georg. But this effect, we must realize, does nothing to affect the illocutionary force of the father's utterance; perlocutionary effects serve to define perlocutions, not illocutions. The father's "sentence" has been effective as a perlocutionary act, but was it also an illocutionary one? Did the father really do something *in* his saying "I sentence you"? Georg's suicide, his apparent acceptance of his father's authority, cannot help us decide the question except perhaps by reminding us that only rhetorical illocutions require the complicity of the addressee.

Given the context of the story—central Europe in the early twentieth century, the home of a well-to-do family—we cannot suppose a social order in which fathers have the sanctioned authority over members of their families to pass judgments of life and death. On the contrary, the setting directly and unmistakably implies that Georg, unlike the son of an ancient Roman paterfamilias, would have the legal and social right to ignore such talk of "sentencing" as delusionary rubbish. He does not do so, however, and not only because he "accepts" the sentence. Georg does not willingly cooperate; something compels him to do so. As soon as the father utters the sentence, Georg "felt himself driven out of the room" and "driven to the water."[30] It is as if the father indeed had authority, not just over Georg but also over the forces that control Georg's behavior. That these forces reside within Georg himself does not make the compulsion any less real.

The father's sentence must be understood as rhetorical, then, be-

---

29. *CS* 87; *SE* 32: "Jetzt weißt du also, was es noch außer dir gab, bisher wußtest du nur von dir! Ein unschuldiges Kind warst du ja eigentlich, aber noch eigentlicher warst du ein teuflischer Mensch!—Und darum wisse: Ich verurteile dich jetzt zum Tode des Ertrinkens!"

30. *CS* 87–88; *SE* 32: "Georg fühlte sich aus dem Zimmer gejagt . . . zum Wasser trieb es ihn."

cause the status of its speaker firmly contradicts its performative status. Its rhetoricity is effectively doubled by the rhetorical origin of its existence in the narrative. As Stanley Corngold has observed the father's act of sentencing (*verurteilen*) represents a rhetorical transformation of the judgment (*Urteil*) Georg sought from his father about informing his friend in Russia about the engagement.[31] Surprising as it is, the father's act of sentencing does not come out of nowhere: it comes from a radical rereading of the meaning of the word *Urteil* and thus from Georg himself. Georg has in a sense given the father the authority to deliver verdicts and sentences (*Urteile*) by virtue of his initial request. But of course he has only done so rhetorically. This rhetoricity, however, does not prevent the sentence from having precisely those perlocutionary effects we would expect of a genuine, unambiguous act of sentencing. The utterance carries authority, even if the speaker does not. Georg is executed, even though no one has "really" sentenced him, just as the Cyclops is blinded, even though "Noman" drove a stake through his eye. "Noman" arrested K., and yet he is arrested. Rhetorical antecedents have real consequences. Kafka's rhetorical moment initiates an action with no definable origin, no *arche*, even though it may have a definite (and horrifying) *telos*. It arises from a void, a rhetorical atopia, but then follows a path of genuine pain through a depressingly real universe.

Kafka became something of a specialist in showing how painful human situations could arise from rhetorical moments. Although at times he could spin a lengthy narrative such as *The Trial* or *The Castle* from a rhetorical aporia or set thereof, he could also content himself with the rhetorical moment itself. The little story "Give It Up!" which I have already discussed in detail in the opening chapter, centers our attention on a moment of reading in which it is impossible to decide what sort of illocutionary act is taking place. The policeman's reply to the man who has lost his way presupposes a request of the form "Please tell me the way," a phrase that is readily understood as a figurative request for philosophical or theological enlightenment. But if the man used these same words in an attempt to get directions to the station, his request would be uselessly vague, the functional equivalent of "I hereby promise you something." Were such illocutions to exist—as the story indirectly assumes they do—they would have to be

31. Stanley Corngold, "Kafka's 'The Judgment' and Modern Rhetorical Theory," *NKSA* 7 (June 1983), 15–21.

considered paradigmatic cases of rhetoricity. Promising "something"
would be an act simultaneously affirming and denying its illocutionary mode, affirming it by saying "I promise" and denying it by declin-
ing to say just what is promised. The contradiction thereby arising is
the very thing that makes "Give It Up!" able to catch and hold our
attention, as so many of Kafka's intriguing stories do.

Such a contradiction would surely also arise in a society governed
by injunctions of the form "You are hereby commanded to—something." Although such a locutionary form is not possible, we have seen
in "Give It Up!" that reports of illocutions can readily be construed to
presuppose such indefinite illocutions. Although a speaker would ordinarily use the statement "He promised her something" to report the
promise of something real and specific, the structure of the language
(German or English) does not prevent the hearer from imagining that
the report refers back to an utterance of the form "I hereby promise
you something." That indeed is what the policeman apparently imagined in "Give It Up!" Other statements can produce the same effect in
less direct ways. Someone might say, "You know, there's a law governing the use of pesticides." Such a statement is the equivalent of reporting an illocutionary act of commanding by the authorities: in other
words, "You are commanded something about pesticides." The listener can only respond to such news with anxiety and bewilderment,
and unless someone explains just what this law says, that anxiety will
grow.

Kafka's story "The Problem of Our Laws" ("Zur Frage der Gesetze")
describes precisely this situation. "Our laws are not generally known,"
it begins; "they are kept secret by the small group of nobles who rule
us."[32] Actually, as the narrator notes later, the situation may be even
more problematic: "The very existence of these laws, however, is at
most a matter of presumption. There is a tradition that they exist and
that they are a mystery confided to the nobility, but it is not and
cannot be more than a mere tradition sanctioned by age, for the
essence of a secret code is that it should remain a mystery."[33] If one

---

32. *CS* 437; *SE* 314: "Unsere Gesetze sind nicht allgemein bekannt, sie sind
Geheimnis der kleinen Adelsgruppe, welche uns beherrscht."
33. *CS* 437; *SE* 314: "Übrigens können auch diese Scheingesetze eigentlich nur
vermutet werden. Es ist eine Tradition, daß sie bestehen und dem Adel als
Geheimnis anvertraut sind, aber mehr als alte und durch ihr Alter glaubwürdige
Tradition ist es nicht und kann es nicht sein, denn der Charakter dieser Gesetze
verlangt auch das Geheimhalten ihres Bestandes."

could be certain of the content of the laws—know, that is, just what is "commanded"—there would be no problem; if, on the other hand, one could be certain that no laws exist, that no illocutionary act of commanding ever took place, there would be no problem either. In Kafka's story, however, the people can be certain of neither:

> Some of us among the people have attentively scrutinized the doings of the nobility since the earliest times and possess records made by our forefathers—records which we have conscientiously continued—and claim to recognize amid the countless number of facts certain main tendencies which permit of this or that historical formulation; but when in accordance with these scrupulously tested and logically ordered conclusions we seek to adjust ourselves somewhat for the present or future, everything becomes uncertain, and our work seems only an intellectual game, for perhaps these laws we are trying to unravel do not exist at all. There is a small party who are actually of this opinion and who try to show that, if any law exists, it can only be this: The Law is whatever the nobles do. . . . Actually one can express the problem only in a sort of paradox [*Widerspruch*]: Any party that would repudiate not only all belief in the laws, but the nobility as well, would have the whole people behind it; yet no such party can come into existence, for nobody would dare to repudiate the nobility. We live on this razor's edge. A writer once summed the matter up this way: The sole visible and indubitable law that is imposed on us is the nobility, and must we ourselves deprive ourselves of that one law?[34]

The law of the nobility means nothing more or less than a law of the form "You are hereby commanded to something," a law that the

---

34. *CS* 437–438; *SE* 314–315: "Wenn wir im Volk aber seit ältesten Zeiten die Handlungen des Adels aufmerksam verfolgen, Aufschreibungen unserer Voreltern darüber besitzen, sie gewissenhaft fortgesetzt haben und in den zahllosen Tatsachen gewisse Richtlinien zu erkennen glauben, die auf diese oder jene geschichtliche Bestimmung schließen lassen, und wenn wir nach diesen sorgfältig gesiebten und geordneten Schlußfolgerungen uns für die Gegenwart und Zukunft ein wenig einzurichten suchen—so ist alles unsicher und vielleicht nur ein Spiel des Verstandes, denn vielleicht bestehen diese Gesetze, die wir hier zu erraten suchen, überhaupt nicht. Es gibt eine kleine Partei, die wirklich dieser Meinung ist und die nachzuweisen sucht, daß, wenn ein Gesetz besteht, es nur lauten kann: Was der Adel tut, ist Gesetz. . . . Man kann es eigentlich nur in einer Art Widerspruch ausdrücken: Eine Partei, die neben dem Glauben an die Gesetze auch den Adel verwerfen würde, hätte sofort das ganze Volk hinter sich, aber eine solche Partei kann nicht entstehen, weil den Adel niemand zu verwerfen wagt. Auf dieses Messers Schneide leben wir. Ein Schriftsteller hat das einmal so zusammengefaßt: Das einzige, sichtbare, zweifellose Gesetz, das uns auferlegt ist, ist der Adel, und um dieses einzige Gesetz sollten wir uns selbst bringen wollen?"

people find it difficult to live with but impossible to live without. The only law available to them is a rhetorical law that bewilders and disquiets them, but they prefer a rhetorical law to none at all. They live in the gap (or on the razor's edge) created by this contradiction.

The rhetoricity of such reported (and thus implied) illocutions as "Please tell me the way" and "You are hereby commanded to something" is the result of vagueness, of the absence of information required by the illocutionary intention. The utterance thereby denies itself and paralyzes its addressee in a state of anxiety and uncertainty. The logical extreme of such a rhetoricity would be an illocution with no locutionary form at all, one not even specifying the illocutionary mode itself (commanding, asking, and so forth). Kafka articulates this seemingly impossible construction in one of his most poignant parables, "An Imperial Message" ("Eine kaiserliche Botschaft"):

> The Emperor, so it runs, has sent a message to you . . . ; the Emperor from his deathbed has sent a message to you alone. He has commanded the messenger to kneel down by the bed, and has whispered the message to him . . . . The messenger immediately sets out on his journey; a powerful, an indefatigable man . . . the way is made easier for him than it would be for any other. But the multitudes are so vast; their numbers have no end. If he could reach the open fields how fast he would fly, and soon doubtless you would hear the welcome hammering of his fists on your door. But instead how vainly does he wear out his strength . . . . Nobody could fight his way through here even with a message from a dead man. But you sit at your window when evening falls and dream it to yourself.[35]

The story asserts that the message exists, that it came from the dying Emperor himself, that he intended it for you alone, and that it will never arrive. All that is left of this (reported) utterance is "I . . . you." Most of the narrative describes the messenger and the impossibility of his task. In other words, the gap between "I" and "you," a gap that has

35. CS 4–5; SE 138–139: "Der Kaiser—so heißt es—hat Dir . . . gerade Dir hat der Kaiser von seinem Sterbebett aus eine Botschaft gesendet. Den Boten hat er beim Bett niederknien lassen und ihm die Botschaft ins Ohr zugeflüstert. . . . Der Bote hat sich gleich auf den Weg gemacht; ein kräftiger, ein unermüdlicher Mann . . . er kommt auch leicht vorwärts, wie kein anderer. Aber die Menge ist so groß; ihre Wohnstätten nehmen kein Ende. Öffnete sich freies Feld, wie würde er fliegen und bald hörtest Du das herrliche Schlagen seiner Fäuste an Deiner Tür. Aber statt dessen, wie nutzlos müht er sich ab. . . . Niemand dringt hier durch und gar mit der Botschaft eines Toten.—Du aber sitzt an Deinem Fenster und erträumst sie Dir, wenn der Abend kommt."

become infinite and unbridgeable, makes up the space of the fiction, but in that gap powerful forces are ceaselessly at work. Something is happening there, even though it can never link speaker and addressee. This utterance of indeterminate locutionary form and uncertain illocutionary status has significant perlocutionary effects, even on the "you" who will never hear its words. "You" try to construct its form by an act of imagination, try to bridge the gap from your side as the messenger tries from his.

That gap is the locus of much of Kafka's fiction. The rhetorical moment that generates the narratives also sustains them and clears a place for them. Kafka's world rests on a foundation of rhetoric, on language that is readable as either figurative or not, performative or not. His characters constantly strive to interpret discourse that looks like one thing but might well be another—assertions, requests, commands, and so on that do not assert, request, or command anything in particular but nevertheless direct their lives by continuing to assert, request, and command *urgently*. It is a world generated both from a profound consideration of problematic language and from such problematic language itself.

Chapter 4

TWO READINGS OF READING

Because I focus my investigation of Kafka's writing on his activity as a reader, it will be helpful to devote some effort toward understanding Kafka's view of the reading process. This project might at first seem somewhat quixotic, as Kafka wrote hardly anything that could be considered literary criticism, not to mention hermeneutic theory. And although he made a few scattered comments in his letters and diaries about reading, he appears on the whole to have been much more concerned with the problematic of writing, of literary production, than with reception. Even in his fiction this same situation appears to exist. Stories such as "A Hunger Artist" ("Ein Hungerkünstler"), "Josephine the Singer" ("Josefine die Sängerin"), "First Sorrow" ("Erstes Leid"), and others dealing with art and artists seem entirely devoted to the issue of how art is produced and who produces it. And then there is the famous story "In the Penal Colony" ("In der Strafkolonie"), wherein the process of writing, as figured by the formidable execution machine, takes center stage. Where, in all of these writings, is there anything from which we can learn about Kafka's attitude toward reading? And how should we interpret this attitude once we have found it?

The relative paucity of material proves to be the lesser problem. The little there is that directly treats the issue of reading speaks in such powerful terms as to compel attention and alert us to the possibilities for the fictional treatment of the theme of reading that we might not otherwise have suspected. When we combine these fictional treatments with the statements in diaries and letters, we find ourselves with a substantial body of material by which to judge Kafka's conception of the reading process. The greater problem proves to be assessing the find. Kafka seems to propose in fact two radically different views of the reading process, two conflicting readings of reading that interact in complex ways.

My assessment will be aided by some terms and distinctions introduced by Jacques Derrida in his essay "Structure, Sign, and Play in the Discourse of the Human Sciences." Derrida proposes that indeed there exist—both as logical possibilities and as historical facts—"two interpretations of interpretation," two ways of understanding the nature of signification, two readings of the process of reading. "The one seeks to decipher, dreams of deciphering a truth or an origin which escapes play and the order of the sign, and which lives the necessity of interpretation as exile. The other, which is no longer turned toward the origin, affirms play and tries to pass beyond man and humanism, the name of man being the name of that being who, throughout the history of metaphysics or of ontotheology—in other words, throughout his entire history—has dreamed of full presence, the reassuring foundation, the origin and the end of play." Derrida associates the second interpretation of interpretation with Nietzsche, particularly with his "joyous affirmation of the world and of the innocence of becoming, the affirmation of a world of signs without fault, without truth, and without origin which is offered to an active interpretation."[1] The first, the "humanistic" reading of reading, is associated in "Structure, Sign, and Play" with Lévi-Strauss, but in other essays, especially "Freud and the Scene of Writing," with Freud and with Plato. I argue below that Kafka's interest in the problematic of reading parallels in essence the structure of Derrida's distinction between the two views of interpretation. This similarity is perhaps nowhere as clear as in the story "In the Penal Colony."[2]

1. W&D, 297.
2. My treatment of this story departs from the main line of criticism devoted to it. The following essays take approaches to the story on the whole closer to the scholarly consensus: E. R. Davey, "The Broken Engine: A Study of Franz Kafka's In der Strafkolonie," Journal of European Studies 14:4 (1984), 271–283; Dale Kramer, "The Aesthetics of Theme: Kafka's 'In the Penal Colony,'" Studies in Short Fiction 5 (1969), 362–367; Ernst Loeb, "Kafkas 'In der Strafkolonie' im Spiegel 'klassischer' und 'romantischer' Religion," Seminar 21:2 (May 1985), 139–141 (English version in CT); Ulrich Schmidt, "Von der 'Peinlichkeit' der Zeit: Kafkas Erzählung In der

The fabulous execution machine that is the center of attention in "In the Penal Colony" stands in a "small sandy valley surrounded on all sides by naked crags."[3] At the time represented by the narration, this natural theater is almost empty: no one is there except the principal performers themselves, the officer, the traveler, the condemned prisoner, and the soldier in charge of the prisoner. But such performances as the one about to take place did not always attract so small an audience, the officer explains to the traveler: "How different an execution was in the old days! A whole day before the ceremony the valley was packed with people; they came only to look on . . . . Before hundreds of spectators—all of them standing on tiptoe as far as the heights there—the condemned man was laid under the Harrow by the Commandant himself."[4] The theatrical character of the proceeding is clearly stressed, and the "spectators" are clearly represented as the audience of a kind of performance in which the death of the chief performer is the climactic—though not central—action. The central action of a proper execution as described by the officer in Kafka's tale is an act of reading.

At one time it would have been almost certain that a substantial number of Kafka's readers would have objected to this claim and insisted that *writing*, not *reading*, is at issue here. Is the attention of the story's reader not, after all, focused on the mechanism whereby the machine writes upon the body of the condemned prisoner, and does the process of inscription not receive far more verbal space in the narration than the process of decipherment? Such objections may still be heard, of course, for they are neither uninformed nor illogical. But a case may be made that this inscription is simply the reproduction of an act of writing that has taken place long before the time of the

---

Strafkolonie," Jahrbuch der Deutschen Schiller-Gesellschaft 28 (1984), 407–445; Marion Sonnenfeld, "Eine Deutung der *Strafkolonie*," in Marion Sonnenfeld, ed., *Wert und Wort* (Aurora, N.Y.: Wells College, 1965), 61–68; J. D. Thomas, "The Dark at the End of the Tunnel: Kafka's 'In the Penal Colony,'" *Studies in Short Fiction* 4 (1966), 12–18; and Arnold Weinstein, "Kafka's Writing Machine: Metamorphosis in *The Penal Colony*," *Studies in Twentieth Century Literature*, 7:1 (1982), 21–33.

3. *CS* 140; *SE* 100: "In dem tiefen, sandigen, von kahlen Abhängen ringsum abgeschlossenen kleinen Tal."

4. *CS* 153; *SE* 111: "Wie war die Exekution anders in früherer Zeit! Schon einen Tag vor der Hinrichtung war das ganze Tal von Menschen überfüllt; alle kamen nur um zu sehen. . . . Vor hunderten Augen—alle Zuschauer standen auf den Fußspitzen bis dort zu den Anhöhen—wurde der Verurteilte vom Kommandanten selbst unter die Egge gelegt."

narration and that as such it is the embodiment of the intellectual reproduction that we ordinarily call "reading." The groundwork for
such an argument has been laid in part by Derrida's analysis of the
figuration of writing and reading in the Western philosophical tradition, particularly in essays such as "Plato's Pharmacy" and "Freud and
the Scene of Writing." To one sympathetic to Derrida's deconstructive
practice as it bears on the imagery of inscription, the story of Kafka's
act of writing "In the Penal Colony" ought to be titled "Kafka and the
Scene of Reading."

The comparison implied by the play on Derrida's title is not, I want
to stress, between the enterprise in which I am engaged and Derrida's
but between Kafka's myth and the myth of inscription discussed in
"Freud and the Scene of Writing." The object of attention in both
Kafka's story and Derrida's essay is a machine involved in the process
of writing and reading. Derrida is particularly interested in an analogy Freud had drawn between the operation of the perceptual apparatus and a device called the Mystic Writing-Pad, familiar to American
children as a "Magic Slate." Near the end of the "Note on the Mystic
Writing-Pad," Freud noted: "If we imagine one hand writing upon
the surface of the Mystic Writing-Pad while another periodically
raises its covering sheet from the wax slab, we shall have a concrete
representation of the perceptual apparatus of our mind" (W&D 226).
Freud seems to have assumed that the "writing machine" needs external assistance to run. "That the machine does not run by itself means
. . . a mechanism without its own energy," comments Derrida. "The
machine is dead. It is death. . . . A pure representation, a machine,
never runs by itself" (W&D 227). A machine that *did* run by itself—
what would that be? No longer a pure representation, it would deconstruct the very notion of a "machine." A machine running by itself,
especially a reading/writing machine, would deconstruct itself. Perhaps it would also self-destruct.

Derrida is also interested in the sexual terms of Freud's mechanical
metaphors, especially because they are also terms of aggression and
even rape. He speaks of "metaphors of path, trace, breach, of the
march treading down a track which was opened by effraction through
neurons, light or wax, wood or resin, in order violently to inscribe
itself in nature, matter, or matrix," and he quotes Freud's own description of *Bahnung*, pathbreaking, mentioning particularly Freud's
equation of "all complicated machinery" with the male genitalia and
of writing with a forbidden sexual act (W&D 229).

The sexual aspect of Kafka's execution machine is far more overt than that of Freud's metaphor of psychic writing, as Derrida sees it. The device is designed in such a way as to make the process of execution an unmistakable travesty of copulation. The condemned prisoner is laid out, naked, on a platform covered with a layer of cotton and named "the Bed," while the Harrow, a mechanism shaped exactly like a human body, is placed in contact with him. Here is the description the story provides:

> The Bed and the Designer were of the same size and looked like two dark wooden chests. The Designer hung about two meters above the Bed; each of them was bound at the corners with four rods of brass that almost flashed out rays in the sunlight. Between the chests shuttled the Harrow on a ribbon of steel. . . . "As you see, the shape of the Harrow corresponds to the human form; here is the harrow for the torso, here are the harrows for the legs. For the head there is only this one small spike. . . . When the man lies down on the Bed and it begins to vibrate, the Harrow is lowered onto his body. [The Harrow is covered with needles pointing downward.] It regulates itself automatically so that the needles barely touch his skin; once contact is made the steel ribbon stiffens immediately into a rigid band. . . . So that the actual progress of the sentence can be watched, the Harrow is made of glass. Getting the needles fixed in the glass was a technical problem . . . there are two kinds of needles arranged in multiple patterns. Each long needle has a short one beside it. The long needle does the writing, and the short needle sprays a jet of water to wash away the blood and keep the inscription clear."[5]

In this copulation of man and machine, however, the male sexual role is reserved entirely for the machine. Not only is it covered with hundreds of penetrating and spraying organs, but it also performs a grotesque parody of sexual excitement: "strafft sich sofort dieses

5. CS 143–147; SE 102–106: "Das Bett und der Zeichner hatten gleichen Umfang und sahen wie zwei dunkle Truhen aus. Der Zeichner war etwa zwei Meter über dem Bett angebracht; beide waren in den Ecken durch vier Messingstangen verbunden, die in der Sonne fast Strahlen warfen. Zwischen den Truhen schwebte an einem Stahlband die Egge. . . . 'Wie Sie sehen, entspricht die Egge der Form des Menschen; hier ist die Egge für den Oberkörper, hier sind die Eggen für die Beine. Für den Kopf ist nur dieser Stichel bestimmt. . . . Wenn der Mann auf dem Bett liegt und dieses ins Zittern gebracht ist, wird die Egge auf den Körper gesenkt. Sie stellt sich von selbst so ein, daß sie nur knapp mit den Spitzen den Körper berührt; ist die Einstellung vollzogen, strafft sich sofort dieses Stahlseil zu einer Stange. . . . Um es nun jedem zu ermöglichen, die Ausführung des Urteils zu überprüfen, wurde die Egge aus Glas gemacht. Es hat einige technische Schwierigkeiten verursacht, die Nadeln darin zu festigen. . . . Sie sehen . . . zweierlei Nadeln in vielfacher Ordnung. Jede lange hat eine kurze neben sich. Die

Stahlseil zu einer Stange" could be rendered by "this steel band stiffens immediately into a rod." In the world of the penal colony ("Strafkolonie") there is little difference between a "straffe Stange," an "erect rod," and a *Straf-stange*, a rod used for punishment. Thus the *Straffheit* of the machine, which is just a reflection of the *Straffheit* of the Old Commandant and his ethic, an ideal of "straffe Zucht," "rigid discipline," is both sexual and authoritarian.

Kafka's machine and Derrida's conception of Freud's machine are comparable, then, in a number of ways. To note this similarity seems to me proper to this inquiry, not because I imagine Kafka to have been influenced by Freud's "Note on the Mystic Writing-Pad" or Derrida to have been influenced by Kafka's story, but because all three represent treatments of the theme of inscription. Just as Derrida sees in Freud's metaphors of writing an approach to the problematic of writing that lies as the heart of our philosophical tradition, so do I wish to examine Kafka's story, and particularly its central metaphor, as a direct confrontation with the issue of the relation between a text and the soul upon which it seeks to inscribe itself. This relation is regularly described as "reading."

There is good evidence that Kafka was concerned with this issue, in these or analogous terms, from sources other than "In the Penal Colony." Over and over again in his writings—the diaries provide several examples—we find an attitude toward the act of reading in which eagerness is mixed with a high level of anxiety, in which the reader is viewed as one who suffers something to be done to him. Such a mixture of fear and anticipation is evident in his description of his reading of Dickens in a diary entry of August 1911:

> Is it so difficult and can an outsider understand that you experience a story within yourself from its beginning, from the distant point up to the approaching locomotive of steel, coal and steam, and you don't abandon it even now, but want to be pursued by it and have time for it, therefore are pursued by it and of your own volition run before it wherever it may thrust and wherever you may lure it.[6]

---

lange schreibt nämlich, und die kurze spritzt Wasser aus, um das Blut abzuwaschen und die Schrift immer klar zu erhalten.'"

6. *DI1* 61; *TB* 60: "Ist es so schwer und kann es ein Außenseiter begreifen, daß man eine Geschichte von ihrem Anfang in sich erlebt, vom fernen Punkt bis zu der heranfahrenden Lokomotive aus Stahl, Kohle und Dampf, sie aber auch jetzt noch nicht verläßt, sondern von ihr gejagt wird und aus eigenem Schwung vor ihr läuft, wohin sie nur stößt und wohin man sie lockt."

Even here we see the beginnings of an imagery of reading in which the reader is pursued by a powerful machine that is the text he reads. The text is bigger and stronger than the reader, and it is frightening, even though one may *want* to "run before it." This machine is also figuratively a hunter (the verb Kafka uses is *jagen*) pursuing the reader as prey; at the same time, however, the reader seems to be the hunter, "luring" the text into its pursuit. Similar imagery appears in a letter to Max Brod about a story by Hamsun that they had been discussing: "This last phrase, you know, is a point at which the story, before the reader's eyes, destroys itself or at least obscures itself, no, diminishes, moves away, so that the reader, in order not to lose it, must walk into the obvious trap."[7] Reading is a dangerous game. Destruction is threatened at every moment, with the text and the reader equally threatened. The text has its greatest success, however, when it can overcome the reader, "trap" him, even at the price of the text's own (apparent) suicide. Kafka's comments on Hamsun's story happen to describe very well the relation between the machine and the officer in the "Penal Colony." When we finally see it function, the machine destroys both itself and the officer, both the text and its most devoted reader.

Another description of the reading process whose imagery closely parallels that of the "Penal Colony" occurs in a letter Kafka wrote to his friend Oskar Pollak in 1904, a full decade before "In the Penal Colony" was written:

> I think we ought to read only the kind of books that wound and stab us. If the book we're reading doesn't wake us up with a blow on the head, what are we reading for? So that it will make us happy, as you write? Good Lord, we would be happy precisely if we had no books, and the kind of books that make us happy are the kind we could write ourselves if we had to. But we need the books that affect us like a disaster, that grieve us deeply, like the death of someone we loved more than ourselves, like being banished into forests far from everyone, like a suicide. A book must be the axe for the frozen sea inside us. That is my belief.[8]

7. *LE* 53–54; *BR* 68: "Dieser letzte Satz, das ist doch eine Stelle, wo die Geschichte in der Gegenwart des Lesers sich selbst zerstört oder wenigstens verdunkelt, nein verkleinert, entfernt, so daß der Leser, um sie nicht zu verlieren, in die offenbare Umzingelung hineingehen muß."

8. *LE* 16; *BR* 27–28: "Ich glaube, man sollte überhaupt nur solche Bücher lesen, die einen beißen und stechen. Wenn das Buch, das wir lesen, uns nicht mit einem Faustschlag auf den Schädel weckt, wozu lesen wir dann das Buch? Damit

The kind of reading that conjures up such images of violence, of blows to the head, of wounding and stabbing, is *good* reading, from Kafka's viewpoint. There is no threat associated with bad reading or with nonreading; quite the contrary, they are ways of achieving happiness. But happiness is not the goal Kafka envisions for reading; he participates fully here in the tradition that equates successful reading with the penetration of the reader by the text or by the authority that the text represents. The text must stab the reader to succeed, an image that is acted out with brutal precision by the Old Commandant's machine. Ultimately the book should plunge deep into the psychic interior, where its sharp edge can hack open something that has been frozen shut.

Derrida sees a tendency in the first, humanistic reading of reading to "live the necessity of interpretation as exile," and the young Kafka sees it, too, invoking the imagery of banishment. The text is most effective when it makes the reader painfully aware of his distance from its (the text's) origin, which it will do when it seems most true. The present text becomes a reminder of the absence of that for which the text stands, and the more "truthful" the book is, the more urgent the reminder will be. The reader who desires the truth from his reading will positively desire to feel exiled, because he will want to be reminded of something that is necessarily distant from him and from the book he reads. Thus the necessity of banishment implicit in "good" reading calls forth no lament in this passage; instead, the exile into "forests far from everyone" seems desirable even if, even because, it is painful, because it advances the cause of truth.

The exile of "good" reading also advances the attack on the "frozen" self. Kafka's rhetoric makes clear that the goal of this sort of reading, the reading he most urgently wants, is the effacement of something lying at the core of the self by a powerful instrument, an axe. The book as axe hews apart the present structure of the self both to make an entry for itself and to make the reader into a matrix upon which it can impose its own form. That is why we read, Kafka implies: we want

---

es uns glücklich macht, wie Du schreibst? Mein Gott, glücklich wären wir eben auch, wenn wir keine Bücher hätten, und solche Bücher, die uns glücklich machen, könnten wir zur Not selber schreiben. Wir brauchen aber die Bücher, die auf uns wirken wie ein Unglück, das uns schmerzt, wie der Tod eines, den wir lieber hatten als uns, wie wenn wir in Wälder verstoßen würden, von allen Menschen weg, wie ein Selbstmord, ein Buch muß die Axt sein für das gefrorene Meer in uns. Das glaube ich."

to be opened up and re-formed. If we wanted to stay as we are, there would be no need for books.

The powerful text penetrates the reader. Kafka describes his reading of *Karl Stauffers Lebensgang* as being "caught up and held fast by the powerful impression forcing its way into that inner part of me which I listen to and learn from only at rare intervals."[9] Later he says of the same work:

> If one patiently submits to a book . . . no matter by whom . . . one doesn't make it one's own by main strength . . . but one suffers oneself to be drawn away—this is easily done, if one doesn't resist—by the concentrated otherness of the person writing and lets oneself be made into his counterpart. Thus it is no longer remarkable, when one is brought back to oneself by the closing of the book, that one feels better for the excursion and the recreation, and, with a clearer head, remains behind in one's own being, which has been newly discovered, newly shaken up and seen for a moment from the distance.[10]

In the theory of reading implicit here, the reader does not act upon the text, but rather the text takes the initiative and acts upon the reader. The reader submits, and this submission is all the reader needs to do. The book then takes charge and both picks up the reader and forces its way inside him. The text writes upon the reader and even makes him into a kind of copy of itself.

Kafka's scene of writing, then, is really just as much a scene of reading. There is, in fact, little distinction to be made between writing and reading in this mythology, wherein reading is understood to be the passive reception of an aggressive and powerful text. Writing is the creation of a template that directs an act of inscription, and reading is the suffering of that inscription upon the reader's psyche. Obviously, what is needed is a mechanism to mediate, to bring the writ-

9. *DI₁* 168; *TB* 180: "[ich] bin von diesem großen, in mein nur in Augenblicken erhorchtes Innere dringenden Eindruck so befangen und festgehalten."

10. *DI₁* 173–174; *TB* 186: "Wenn man über einem Buch . . . gleichgültig von was für einem Menschen . . . still hält, nicht aus eigener Kraft in sich zieht . . . sondern hingegeben—wer nur nicht Widerstand leistet, dem geschieht es bald—von dem gesammelten fremden Menschen sich wegziehn und zu seinem Verwandten sich machen läßt, dann ist es nichts Besonderes mehr, wenn man durch Zuschlagen des Buches, wieder auf sich selber gebracht, nach diesem Ausflug und dieser Erholung sich in seinem neu erkannten, neu geschüttelten, einen Augenblick lang von der Ferne aus betrachteten eigenen Wesen wieder wohler fühlt und mit freierem Kopfe zurückbleibt."

er's template text into contact with the reader's psychic matrix. Kafka's machine has just this function. It does not *record* the words of the Old Commandant; rather it makes those words, previously recorded on paper, sensible to the condemned prisoner. The officer possesses the holograph manuscript of what represents to him the most sacred scripture: "'I am still using the guiding plans drawn by the former Commandant. Here they are'—he extracted some sheets from the leather wallet—'but I'm sorry I can't let you handle them, they are my most precious possessions.'"[11] The task of the machine is not simply to write the commandments of paternal authority—the Old Commandant has in fact already written them, all of them, and given them to the officer—but to make that writing legible to the victim. Kafka is careful to make clear that, as marks on paper, the writing of the Old Commandant is not legible at all: "The explorer would have liked to say something appreciative, but all he could see was a labyrinth of lines crossing and recrossing each other, which covered the paper so thickly that it was difficult to discern the blank spaces between them. 'Read it,' said the officer. 'I can't,' said the explorer. 'Yet it's clear enough,' said the officer."[12] This scripture,[13] then, already exists in the documents preserved by the officer. It has already been written. The function of the machine is to make the scripture comprehensible to the prisoner. In other words, its chief job is to serve as the means by which one may read what is written. And this reading takes time. "Man muß lange darin lesen." The machine ensures that the condemned man will spend an average of twelve hours in continuous study, at the end of which time he will be dead.

I do not mean that understanding itself is necessarily deadly in Kafka's fictional world. Rather the process of the painful opening up

11. *CS* 148; *SE* 107: "'Ich verwende noch die Zeichnungen des früheren Kommandanten. Hier sind sie,'—er zog einige Blätter aus der Ledermappe—'ich kann sie Ihnen aber leider nicht in die Hand geben, sie sind das Teuerste, was ich habe.'"

12. *CS* 148; *SE* 107: "Der Reisende hätte gerne etwas Anerkennendes gesagt, aber er sah nur labyrinthartige, einander vielfach kreuzende Linien, die so dicht das Papier bedeckten, daß man nur mit Mühe die weißen Zwischenräume erkannte. 'Lesen Sie,' sagte der Offizier. 'Ich kann nicht,' sagte der Reisende. 'Es ist doch deutlich,' sagte der Offizier."

13. As Heinz Politzer and others have noted, the script of the former Commandant is called *Schrift*, the name that is used for holy scripture. Politzer also reminds us of the remark Kafka made to Janouch later in his life: "It is not by chance that the Bible is called *die Schrift*." See Politzer, *Franz Kafka: Parable and Paradox* (Ithaca: Cornell University Press, 1962), 106.

of the self—a process, that is, of reading in the "humanistic" mode—seems inevitably destructive. If understanding could be achieved directly by some less complicated means, it would be not painful but glorious and thrilling. Kafka creates a myth of the loss of the possibility of such direct and happy access to understanding and its replacement by reading in the important little story "The New Advocate" ("Der neue Advokat"). The story tells how the former battle steed of Alexander the Great, Bucephalus, takes up the legal profession after the death of his master. Both Bucephalus and the bar must go through a difficult period of transition. The bar must accept the new colleague, in spite of the fact that every now and then little things remind them that he is—or was—a horse. Bucephalus himself has an even harder time adjusting. Alexander the Great is dead, and no one is left to hold the reins, to point the way to India as the conqueror once did. With Alexander on his back, Bucephalus had once reached the "unreachable" gates of India. Now those gates are further away than ever; they have "receded to remoter and loftier places."[14] Bucephalus has therefore probably done the best he could by turning to the law books. "In the quiet lamplight, his flanks [*Seiten*] unhampered by the thighs of a rider, free and far from the clamor of battle, he reads and turns the pages of our ancient tomes."[15]

The impossibly great distance between Macedonia and India cited in the story is equivalent to the distance between the psyche and truth, between man and God, between the present and the absent. In Kafka's mythology there exists a former time, a golden age now past, when that distance was smaller and could be bridged by heroic but nonetheless conceivable efforts. Now, today, not even those such as Bucephalus who once achieved the impossible, crossed the infinite gap, can do so again. It is of particular importance that reading is presented as the best (*faute de mieux*) alternative to the conquest of India. Bucephalus's study of the old law books is not, as one might easily suppose, a sign of his having utterly abandoned the quest that Alexander represented. There would have been many far easier ways to abandon the search for the gates of India than by transforming oneself from war-horse to human student of law. No, the meta-

14. *CS* 415; *SE* 123–124: "Heute sind die Tore ganz anderswohin und weiter und höher vertragen."

15. *CS* 415; *SE* 124: "Frei, unbedrückt die Seiten von den Lenden des Reiters, bei stiller Lampe fern dem Getöse der Alexanderschlacht, liest und wendet er die Blätter unserer alten Bücher."

morphosed battle-charger is engaged in the same activity as before, but he must now work through a less direct and, certainly, less satisfactory means. What was easy for Alexander's horse is difficult, perhaps even impossible for a human reader, but there is no better alternative. The task entails a loss of selfhood for Buchephalus, who must deny his nature as horse, animal, *alogon*, in order to pursue this special activity that is the particular province of humankind. All that remains to him of his old self is his high-stepping gait, a characteristic that is admirable in a horse but more than slightly grotesque in a man. Reading, then, is a costly and perhaps hopeless compromise whose goal is to attain the otherwise unattainable.

Alexander's method for attaining the gates of India and thereby abolishing the otherwise infinite distance between the mind and the truth is an act of violence and rebellion against paternal authority. The story stresses that Alexander had cursed the father, Philip. This curse in itself is not enough to make India attainable, as the story makes clear, but it was an important element in Alexander's success. Alexander had usurped paternal authority so that he might possess authority himself, a usurpation Kafka knew to be essential for establishing personal independence. Alexander had succeeded in making himself a paternal power, a rider of horses and wielder of riding whips. Bucephalus has achieved the same thing Alexander had achieved—he had reached the gates of India—but by an opposite strategy. He had acquiesced fully and gladly to the role of adjunct and subject subservient to the riding whip that Alexander had, in a very real sense, taken over from Philip.

The turn to reading in "The New Advocate" thus represents not as great a change as it might seem. The prisoner about to be executed in "In the Penal Colony" has been condemned for having failed to perform his duty "to get up every time the hour strikes and salute the captain's door. Not an exacting duty, and very necessary."[16] As one might expect, the prisoner had been unable to stay awake and was discovered sleeping by the captain, who lashed the man across the face with his riding whip. "Instead of getting up and begging pardon, the man caught hold of his master's legs, shook him, and cried: 'Throw that whip away or I'll eat you alive.'"[17] By using the whip, the

16. *CS* 145–146; *SE* 105: "Er hat nämlich die Pflicht, bei jedem Stundenschlag aufzustehen und vor der Tür des Hauptmanns zu salutieren. Gewiß keine schwere Pflicht und eine notwendige."

17. *CS* 146; *SE* 105: "Statt nun aufzustehen und um Verzeihung zu bitten, faßte

captain tries to place the prisoner in the role of ridden animal. The prisoner rebels but in a sense confirms the captain's suggestion with his threat to eat him alive—the most animalistic sort of behavior imaginable. The role of ridden animal is definitively thrust upon the prisoner by the execution machine, which not only rides him but even penetrates his flesh, makes him even less than an animal, makes him an object upon which to inscribe commandments, a matrix upon which is to be impressed the stamp of rigid authority. The imagery of reading in "In the Penal Colony" thus connects the role of reader with the role of servant and animal and even suggests the comparison between reader and horse through the riding whip of the captain and the way in which the victim is ridden by the harrow. Bucephalus's transformation from horse to reader is, in terms of such imagery, a transformation only from the literal to the figurative position of beast of burden, of "ridden" thing.

The goal of reading, the abolition of the distance between the human mind and what Wilhelm Emrich has called "the Whole,"[18] is at once a thing impossible of attainment *and* the only thing worth pursuing. Because it is "no longer" possible (since the end of the golden age of Alexander) actually to cross this distance, we are compelled to adopt the alternative of crossing it figuratively, by means of traces. Kafka has provided in "The Problem of Our Laws" additional material on this theme. There is substantial doubt among the people described there about the existence of the text whose reading is the central activity of their culture. They have only interpretations of the laws and interpretations of these interpretations, regressing forever toward a text that may not exist. But in a manner typical of Kafka's fiction, the narrator and his people do not find this a cause for despair or for abandonment of belief in the laws. To be sure, there is a party "who try to show that, if any law exists, it can be only this: The Law is whatever the nobles do," but this group is a small minority. The people look forward to a time when the law will belong to them and even indulge in self-hatred because they do not feel themselves "worthy of being entrusted with the laws."[19] The narrator sums up the issue with his closing comment that the people live on a razor's edge

---

der Mann seinen Herrn bei den Beinen, schüttelte ihn und rief: 'Wirf die Peitsche weg, oder ich fresse dich.'"

18. Wilhelm Emrich, *Franz Kafka: A Critical Study of His Writings*, trans. Sheema Zeben Buehne (New York: Ungar, 1968), 64 and elsewhere.

19. *CS* 438; *SE* 315: "Eher hassen wir uns selbst, weil wir noch nicht des Gesetzes gewürdigt werden können."

between an uncertain law (the apparently arbitrary whims of the nobility) and no law at all (repudiating the nobility). Alexander may have been able both to curse the father, Philip, and still to attain direct access to "the Whole," but the people of the problematic laws cannot do so because the authority of the paternal(istic) nobility is the only tangible link they possess to the absent text of their "Whole," the law. They must continue to believe in the nobility because they want to believe in the law.

The traveler in "In the Penal Colony" finds himself in the position of being able (or, from another point of view, required) to repudiate all belief in the laws as they are explained to him by the officer. The central issue of the story is that belief, and the climax occurs when the traveler's 'disbelief causes the officer to review his course of action:

> "So you did not find the procedure convincing," he said to himself and smiled, as an old man smiles at childish nonsense and yet pursues his own meditation behind the smile.
>
> "Then the time has come," he said at last . . . .
>
> "You are free," said the officer to the condemned man in the native tongue. The man did not believe it at first. "Yes, you are set free," said the officer.[20]

The traveler's disbelief in the system of reading advocated by the Old Commandant and the officer has the immediate effect of freeing the prisoner from the deadly obligation of reading. The prisoner escapes the fate of being the medium of inscription whereupon, by a deadly act of violence, the world is forced into conformity with a powerful text. The prisoner's momentary disbelief in his own good fortune reflects the fact that he has not had the slightest idea of what has been happening to him, except of course that it has been bad. The entire conversation between the traveler and the officer has been conducted in French, "and certainly neither the soldier nor the prisoner understood a word of French."[21] Understanding was meant to come to him only as a result of the inscription on his body.

---

20. *CS* 160; *SE* 117. "'Das Verfahren hat Sie also nicht überzeugt,' sagte er für sich und lächelte, wie ein Alter über den Unsinn eines Kindes lächelt und hinter dem Lächeln sein eigenes wirkliches Nachdenken behält. 'Dann ist es also Zeit,' sagte er schließlich . . . . 'Du bist frei,' sagte der Offizier zum Verurteilten in dessen Sprache. Dieser glaubte es zuerst nicht. 'Nun, frei bist du,' sagte der Offizier."

21. *CS* 142; *SE* 102: "Der Offizier sprach französisch und französisch verstand gewiß weder der Soldat noch der Verurteilte."

The prisoner is to be initiated into the mysteries of the officer's system of belief by the process of his execution. As Heinz Politzer has noted, the officer's ability to read the labyrinthine script of the Old Commandant is a sign of his participation in a system of belief: "For the outsider it remains unintelligible, unreadable, and thoroughly confusing. The officer experiences as reality what for the Explorer is at best a successful artifice. In other words, the officer still belongs to a system of belief—whatever the merits of this system and the creed of this belief may be."[22] One of the cornerstones of that creed is certainly the injunction intended for the body of the prisoner: "Honor your superior!" The act of reading demanded by the Old Commandant's system is an act of obedience, of honor to one's superior, for it is an act that acknowledges the absolute authority of the "superior" text and its author. Honor to superiors is equivalent to honor for the laws that those superiors promulgate. Indeed, just as in "The Problem of Our Laws" it is impossible to distinguish between the laws themselves and the nobility who interpret and administer them, so too here it is impossible to distinguish personal, human, paternal authority from the injunctions of that authority. The Old Commandant exists now only as the inscription of his laws.

The prime function of the *Vorgesetzter*, one of the "superiors," is the administration of the law. When he carries out this function properly, he may be called just. If the principal injunction for subjects is "Honor your superiors," then surely the first commandment for superiors is "Be just." Indeed, there is no reason to believe that any commandments other than these are necessary in order to regulate a society based on the reading of the law, and it may well be that the officer has no other inscriptions in his leather wallet. In this system, both subject and superior have a certain absolute authority over the other: the superior has absolute power to interpret the law and to pass judgment, even according to such a principle as the officer's "Guilt is never to be doubted," and the subject has absolute authority over the legitimacy of the superior's power, over his claim to being just. As is clear from "The Problem of Our Laws," the "small group of nobles" who rule retain power only because the subject people continue to believe in them.

The situation in "In the Penal Colony" reflects a social order in which belief in the justice of the superiors has all but died out. The

22. Politzer, *Parable and Paradox*, 105.

scene of reading that once attracted huge audiences now takes place in a nearly empty theater: "During the Old Commandant's lifetime the colony was full of his adherents; his strength of conviction I still have in some measure, but not an atom of his power; consequently the adherents have skulked out of sight, there are still many of them but none of them will admit to it."[23] A key concept here is that of *Überzeugung* (conviction, belief), something that the officer has in abundance and that he wishes to convey to others, particularly the traveler, who represents the officer's last hope of perpetuating his claim to legitimacy as judge of the colony. *Überzeugungskraft*, "strength of conviction," is also persuasive power, the virtue most prized by the orator, the practitioner of rhetoric. It is something for which the Old Commandant was especially known and which has been preserved as much by his machine as by the officer. Torture apparatus has even been found an effective way of exercising persuasive power, but here the power is apotheosized into a means for effecting both transfiguration (*Verklärung*) and salvation (*Erlösung*). The persuasive power of the Old Commandant is not matched by that of the officer, however. He is able to generate no conviction in the new ruling elite or in the traveler himself. "Das Verfahren hat Sie also nicht überzeugt" are the officer's climactic words. "The procedure has not convinced you, then." It is the procedure's central function to be convincing, to enforce belief. If the procedure cannot do it, "then the time has come."

The officer tells the traveler of former successful scenes of reading, but the story offers no evidence that the "transfiguration" of which he speaks testifies to anything more than his own faith in the system. He detects signs of the prisoner's dawning understanding at the sixth hour of torture, but did the prisoner really experience such understanding? By the very nature of the deadly process of reading, it is impossible to interrogate the prisoner to find out.

Even though the officer accepts the traveler's disbelief in his system of justice as a condemnation of the entire procedure and as a death sentence for himself and that system, his conviction is unaffected. The officer cannot escape, as the condemned prisoner has, through the traveler's disbelief, for *his* belief is unshaken. Indeed, he sentences himself precisely in terms of the principles of his system, for only such

23. *CS* 153; *SE* 110–111: "Als der alte Kommandant lebte, war die Kolonie von seinen Anhängern voll; die Überzeugungskraft des alten Kommandanten habe ich zum Teil, aber seine Macht fehlt mir ganz; infolgedessen haben sich die Anhänger verkrochen, es gibt noch viele, aber keiner gesteht es ein."

a notion as "Guilt is never to be doubted" could justify taking one man's doubt as the occasion for self-execution. The fact that the traveler is unconvinced represents an accusation, but by the rules under which the officer and Old Commandant judged others, such an accusation is always enough to produce a verdict of "guilty." Because the traveler has in effect accused the officer of failing to obey the central injunction given to superiors, he cannot fail to sentence himself to suffer "Be just" to be written on him by his own machine.

The officer's act of self-execution is, therefore, as much an act of defiance of the traveler's opinion as an acceptance of his judgment. The officer asserts thereby the authority of the law and of the law's injunctions as the trace of an absent father. If he has failed to convince others, if he has been lacking in the power of persuasion, he must touch the source of all power, which is embodied in the text. He must read the law. And to do so, he must first do to himself what other condemned prisoners have had done to them: he must renounce his male role of authority and power to become a female matrix upon which the father may write. For this reason he engages in an elaborate act of divestiture and symbolic self-emasculation: after taking off all his clothes, his uniform with its braid and tassles, he breaks his sword and throws its pieces, along with the rest of his things, into the pit. Now the officer is ready to receive the inscription, and it soon becomes clear that the machine is itself ready to take him as its last victim.

I would like to pause here and look back a moment to the relation that has been tentatively established between the narration of "In the Penal Colony" and its readers. Thus far the events represented have been bizarre, to be sure, but nothing has happened to disturb the notion that what is related here is *convincing* in the Aristotelian sense of *eikos*. We do not suppose that these events have happened or that we would be very likely to hear of them happening, but they are not so outrageous that we are prevented from thinking that they could happen. The technology of the machine is uncertain and comes close to the bounds of credibility, but it does not cross those bounds. The narration itself, in other words, has not solicited the reader's disbelief. Once the officer begins the progress of his own execution, however, the nature of the narration changes: the events reported pass over from the realm of the merely bizarre into atopia, the land of the outlandish. The machine suddenly begins to act like a living creature:

The officer, however, had turned to the machine. It had been clear enough previously that he understood the machine well, but now it was almost staggering to see how he managed it and how it obeyed him. His hand had only to approach the Harrow for it to rise and sink several times till it was adjusted to the right position for receiving him; he touched only the edge of the Bed and already it was vibrating; the felt gag came to meet his mouth, one could see that the officer was reluctant to take it but he shrank from it only a moment, soon he submitted and received it. Everything was ready . . . as soon as the straps were fastened the machine began to work; the Bed vibrated, the needles flickered above the skin, the Harrow rose and fell. The explorer had been staring at it quite a while before he remembered that a wheel in the Designer should have been creaking; but everything was quiet, not even the slightest hum could be heard.[24]

The traveler's disbelief, having set the prisoner free from the obligation of reading the deadly script—writing "en tei psuchei"—seems simultaneously to liberate the narration from the obligation of verisimilitude and the machine from the dead world of the mechanical. Thus far the machine, like Freud's Mystic Pad, could not run by itself; now it begins to develop or manifest its own volition, its own animus. It does so only now because the system of writing and reading in which it was a crucial figure could not accommodate a machine that runs by itself or a narration in which the story departs from the norms of experience. Now that that system is no longer credited, the machine may act on its own—though its act must necessarily be one of self-destruction.

The machine, liberated by the traveler's disbelief, destroys itself by rebelling against the condition of its existence, which stipulates that

24. *CS* 163–164; *SE* 119–120: "Der Offizier aber hatte sich der Maschine zugewendet. Wenn es schon früher deutlich gewesen war, daß er die Maschine gut verstand, so konnte es jetzt einen fast bestürzt machen, wie er mit ihr umging und wie sie gehorchte. Er hatte die Hand der Egge nur genähert, und sie hob und senkte sich mehrmals, bis sie die richtige Lage erreicht hatte um ihn zu empfangen; er faßte das Bett nur am Rande, und es fing schon zu zittern an; der Filzstumpf kam seinem Mund entgegen, man sah, wie der Offizier ihn eigentlich nicht haben wollte, aber das Zögern dauerte nur einen Augenblick, gleich fügte er sich und nahm ihn auf. Alles war bereit . . . kaum waren die Riemen angebracht, fing auch schon die Maschine zu arbeiten an; das Bett zitterte, die Nadeln tanzten auf der Haut, die Egge schwebte auf und ab. Der Reisende hatte schon eine Weile hingestarrt, ehe er sich erinnerte, daß ein Rad im Zeichner hätte kreischen sollen; aber alles war still, nicht das geringste Surren war zu hören."

such a machine may not run by itself. The apparatus transcends its own nature by its act of self-destruction, for in doing so it ceases simply to represent the system of reading and writing the law. The officer, on the other hand, remains until his death—and even beyond—the representative (*Vertreter*) of the "heritage of the Old Commandant" that he claimed to be. His face in death "was as it had been in life; no sign was visible of the promised redemption; what the others had found in the machine the officer had not found; the lips were firmly pressed together, the eyes were open, with the same expression as in life, the look was calm and convinced, through the forehead went the point of the great iron spike."[25] The dead officer's face thus testifies to the inefficacy of the system he championed and his absolute faith in it efficacy. Even as a corpse he retains his Überzeugung.

In the play that is acted out upon this scene of reading, the principal figures are indeed "representations" of others: the machine stands for the procedure of administering justice in which it plays such a prominent role; the officer represents, as best he can, the Old Commandant and his tradition; and the traveler, the emissary from the West, finds himself in the role of sole and final judge of the procedure he witnesses. The officer feels honored by his role, though he acknowledges his shortcomings when he is compared to the Old Commandant himself. The traveler evidently feels uncomfortable with the role thrust upon him, realizing as he must that by making his opinion known the officer will understand that he is taking over the officer's role. The machine, when the time comes for it to perform, throws away the script and behaves in a manner completely different from that assigned to it by the Old Commandant's system. It neither delivers the promised transfiguration to the officer nor behaves like a proper machine.

The bulk of the narrative of "In the Penal Colony" is taken up with the officer's scenarios. The principal scenario, of course, is the process of execution by inscription, the telling of which takes up much of

25. *CS* 166; *SE* 121: "Es war, wie es im Leben gewesen war; (kein Zeichen der versprochenen Erlösung war zu entdecken;) was alle anderen in der Maschine gefunden hatten, der Offizier fand es nicht; die Lippen waren fest zusammengedrückt, die Augen waren offen, hatten den Ausdruck des Lebens, der Blick war ruhig und überzeugt, durch den Stirn ging die Spitze des großen eisernen Stachels."

the text, but another, the description of the triumph of the Old Commandant's system by way of its defense by the traveler before the new Commandant, is also elaborated at some length and in several variants. The officer is forever writing scripts—though in this he is only a representative of that *arche* scriptwriter, the Old Commandant. But the actors available to him regularly fail to follow the text given them: the traveler is unwilling to participate in the defense of the Old Commandant's system and offers an alternative scenario that the officer rejects by ignoring it, and of course the machine itself fails to perform the role assigned to it in the great play conceived by the Old Commandant. The system of reading, which is both reading the law and reading the script, has broken down utterly.

The theatrical metaphor proposed at the opening of the story by the theaterlike setting of the scene of action is centrally relevant to the issue of reading that is at stake in Kafka's tale. The drama as we have understood it since classical times is a form of action that is impossible without an authoritative text to which all the actors adhere scrupulously. Ad-libbing (that is, free speaking and free acting) must be held to a very small minimum. The performance of a play is a kind of communal act of reading, and if the play is well known, the audience will inevitably make judgments about the adequacy and appropriateness of the reading that the performance has given. We talk quite intelligibly and correctly of an actor's "reading" of a part, even though he has memorized his lines and does no actual reading on the stage. The acting out of a drama is thus a way of making the world—a small part of the world, that is, and an artificially controlled part at that— conform to the word of the script. The actor, like the subject, must obey his superior. Acting in a play and being a citizen in a society governed by the law are two forms of essentially the same activity.

It is not only the condemned prisoner who escapes from the torture of reading: both the traveler and the machine escape by refusing to play the roles assigned to them by the officer's scripts. This possibility of escape suggests that Kafka might have envisioned a second mode of reading in which one could avoid submitting to an overwhelmingly powerful text. The Old Commandant and his spokesman the officer seem to represent what we might call Kafka's first reading of reading, something akin to what Derrida calls "humanistic" and associates with Plato, Lévi-Strauss, and Freud and with the orthodox tradition of "good" reading that they represent. This mode is, to use a notion

developed in another context,[26] "alethetic": that is, it assumes that the
goal of reading any text, no matter how trivial or incredible the text
may seem, is the discovery of some truth. But if the Old Commandant
and the officer—as well as numerous passages in Kafka's letters and
diaries—insist on a form of violent reading in which the reader is
opened up in order that the text of authority inscribe itself upon his
or her interior, the possibility of escape raised by the traveler's rejection suggests that another reading of reading avoids such violence.
This would be a "lethetic" concept of reading, which supposes that, no
matter what the text intends, the reader may ignore that intention
and do with the text what he will. Lethetic reading allows the reader
the option of keeping himself apart from what he reads, safe from
any threat the text might present.

It is worth departing from the discussion of "In the Penal Colony"
for a time to examine this other, lethetic mode of reading as it appears
in Kafka's writing, for example, in the following passage from a letter
Kafka wrote to Oskar Baum in 1921: "I am happy to be reading the
book again. For reasons that in a certain sense will not bear inspection, it is one of my favorites among your books. It is so good to live in
it, warm; it's as though the reader were crouching forgotten in a
corner of a room where he can participate all the more intensely in
what is happening there."[27] The text forgets the reader, neither pursues nor penetrates nor traps him, but at the same time does not
exclude him. Here there is no text hacking its way to the center of the
reader's self; instead, the reader dwells unnoticed, warm, in the center of the book. He remains on the margin ("forgotten in a corner of a
room") yet at the same time somehow right in the middle, participating intensely in activities that can do him no harm. He can participate
in the text's action precisely because that action does not concern him.
It is as if the power of the book, the great capacity to obliterate the self
of which Kafka is so aware in other contexts, had been redirected
away from the "forgotten" reader. It is as if the text would part in the
middle to let the reader pass through it untouched.

26. Clayton Koelb, *The Incredulous Reader* (Ithaca: Cornell University Press,
1984), esp. 28–40.

27. *LE* 276; *BR* 321: "Das Buch freue ich mich wieder zu lesen, es ist aus
Gründen, die in einem gewissen Sinne unkontrollierbar sind, eines meiner
Lieblinge unter Deinen Büchern, es ist so gut darin zu leben, warm, wie in der
Ecke eines Zimmers, wo man vergessen ist und um so stärker alles miterleben
kann, was geschieht."

In Kafka's early fragment, "Wedding Preparations in the Country," the character Raban proposes just this analogy:

> I was only going to say that books are useful in every sense and quite especially in respects in which one would not expect it. For when one is about to embark on some enterprise, it is precisely the books whose contents have nothing at all in common with the enterprise that are the most useful. For the reader who does after all intend to embark on some enterprise, that is to say, who has somehow become enthusiastic (and even if, as it were, the effect of the book can penetrate only so far as that enthusiasm), will be stimulated by the book to all kinds of thoughts concerning his enterprise. Now, however, since the contents of the book are precisely something of utter indifference, the reader is not at all impeded in those thoughts, and he passes through the midst of the book with them, as once the Jews passed through the Red Sea, that's how I should like to put it.[28]

The "intense participation" of the previous quotation is replaced here by "enthusiasm" but an enthusiasm that has nothing to do with the matter of the text. Where the previous quotation spoke of intense participation in the world of the book, this passage speaks of enthusiasm, but we now see that this intense feeling need not be directly connected to the matter of the text. The powerful feelings associated with the reading process are separable from the material being read. We notice also that Kafka's imagery of reading still implies the threat of violence: the Jews who passed through the Red Sea were in great danger, not only from the troops pursuing them but also from the waters that threatened to drown them if only God's miraculous favor were withdrawn. Reading, according to such a metaphor, is an extremely dangerous activity because the reader is threatened with drowning, of being flooded, of being in-fluenced in the root sense of that term. Raban thinks of his (lethetic) reading as an escape from the

---

28. CS 75; SE 251: "Ich meinte nur, Bücher sind nützlich in jedem Sinn und ganz besonders, wo man es nicht erwarten sollte. Denn wenn man eine Unternehmung vorhat, so sind gerade die Bücher, deren Inhalt mit der Unternehmung gar nichts Gemeinschaftliches hat, die nützlichsten. Denn der Leser, der doch jene Unternehmung beabsichtigt, also irgendwie (und wenn förmlich auch nur die Wirkung des Buches bis zu jener Hitze dringen kann) erhitzt ist, wird durch das Buch zu lauter Gedanken gereizt, die seine Unternehmung betreffen. Da nun aber der Inhalt des Buches ein gerade ganz gleichgültiger ist, wird der Leser in jenen Gedanken gar nicht gehindert und er zieht mit ihnen mitten durch das Buch, wie einmal die Juden durch das Rote Meer, möchte ich sagen."

threat of being overwhelmed by a text that, approached alethetically, would surely be powerful enough to flood him.

Kafka felt the threat of drowning in a text on more than one occasion, as may be observed in one of the conversations that Gustav Janouch reports having had with Kafka. They were talking about a set of five volumes on the subject of Taoism that Kafka had in his possession:

> "That's a mighty treasury," I said, as I placed the books back on top of the desk.
> "Yes," said Kafka, "the Germans are thorough. They make a museum out of everything. These five volumes are only half of the complete set."
> "Will you get the others?"
> "No. What I have is enough for me. They are a sea in which one can easily drown."[29]

In itself this comment would seem little more than a near cliché on the sheer volume of material available. Seen together with the passage cited from "Wedding Preparations," though, it suggests the terms of a consistent metaphor of one sort of reading. One need not be a disciple of Harold Bloom to recognize that the anxiety of being flooded properly belongs to "good" reading as our culture understands it ("every good reader properly *desires* to drown").[30] The "good" reader is submissive to the authority of the author and wants nothing more than to be flooded by that author's discourse; in the same way the reader in the penal colony is to be obliterated as he is turned into a surface upon which may be inscribed the texts of absolute, though absent, authority. To drown in the text of authority is exactly what the first (alethetic) interpretation of interpretation expects of us.

But in this second, lethetic mode of reading, the text that threatens to drown the reader in fact never does so. The reader passes unharmed through the text by paying strict attention to his own thoughts and ignoring utterly the matter being read. If this sort of lethetic reading is valuable, as Raban says it is, then we might expect texts that allow or even encourage an oblivious reading to be highly prized. And indeed we find Kafka (the Kafka, that is, of the second reading of reading) maintaining precisely the high value of texts that

---

29. Gustav Janouch, *Conversations with Kafka*, trans. Goronwy Rees (New York: New Directions, 1971), 153.

30. Harold Bloom, *The Anxiety of Influence* (New York: Oxford University Press, 1973), p. 57.

encourage a certain misreading. The following remarkable passage from one of the letters to Felice proposes just such a view:

> [Stoessl] writes about my book [*Meditation*], but with such complete lack of understanding that for a moment I thought the book must really be good, since—even in a man as discerning and experienced in literary matters as Stoessl—it can create the kind of misunderstanding one would consider impossible with books and possible only with living, hence complex, human beings. There is only one explanation: either that he read the book superficially, or only parts of it, or (though the impression of good faith his personality creates with every word makes it unlikely) that he didn't read it at all.[31]

The surprising position Kafka takes here is that it would be strong evidence in favor of the high quality of his book if Stoessl failed to understand it and in fact remained in all important respects untouched by it. Such a book, capable of being misread, its meaning ignored or unseen, would have the complex, ambiguous (*vieldeutig*) quality of persons, not the deadly mechanical character of an apparatus. It would be a "good" book of a very different sort from the one that, enforcing its thought upon the reader, hacks open the frozen sea of the human psyche.

As strongly stated as this position is, however, we must realize that Kafka's ambivalence about the two modes of reading hardly wanes. In the very same paragraph in which he equates the possibility of misunderstanding with a complex and "living" form of reading, he goes out of his way to impress upon Felice the reading of Stoessl that Kafka considers to be proper: "I am copying the relevant passages for you, because his writing is quite illegible, and even if after much effort you thought you could decipher it, you would undoubtedly be reading with misleading interpretations."[32] How does Kafka know that *he* has

31. *LB* 177; *BF* 278: "Er schreibt auch über mein Buch, aber mit so vollständigem Mißverständnis, daß ich einen Augenblick geglaubt habe, mein Buch sei wirklich gut, da es selbst bei einem so einsichtigen und literarisch vielgeprüften Mann wie Stoessl solche Mißverständnisse erzeugen kann, wie man sie Büchern gegenüber für gar nicht möglich halten sollte und wie sie nur gegenüber lebenden und deshalb vieldeutigen Menschen möglich sind. Als einzige Erklärung bleibt, daß er das Buch flüchtig oder stellenweise oder (was allerdings bei dem Eindruck der Treue, die sein Wesen in jeder Äußerung macht, unwahrscheinlich ist) gar nicht gelesen hat."

32. *LB* 177–178; *BF* 278–279: "Ich schreibe hier die betreffende Stelle für Dich ab, seine Schrift ist nämlich ganz unlesbar und wenn Du nach vieler Mühe auch glauben würdest, sie lesen zu können, würdest Du gewiß mit mißverständlichen Deutungen lesen."

managed to decipher the "illegible" text of Stoessl's letter without misunderstandings of his own? Is his concern here that Felice understand Stoessl's writing and therefore find it bad while suggesting to her that his own might be unintelligible and thus good? More likely, I think, is that Kafka simply cannot decide what sort of reading one ought to value and is not sure in his own mind whether "misleading interpretations" should be encouraged or expunged. At such times he wants it both ways at once.

Still, the notion expressed in the letter that his own writing might be proven "good" if it is shown to foster misunderstanding is strikingly similar to the view propounded by Raban in his discourse on the usefulness of books. And Raban's view is very similar to one proposed by Edgar Allan Poe in his *Marginalia*, a little book centrally concerned with the potential value of marginal glosses and thus with the theory of reading. Though Poe's concerns ultimately differ from Kafka's, his lethetic approach to certain books is very similar to that of Raban. Concerning a book by Mercier, Poe wrote: "In reading some books we occupy ourselves chiefly with the thoughts of the author; in perusing others, exclusively with our own. . . . It makes little difference, after all. In either case the true book-purpose is answered."[33] Kafka would not likely agree that it makes little difference: it makes all the difference in the world to the reader, who in one case is hewn open by an axe text or drowned by an ocean text but in the other escapes untouched. Yet there does seem to be an area of agreement between Kafka's second reading of reading and Poe's interpretation of the value of the marginal gloss. Instead of restraining the free play of intellect and channeling it into the grooves inscribed by the author, this other sort of reading allows that play to go on unchecked. Poe contends in *Marginalia* that "purely marginal jottings, done with no eye to the Memorandum Book, have a distinct complexion, and not only a distinct purpose, but none at all; this it is which imparts to them a value."[34]

The margin is the locus of that which has no purpose and is thus the place of an unrestricted intellectual play. The reader, exiled to the margin, lives the experience of his exile quite unlike the reader proposed by Kafka in the letter to Pollak. This sort of reader imagines himself separated from the authority represented by the text, a separation that can be overcome only by a horrifying process of hewing

33. *Marginalia—Eureka* (New York: Thomas Y. Crowell, n.d.), 36–37.
34. Poe, *Marginalia*, 1.

open the psyche. This other reader, freed from the authority of the text proper, becomes his own authority, a monarch unto himself. Poe quotes Sallust as having "the same free-and-easy idea": "Impune quae libet facere, id est esse regem" ("To be a king is to do what you want with impunity"). The text proper will retain its purposive character—unless it can be transformed into a kind of margin. Poe effects just this transformation in the body of his *Marginalia*, as for example in the note about Mercier quoted above, for the only mention of Mercier and the title of his book occurs in a footnote appended to Poe's gloss. Poe and the Kafka of "Wedding Preparations" imagine a reading process utterly different from that worked out with such frightening rigor in "In the Penal Colony." Here the reader escapes the threat that the text, understood as the repository of authority, holds over him. A marginal text, or a text displaced to the margin, is divested of the very purpose that gives it the power to penetrate the reader.

This notion of an escape from the perils of reading appears elsewhere in Kafka's fiction as well. The little parable called "The Truth about Sancho Panza" ("Die Wahrheit über Sancho Pansa") provides an example of a rather different sort from those I cited hitherto. The entire story consists of these two sentences:

> Without making any boast of it Sancho Panza succeeded in the course of years, by feeding him a great number of romances of chivalry and adventure in the evening and night hours, in so diverting from himself his demon, whom he later called Don Quixote, that this demon thereupon set out, uninhibited, on the maddest exploits, which, however, for the lack of a preordained object, which should have been Sancho Panza himself, harmed nobody. A free man, Sancho Panza philosophically followed Don Quixote on his crusades, perhaps out of a sense of responsibility, and had of them a great and edifying entertainment to the end of his days.[35]

Sancho divests himself of the demon that threatens him by satiating it with tales of the marvelous. We can properly understand Sancho's

35. *CS* 430; *SE* 304: "Sancho Pansa, der sich übrigens dessen nie gerühmt hat, gelang es im Laufe der Jahre, durch Beistellung einer Menge Ritter- und Räuberromane in den Abend- und Nachtstunden seinen Teufel, dem er später den Namen Don Quixote gab, derart von sich abzulenken, daß dieser dann haltlos die verrücktesten Taten aufführte, die aber mangels eines vorbestimmten Gegenstandes, der eben Sancho Pansa hätte sein sollen, niemandem schadeten. Sancho Pansa, ein freier Mann, folgte gleichmütig, vielleicht aus einem gewissen Verantwortlichkeitsgefühl, dem Don Quixote auf seinen Zügen und hatte davon eine große und nützliche Unterhaltung bis an sein Ende."

demon as a reader—as the reading part of Sancho—because we are
told about it only that it consumes stories. By externalizing the demon
of reading in the form of Don Quixote and by giving it only the most
incredible texts, Sancho rids himself of the obligation to read "seriously" himself. He is able thus to be "a free man" and to find entertainment in the adventures of the demon that would otherwise have
done him harm. Cervantes's Quixote, we must remember, is depicted
in the novel as the most naive sort of alethetic reader.[36] He opens
himself up to romances of chivalry so thoroughly that they overwhelm him and control all his actions. He has put himself under a
powerful reading/writing machine and has lived through it, but now
he is almost nothing more than a palimpsest under layers and layers
of chivalric inscription. Here Kafka uses the metaphor of ingestion
rather than tearing open, however: Sancho "feeds" his demon the
stories that now dwell inside him and flood him from within. Sancho
Panza has made of his reading a creature apart from himself, a creature who can read and who can drown in the texts he reads while
Sancho somehow remains apart and safe, as Kafka remained safe in a
corner of Baum's book, as the children of Israel remained safe while
the troops of Pharaoh were overwhelmed by the waters of the Red
Sea.

The demonic aspect of reading, put so starkly in the foreground in
the parable of the penal colony, is quite as present in this second
metaphor as in the first. The letter to Baum, with its cozy imagery of
warmth and happiness, might allow us to forget the danger of reading even when the reader is "forgotten in a corner." When the reader
is not at the center, is only a secondary character in the scene of
reading, he may no longer feel threatened, but the threat is still there.
The Sancho parable makes clear that the "great and edifying entertainment" of Don Quixote could easily have been a horrifying experience, a diabolical torment, if Sancho had not been able to displace
himself to the margin and put the demon Don Quixote at the center.
What is an edifying entertainment for Sancho (and for like-minded
readers) is more of a torment if it is taken "seriously" from the point
of view of Quixote himself.

"The Truth about Sancho Panza" suggests that both readings of

36. For an examination of some other aspects of the interaction between Kafka
and Cervantes, see Ritchie Robertson, "Kafka und Don Quixote," *Neophilologus* 69
(January 1985), 17–24.

reading can apply equally well to any given text. Kafka's view is not that of Poe, who suggests that whether our own thoughts or those of the author occupy the reader is a matter of what sort of book we read. Sancho and Quixote are reading the same story. The Hebrews and the Egyptians are crossing the same Red Sea. Whether one is drowned or not is clearly a matter not of what body of water is involved but rather of who one is, of how one approaches the passage.[37]

The matter of how one approaches a passage through a perilous act of interpretation is the subject of one of Kafka's most intriguing short stories, his retelling of the legend of Ulysses's escape from the deadly song of the sirens, "The Silence of the Sirens" ("Das Schweigen der Sirenen"). Kafka gives a new and entirely unexpected twist to his version of the tale, which is, in bare summary: the song of the sirens is powerful beyond all imagining. It can "pierce through anything" ("durchdrang alles"), including of course any conceivable amount of wax in one's ears, and can force those overwhelmed by it to break "far stronger bonds than chains and masts" ("mehr als Ketten und Mast gesprengt"). If the sirens had actually sung to Ulysses, he surely would have heard them, would have burst his bonds, and would have been overcome. But even more powerful than the sirens' song is their silence, which nothing at all can resist, and this weapon they use against Ulysses. "But Ulysses, if one may so express it, did not hear their silence" ("hörte ihr Schweigen nicht"). He had stopped his ears with wax and believed that this childish measure had actually prevented him from hearing their song. Perhaps, however, Ulysses was not so childish after all: perhaps he knew that the sirens were silent but pretended not to notice in order to save himself. The narrator presents the story as "proof that inadequate, even childish measures may serve to rescue one from peril."[38]

Although it may not seem so at first glance, the story as Kafka tells it relates to reading. Its central concern is Ulysses' act of interpretation of a certain utterance (the song/silence of the sirens). That the utterance in question happens to be the absence of utterance, the withholding of song, does not change the fundamental situation and, if anything, makes it more dangerous. The inversion that proposes si-

37. A similar point is made about Francesca's fatal (mis)reading in Dante's *Divine Comedy* by Susan Noakes, "The Double Misreading of Paolo and Francesca," *Philological Quarterly* (1983), 221–239.

38. *CS* 430; *SE* 304: "Beweis dessen, daß auch unzulängliche, ja kindische Mittel zur Rettung dienen können."

lence as a more powerful weapon than actual utterance may seem paradoxical, but it is one of the oldest and most enduring notions belonging to the alethetic mode of reading. One can find examples of this inversion from Plato to Lévi-Strauss. Indeed, Derrida uses the example of Lévi-Strauss's attitude toward the absence of writing among the Nambikwara to show his participation in this tradition.[39] Lévi-Strauss shares the belief that what is fully present does not need expression in words or writing, which are only the traces of the power they stand for. Silence betokens self-presence and power, even in the clichés of everyday speech: "he's the strong, silent type." A literary character who has been at times much admired for his strength and silence may be cited as summing up this position: "Words do not express thoughts very well," says Hermann Hesse's Siddhartha. "They always become a little different immediately they are expressed, a little distorted, a little foolish."[40] Given this enormous and inevitable gap between words and thoughts, the true indicator of intellectual power, according to such a view, must be silence.

Kafka proposes an additional, psychological explanation for the effectiveness of the sirens' silence: "Against the feeling of having triumphed over them by one's own strength, and the consequent exaltation that bears down everything before it, no earthly powers can resist."[41] At stake is submission, whether to the song or to the feeling of having conquered that song "by one's own strength." The act of reading is always, from the traditional point of view, an act of submission: it is, in the root sense of the term, a *passion* (that is, a process of "suffering," as in the "Passion" of Jesus). The note from the diary about *Karl Stauffers Lebensgang* cited earlier makes this very point: the reader "suffers" himself to be made into the counterpart of the author one is reading. One allows oneself to be conquered by the book. That is the normal and accepted way to read. In "The Silence of the Sirens" Kafka proposes that one cannot escape the passion of reading by conquering the text instead of letting it conquer you. The act of conquest brings with it a set of feelings that overwhelm the reader as surely as the text itself would have.

39. See especially *Of Grammatology*, trans. Gayatri Spivak (Baltimore: Johns Hopkins University Press, 1976), 118.
40. Hermann Hesse, *Siddhartha*, trans. Hilda Rosner (New York: New Directions, 1957), 117.
41. *CS* 431; *SE* 305: "Dem Gefühl, aus eigener Kraft sie besiegt zu haben, der daraus folgenden alles fortreißenden Überhebung kann nichts Irdisches widerstehen."

In order to escape the sirens' song one must neither conquer nor be conquered. One must ignore it or pretend to ignore it, as Ulysses does, though it is not certain whether or not he knows what he is doing. Ulysses wants to keep to his own thoughts so as not to be tempted by the (destructive) thoughts that the song of the sirens would impose on him. He wants, in short, to avoid being penetrated (*durchdrungen*) and thus to avoid the fate of "good" readers (drowning). His success is paradoxical only in that his efforts would have failed if the sirens had actually sung. He makes for himself a passage through the terrible sea of the sirens' silence, creating a margin in the middle of a page that he may not realize is blank to begin with. What is genuinely surprising is the suggestion that Ulysses "was so full of guile, was such a fox" ("war so listenreich, war ein solcher Fuchs") that he merely pretended not to notice that the sirens were not singing and that this pretense was just as effective as the reality. Ulysses was not ignorant, in this construction, but oblivious. One might suppose that, if he had noticed that the sirens were not singing, that is, if he had become conscious of their silence, he would have been overwhelmed just as surely as if his ears had been unstopped. That he is not overwhelmed suggests that one can escape the perils of reading not only by displacing oneself to the margin but also by merely pretending to do so. One need not avoid noticing the genuine intentions of a text—those thoughts that the tradition says should be *conceptions* planted within the psyche; one need only act as if they had gone unnoticed.

Ulysses thus seems to act out both interpretations of interpretation, to "live them simultaneously and reconcile them in an obscure economy" (*W&D* 293). But one would have to say that, inasmuch as either way he escapes the sirens, this story would place Ulysses firmly in the camp of the second sort of reading. If Ulysses participated in the first tradition, he would not have desired to escape. Like the Kafka of the letter to Pollak, he would have sought out the experience of a song that had the power to penetrate him, open him up, hack apart the frozen sea of his innermost self.[42] It is not Ulysses, but Kafka himself, and especially Kafka's writing, that inhabits the ground of an undecidability (and a *différance*) between the two readings of reading.

42. Homer's Odysseus does indeed seek out the experience of the sirens' song. This comparison is developed further in Clayton Koelb, "Kafka and the Sirens: Writing as Lethetic Reading," in Clayton Koelb and Susan Noakes, eds., *The Comparative Perspective on Literature: Approaches to Theory and Practice* (Ithaca: Cornell University Press, 1988), 300–314.

Kafka himself does appear to be ambivalent, and this ambivalence is acted out most directly by the traveler in the "Penal Colony." In spite of the ad libitum behavior of both the traveler and the machine, in spite of their spoiling the officer's scenarios, both in the end to some extent play the very roles they have refused. The traveler finds himself being the very judge he has condemned, for his refusal to defend the system is perceived as a verdict against it and a sentence of its death (a slide from *urteilen* to *verurteilen* analogous to that in "The Judgment"). The machine executes the traveler's sentence, destroying both itself and the officer and thereby apparently the system of reading devised by the Old Commandant.

The play acted out on the scene of reading does not end with the death of the officer. After this principal episode there is, as a sort of epilogue, a second. Yet another inscription, another scenario, is left behind in the name of the Old Commandant. After the death of the officer and the destruction of the machine, the traveler returns with the soldier and the prisoner to the town and to the teahouse where the Old Commandant's grave had been placed. Near the back of the building, underneath one of the tables, is a gravestone upon which an inscription foretells the return of the Old Commandant. The demise of the system of reading that the traveler has precipitated and that the reader has witnessed is alleged by this inscription to be only temporary. This scenario calls for the resurrection of the Old Commandant and the reimposition of his system. All that is necessary, in the meantime, is patience and faith: "Have faith and wait!"[43] Belief, as we have seen, is the core of the system, so that the revival of the Old Commandant requires only a sufficiency of belief.

The reading of the gravestone has been a performance before an audience. This audience expects the traveler to make a judgment about what he has read, just as the officer had expected him to judge the local system of justice. But where the officer had expected a favorable interpretation, the patrons of the teahouse expect an unfavorable one. They expect him to share their disbelief, or so it seems to him. But apparently the traveler's disbelief is not so strong as to allow him to dismiss the inscription as ridiculous. Although nothing is said about the traveler's feelings, he is apparently frightened: he wants to leave the island as soon as possible. He goes directly to the harbor to engage a boat to take him out to his steamer, and he man-

43. *CS* 167; *SE* 122: "Glaubet und wartet!"

ages to escape just quickly enough to prevent the soldier and prisoner, he thinks, from trying to escape with him.

The traveler cannot dismiss the inscription on the gravestone even
though he was firm in his disapproval of the machine and in its
method of dispensing justice, for he is not prepared (in the words of
"The Problem of Our Laws") to "repudiate the nobility." In spite of his
aversion for the brutality of the Old Commandant's methods, the
traveler believes in respect for authority. He is prepared to let the
unfortunate prisoner be executed for failure to salute the door of his
superior and only prevents it from happening, as it were, in spite of
himself: "He was neither a member of the penal colony nor a citizen
of the state to which it belonged. Were he to denounce this execution
or actually to try to stop it, they could say to him: You are a foreigner,
mind your own business." He even feels "a dawning interest in the
apparatus," and he admires the officer: "your sincere conviction has
touched me," he tells him, almost apologizing for his own lack of
conviction.[44]

The traveler is threatened by the gravestone, the scenario it proposes, and the injunction it proclaims, because something in him is
unable to find the promised resurrection ridiculous. He belongs to
and believes in an order that values respect for superiors and adherence to the scenarios authorized by society. He has more human
understanding for the officer, who does his duty and has the courage
of his convictions, than for the condemned prisoner, who is not serious and plays like a child with the soldier after his release and shows
childlike curiosity about the machine. This behavior annoys the traveler: "He was resolved to stay till the end, but he could not bear the
sight of these two. 'Go back home,' he said."[45] Actually, the prisoner is
behaving precisely as the officer has said viewers of executions used to
do in the old days, showing great and animated interest in the operation of the machine. But it annoys the traveler because the prisoner
cannot possibly fully understand what is happening, cannot know
what the machine is really supposed to do. He is playing in the same

44. "Er war weder Bürger der Strafkolonie, noch Bürger des Staates, dem sie
angehörte. Wenn er diese Exekution verurteilen oder gar hintertreiben wollte,
konnte man ihm sagen: Du bist ein Fremder, sei still" (CS 151; SE 109). "Der
Reisende war schon ein wenig für den Apparat gewonnen" (CS 143; SE 102).
"Ihre ehrliche Überzeugung geht mir nahe" (CS 160; SE 116).

45. CS 164; SE 120: "Er war entschlossen, hier bis zum Ende zu bleiben, aber
den Anblick der zwei hätte er nicht lange ertragen. 'Geht nach Hause,' sagte er."

sort of half joking way as when he wrestled with the soldier and reclothed himself in his filthy and cut up garments. He does not take it seriously enough. The officer, though the defender of a barbarous system, was serious, and the traveler could understand and sympathize with such seriousness: "he had a feeling that he must now stand by the officer, since the officer was no longer able to look after himself."[46]

Though he rejects the "straffe Zucht" of the Old Commandant, the traveler is not prepared to accept the unlimited playfulness of the condemned man, who indeed shows only the most perfunctory respect for his superiors. His disbelief in the Old Commandant's system is really directed only at the machine itself and the executions it carries out, not at the assumptions about reading that underlie the system. The Old Commandant and the officer have ruthlessly pursued the notion of reading as writing "in the soul" to its ultimate conclusion, something neither the traveler of Kafka's story nor the Freud of Derrida's essay wishes to do. Derrida's Freud wants to conceive of the human psyche as a scene of writing, but he does not want to acknowledge the element of the mechanical—that is, of death—which his analogy would ascribe to the living soul. Kafka's traveler wants to banish death from the scene of reading but not thereby to banish also respect for authority, duty, seriousness. He wants the Old Commandant's principles, but he does not want them applied with the Old Commandant's rigor. And given that ambivalence, he might feel that the resurrection of the Old Commandant was not something to be dismissed as ridiculous after all. The only course of action he can follow is to flee the scene altogether, thus to escape the choice between the deadly seriousness of "straffe Zucht" and the childish playfulness of those who do not read.

"In the Penal Colony" is thus a story of escape, particularly of escape from the deadly rigors of one sort of reading by the timely application of disbelief. Although it is true that the traveler's disbelief is not as rigorous as the system against which it is applied, it is at least temporarily effective. The traveler is able to escape from the problematic choice put to him by the scenario of the gravestone only by the usually unavailable strategy of departing for another world. Kafka's heroes do not often have this option or at least do not often recognize

---

46. *CS* 165; *SE* 121: "Er hatte das Gefühl, als müsse er sich jetzt des Offiziers annehmen, da dieser nicht mehr für sich selbst sorgen konnte."

themselves as having it. It does not occur to Joseph K. that he might simply ignore the court that has put him on trial, nor does Landsurveyor K. seriously consider leaving the Castle village. The reader recognizes these possibilities, to be sure, but the characters do not, or at least do not act upon their recognition. The *Reisender*, however, precisely because he is a traveler, can move, if this place does not suit him, to another spot where the out-of-place (Aristotle's "to atopon") will not be such a commonplace.

If the story has ended in the realm of atopia, with the incredible destruction of the machine, it has begun unquestionably with the topos, the verbal commonplace. Günther Anders, Walter Sokel, Stanley Corngold, Ruth Gross, and others have all contributed to our understanding of this process, whereby the reading of a piece of commonplace discourse becomes the starting point for poetic invention. The entire structure of "In the Penal Colony" can also be understood as an elaboration and gloss upon a certain topos or set of topoi. The proverbial "Am eigenen Leibe etwas erfahren" ("experiencing something on your body") becomes a text to be read, a scenario to be acted out in the fictional narrative. Considered from this point of view, the story itself represents an act of reading but reading precisely in the terms set forth by the Old Commandant's system. This reading brings action into conformity with injunction, the world into conformity with the word, the story into conformity with the proverb, and (ultimately) the endoxa into deadly contact with its opposite, paradox. Kafka's procedure and the Old Commandant's are both based on the necessity of making the reader behave in the manner prescribed by the text. Kafka's reading of the topoi of "feeling on your body" and "writing in the soul" are as rigorously consequential as the Old Commandant could wish. His logomimesis takes these metaphors *seriously*.

It is a curious fact, however, that the rigorous reading of topoi leads to atopia, that taking endoxal statements seriously leads to paradox. Paradox, as Ruth V. Gross has observed, is the opposite of proverbial opinion, indeed its "antidote": "a certain conflict is set up between what is 'contrary to opinion,' the figure of paradox, and the vehicle of opinion, the commonplace or proverb—endoxal knowledge. . . . the commonplace is the 'already-there' of language. Its antidote is paradox."[47] The imagery of the antidote (*alexipharmakon*) is noteworthy

47. Ruth V. Gross, "Rich Text/Poor Text: A Kafkan Confusion," *PMLA* 95:2 (1980), 171.

and entirely proper. Kafka participates completely in the tradition that understands language as *both* poison and antidote, both sense and nonsense, and as capable of generating both lethetic and alethetic readings.

Kafka's attitude toward the possibility of lethetic reading and the unfettered rhetorical freedom it could offer remained necessarily ambivalent—no less so, however, than his attitude toward alethetic reading and the potential for the attainment of truth it presupposes. A combination of idealistic longing and skeptical embarrassment affects his thinking about all versions of the absolute "Whole," including both absolute truth and absolute freedom. The combination of reverence and skepticism animates the narration of "In the Penal Colony" and gives it much of its paradoxical power. Before enacting the scene of the traveler's skepticism, Kafka gives plenty of reason for reverence. The process of reading that leads to the scene of the machine's self-destruction begins with a sacred text, whether we conceive that text as the holy Schrift of the Old Commandant or as the culturally enshrined wisdom of commonplaces. The possibility of escape from the torture of reading and the annihilation of self-destruction exists in a desacralizing act of disbelief, but the possibility is carefully circumscribed. Kafka lets the traveler effect an escape for himself and for the condemned prisoner, but he makes clear at the same time that the escape is a narrow one and that the traveler is teetering on the brink of belief. The Old Commandant may be dead and his machine in ruins, but their resurrection is promised.

"In the Penal Colony" displays this interaction of reverence and skepticism in an especially dramatic way. We recall that, though the traveler may not be able to read the Old Commandant's scripture, he is aware of the sacred nature of the reading machine itself. That this machine is in some kind of communication with the sacred world of "the Whole" is expressed by the imagery of bright sunshine that bathes it and bothers the traveler. "The glare of the sun in the shadeless valley was altogether too strong," and the eyes of the observer cannot focus on it without protection: "He sheltered his eyes from the sun with one hand and gazed up at the structure." The four brass rods at the corners "almost flashed out rays in the sunlight."[48] Kafka

48. "Die Sonne verfing sich allzustark in dem schattenlosen Tal" (*CS* 142; *SE* 101) ". . . die Hand zum Schutz gegen die Sonne über den Augen, sah er an dem Apparat in die Höhe" (*CS* 143; *SE* 102) ". . . in der Sonne fast Strahlen warfen" (*CS* 143; *SE* 102).

follows the easily recognized tradition that associates the sun with power and authority, with the truth untainted, with the highest divinity. The Messenger in "An Imperial Message" carries the sign of the sun on his breast in token of his commission from the highest authority, the Emperor. His mission is to bring the sacred light to "you" who are condemned to sit in the twilight, where perfect light is alloyed with darkness, and dream of that unattainable perfection.

The purpose of the machine, in the orthodox view of the officer, is to put the condemned prisoner in direct touch with the divine light. Its sacred mission is no different from that of the Imperial Messenger, and it is just as hopeless. The impossibility of communication between the human world and the world of absolute completeness, "the Whole," is one of Kafka's constant themes, but his skepticism never appears to have led him to suppose that such an absolute realm does not exist and does not lead him to the affirmation of absolute freedom that such a supposition would have entailed. The poignancy of much of Kafka's fiction lies in his continuing commitment to a sacred realm of truth, law, and epistemological and ethical certainty, with which one cannot make secure contact. The observer writing about Bucephalus never doubts that the gates of India are there or that Alexander reached them, but now they have somehow been moved further away. The message from the Emperor really exists, as all the spectators assembled at his death see, but it just happens that this message can never reach its destination.

Absolute belief in the existence of such a divine source for the authority of texts is in part responsible for the dismal situation to be found in the penal colony, where orthodoxy demands that these texts be written on the soul, by way of the bodies, of the colony's intransigent subjects. If there were no holy scripture, there would be no need to read with one's wounds and thus no need to inflict the wounds required by such a reading process. If one could simply play, as the condemned prisoner does, and remain innocent of the need for seriousness and of contact with an absent and invisible law—if one could read without the need to find in the word of the text a truth that transcends present reality—then perhaps one could escape from the passion of reading and from the problematic of submission to an absent authority that such reading represents. Freedom could be won by the employment of the lethetic mode of reading that Kafka clearly recognizes and elsewhere seems to advocate. It must be granted, though, that the same freedom might be won by the opposite strategy of adopting an unquestioning faith in the supremacy of the word in the manner advocated by the officer. "Scripture" could bring liberation—whether the scripture was the law, holy doctrine, or even literature—*if* we could accept it unconditionally as true, in spite of any apparent discrepancies.

The same view might even be taken of Kafka's parabolic fiction, as has been advocated by Wilhelm Emrich:

> From the point of view of the empirical "real" human being, all of Kafka's writing is meaningless, absurd, useless, incomprehensible [even as the Old Commandant's script is incomprehensible]. It cannot "help" such a person; what is more, it cannot even enlighten him. If, however, empirical man were to "go along with" this literature, take it not only as parable, not only as "literature," but as *the* reality and truth of life, he would be "free."[49]

Such an absolute belief in the truth of fiction is almost indistinguishable from disbelief because it would appear prepared to deal with the apparent lack of congruence between "reality" and the fictional text by simply redefining reality to fit the fiction. This is essentially the Platonic strategy, the "sacralization of fiction" I have discussed elsewhere.[50] Emrich posits that Kafka is the ultimate sacralizer of fiction, in whose works the fiction takes on a reality and truth quite beyond actuality. The text becomes the means whereby reality is given human structure and significance, in the way that Heidegger's "authentic language" is supposed to do: "Only when these literary works are comprehended not simply as 'literature' and fiction, but as concrete representations of our *entire* human existence, do they have liberating significance. Only then does man himself become maker and 'judge' of his own existence, of the totality of his earthly and spiritual existence."[51] It is not surprising that Emrich's approach, which is explicitly Heideggerian, should come to a conception of an aletheia such as that revealed in Kafka's works, but it does not really seem very likely that Kafka shared Heidegger's faith in the power of poetic language to dis-cover the truth or in the ability of such dis-covery to liberate anyone. The case of the officer in "In the Penal Colony" suggests more than a little skepticism in this regard because his indestructible Überzeugung brings neither liberation nor enlightenment.

49. Emrich, *Kakfa*, 109.
50. Koelb, *The Incredulous Reader*, 192–215.
51. Emrich, *Kafka*, 110.

The clear implication is that conviction alone, no matter how potent, cannot make the act of reading into the experience of transfiguration and salvation promised by the Old Commandant's orthodoxy.

Emrich's view of the liberating power of Kafka's fiction, however, comes surprisingly close to advocating a lethetic reading of these stories inasmuch as he urges that a certain sort of disbelief be employed in interpreting them. Indeed, question of belief and disbelief become crucial to his argument. But Emrich's Heideggerian approach cannot tolerate lethetic readers of the kind Kafka himself described, those who sit quietly unnoticed in the corner of the text or who pass through the text untouched by its dangerous power. Emrich finds in Kafka's works a prodigious effort to attain the truth, "access to that which 'is,' which is being unceasingly proclaimed by everything that has Being."[52] Disbelief is essential in order to gain this access, according to Emrich, because man has "forgotten," or believes he has forgotten, the truth. A "pseudo-story," which must be disbelieved but on the whole is believed, blocks and substitutes for the true story:

> In man's consciousness there is another story that cannot be forgotten, one that he definitely remembers, for otherwise he could not confuse it with the genuine one. However, "because" he puts this other story in place of the authentic one and mistakes it for the latter, in this way interposing a substitute, he succumbs to the illusion, nay more, to the honest, actual "belief" that he no longer has any recollection of the genuine story. His awareness of and his belief in a pseudo-story are, therefore, the reason why he seemingly forgets the true story. . . . In reference to this, the word "believe" should be—and actually must be—interpreted in the sense of "being of the opinion," or of "considering as true" . . . . There can be no doubt that the guest's confusion [in "The Hunter Gracchus"] is the confusion of those people who are still letting themselves "be deceived by the words of all the authorities round about," and are putting truth-substitutes in place of the genuine truths. This criticism of everything on earth that is said, thought, believed, and lived cannot be excelled.[53]

It is clear enough from "In the Penal Colony," as well as from other writings, that Kafka was indeed very skeptical about authorities of various kinds that put truth substitutes in place of genuine truths. But this skepticism is perhaps slightly more far-reaching than Emrich would grant; it is clear that at times Kafka thought that all authorities,

52. Ibid., 47.
53. Ibid., 46–47.

all texts *including his own*, could never be more than truth substitutes. At times, the only liberation possible through reading appeared to Kafka to be that attained by strictly ignoring the authority of the text.

A number of texts demonstrate Kafka's suspicion of texts, including his own, as repositories of truth. Indeed, language appears to be inadequate even to convictions:

> Distributing belief rightly between one's words and one's convictions. Not letting a conviction escape like steam in the very moment when one becomes aware of it. Not shifting on to the words the responsibility imposed by the conviction. Not letting convictions be stolen by words, harmony between words and convictions is still not decisive, nor is good faith ["guter Glaube"]. Such words can always ram such convictions in, or dig them up, according to circumstances.
>
> Utterance does not in principle mean a weakening of conviction— that would not be anything to be deplored—but a weakness of conviction.[54]

Particularly remarkable in this passage is the notion that words might be capable of "stealing" convictions. Language is placed in a surprising role here as an agent able to alienate convictions from their proper owner. In this view, "speaking one's mind" would be not a virtue but rather an abandonment of something valuable to an immoral end. Genuinely strong convictions could not, Kafka suggests, be expressed in speech because utterance presupposes their weakness. The conditions for the existence of real convictions is their inexpressibility and thus their unavailability for examination. The paradoxical consequence is that the strongest testimony to the existence of convictions would be a person's utter silence about them.

In a similar vein is the famous fragment from the *Nachlaß* about the nature of another form of truth, confession: "Confession and the lie are one and the same. In order to be able to confess, one tells lies. One cannot express what one is, for that *is* precisely what one is; one can

54. *WP* 84; *HO* 85: "Den Glauben richtig verteilen zwischen den eigenen Worten and den eigenen Überzeugungen. Eine Überzeugung, nicht in dem Augenblick, in dem man von ihr erfährt, verzischen lassen. Die Verantwortung, welche die Überzeugung auflegt, nicht auf die Worte abwälzen. Überzeugungen nicht durch Worte stehlen lassen. Übereinstimmung der Worte und Überzeugungen ist noch nicht entscheidend, auch guter Glaube nicht. Solche Worte können solche Überzeugungen noch immer je nach den Umständen einrammen oder ausgraben. Aussprache bedeutet nicht grundsätzlich eine Schwächung der Überzeugung— darüber wäre auch nicht zu klagen—, aber eine Schwäche der Überzeugung."

communicate only what one is not, that is, the lie. Only in the chorus may be a certain truth."[55] The self, like strong conviction, is not communicable through discourse because the very act of making a discourse belies the nature of the self, apparently by fragmenting it and presenting only one broken piece of the whole. The whole self is therefore unavailable for textual presentation and can be reconstructed only retrospectively by assembling the pieces, the chorus of lies, of many acts of confession. Kafka does not deny the existence of the self or of strong convictions, nor does he deny the possibility of any access to them. He does, however, indicate that any access we have must inevitably falsify, weaken, or destroy the things we are looking for. Any truth we get will always be a fiction, a "lie" in which only the ghost of some distant and now broken contact with the genuine article resides. What remains is "nothing, only an image, nothing else, utter oblivion,"[56] and even this image (*Bild*) is morally suspect. Kafka quotes in these same pages a fragment of the decalog: "Ihr sollt euch kein Bild."[57] The image, imperfect and slight as it is, is all we have, and even this is forbidden to us by the law.

Emrich understands Kafka to be undertaking and recommending the very traditional alethetic strategy of directing one's disbelief against the "reality" of common opinion and of conducting the search for truth by way of fiction. This understanding is not wrong, but it is incomplete. There is little doubt that Kafka did indeed believe in the existence of some transcendent truth that could not be reached by ordinary means, and this belief is evident in much of the fiction. In this sense Kafka certainly belongs to the main line of the Western tradition, inaugurated by Plato, which holds that truth, if it is to be revealed at all, will appear in the structure of fiction. But that last "if" looms large in the world Kafka depicts. We find evidence there of a strong faith both in the existence of truth and in the necessity of the quest for it but evidence also of a radical questioning of the possibility of attaining such truth by means (such as language) available to hu-

---

55. *WP* 338; *HO* 343: "Geständnis und Lüge ist das Gleiche. Um gestehen zu können, lügt man. Das, was man ist, kann man nicht ausdrücken, denn dies ist man eben; mitteilen kann man nur das, was man nicht ist, also die Lüge. Erst im Chor mag eine gewisse Wahrheit liegen." This passage is often commented upon. For a discussion of Kafka's work based upon it, see Ulrich Gaier, "Chorus of Lies: On Interpreting Kafka," *German Life and Letters* 22 (1969), 283–296.

56. *WP* 344; *HO* 349: "Nichts, nur Bild, nichts anderes, völlige Vergessenheit."

57. *HO* 352; *WP* 348. "Thou shalt not make any [graven] image."

man beings. Gods like Alexander and animals like Bucephalus, the ape in "Report for an Academy," and others may do so, but ordinary persons may not. "Plenty of hope—for God—no end of hope—only none for us," he remarked in a famous conversation with Max Brod.[58] Bucephalus's best hope, now that he is no longer Alexander's horse, is to read old books, but there is no reason to think that success is any more certain by this method than by sitting at your window and dreaming. One might hit the truth by either method, but one could never be certain.

Certainty is always lacking, and this is surely one of the reasons why the process of reading the law should turn out to be so painful and ultimately so deadly. Absolute certainty can only come, the officer claims, to a human soul that has crossed the boundary into the realm of the dead, after the "sixth hour" when death itself is the greatest certainty. The existence of a sacred text and the belief in it are not sufficient to liberate us, contrary to Emrich's proposal, but appear on the contrary to subject us to the most horrible torture and finally to kill us. And were our faith sufficient to lead us to genuine certainty, there is no guarantee that such certainty would not itself be enslaving rather than liberating. The officer possesses an absolute principle, "Guilt is never to be doubted." Joseph K. finds a "universal principle" (*Weltordnung*) in the Chaplain's reading of the parable "Before the Law": "Falsehood is made the order of the universe."[59] But such certainties are neither liberating nor salvific.

Lethetic reading, on the other hand, could be liberating and indeed is liberating for some of Kafka's characters and for Kafka himself some of the time.[60] But Kafka could not or did not want to sustain the disbelief necessary for lethetic reading over the long term. Although he has a certain nostalgia for the unauthorized playfulness of children (the condemned prisoner, the balls in "Blumfeld"), he has no little horror of it as well. Such playfulness represents a complete divorce from any serious engagement with those traces of the transcendent "Absolute"[61] available to us, a divorce Kafka was unwilling to sanction.

58. Max Brod, *Franz Kafka: A Biography* (New York: Schocken, 1963), 75. Brod made a record of the conversation, noting that it occurred on February 28, 1920.

59. *TR* 276; *RO* 439 (translation mine): "Die Lüge wird zur Weltordnung gemacht."

60. On Kafka's employment of the lethetic mode, see Koelb, "Kafka and the Sirens: Writing as Lethetic Reading."

61. The term is used by Brod in his *Biography* and has a meaning similar to Emrich's "Whole."

And though he understands that the serious treatment of language becomes indistinguishable from play, that the opposition between seriousness and play deconstructs itself when examined rigorously, he is not prepared to relinquish the opposition. He wants to read texts rigorously and alethetically, even though such a reading may in the end drive these texts to atopia, as happens with proverbial language in "In the Penal Colony" and with the parable in *The Trial*. The process creates a new text that resembles a tale of the marvelous, a lethetic fiction soliciting disbelief.

But although Kafka occasionally engages in lethetic reading, he does not write lethetic fictions. His stories are meant to engage the reader in the problematic of reading, of interpreting traces of something that is both absolutely important and absolutely unattainable; they are meant to put the reader in a torture machine and stretch him out on the rack of this tough word. It is no fun for him and an odd kind of fun for us: these stories are "no calligraphy for schoolchildren." The possibility for relief, for salvation and escape from such reading through disbelief, is offered at the end of the "Penal Colony" only to be withdrawn again as premature and partial. The Old Commandant may rise again at any moment and regain control of the colony, or so the gravestone promises. Those who can pass through this text as Odysseus passed through the song of the sirens would have nothing to fear from it, of course, but Kafka implies that this trick is very difficult to bring off. And perhaps we ought not to want to bring it off, at least not very often. Kafka more often chooses the rigors of alethetic reading over the escape of the lethetic. He does so, however, with a full knowledge of the implications of his choice. Like the officer, he retains his conviction, but his eyes remain open to the threat of destruction that such convictions carry with them.

Kafka proposed no solutions to the conflict between the two approaches to reading. They are probably, as Derrida suggests, absolutely irreconcilable, though it remains urgently necessary to reconcile them. What Kafka accomplished was to make explicit the terms of their opposition and, what is more important, the ground common to both. "In the Penal Colony" shows as clearly as any text in the Western canon the reversibility of rhetorical construction. We discover that commonplaces taken seriously, their metaphors pursued conscientiously in all their implications, turn into the very agents most effective in neutralizing commonplaces. Topoi are the antidote to topoi. Just as the officer must follow even to his own death the paradoxical requirements of his system, a system that commands officers to be just and at the same time assumes that guilt is never to be doubted, so does Kafka follow the requirements of an analogous system in which language must be taken seriously even though in he process it turns inevitably into a kind of play—wordplay. The act of alethic reading discloses the embarrassing but irrepressible and indeed inevitable possibility of lethetic reading.

Chapter 5

THE RHETORIC OF REALISM

In spite of the fact that he wrote fantasy, and sometimes wildly outlandish fantasy at that, Kafka is regularly admired as a writer deeply perceptive about the reality of modern life and of the human condition.[1] Although I do not wish to dispute this view, I believe it needs substantial complication, for much of Kafka's "realism" depends to a large extent less on his accurate perception and reproduction of the observed world than on a verbal imagination that looks to language itself for its principal impetus, its rhetorical moment. If we value Kafka's writing for its insightfulness, its unsparing candor, and its dedication to the pursuit of truth—and we do and we should—we must recognize that these qualities are deeply and closely related to another, a rigorous attention to the verbal structure of preexisting discourse.

The question of the way in which realism relates to the verbal imagination is a crucial one for the study of Kafka, but it is of considerable consequence for the study of other writers as well. In Kafka's case the issue is somewhat blurred by the prominence of the fantastic in his fiction, and so it is perhaps best to introduce the topic

1. Emrich, to take one prominent example, observes that "Kafka's writing . . . reveals startlingly clairvoyant insights into the actual social life of the present time and describes the reality of our social-political life with bold exactitude and *realism*" (*Franz Kafka: A Critical Study of His Writings*, trans. Sheema Zeben Buehne [New York: Ungar, 1968], 30; emphasis mine).

by briefly considering another writer, one almost universally admired for the vividness of his realism, Stephen Crane. Superficially there would seem to be little reason for comparing Crane and Kafka and less reason still for hoping to clarify Kafka by using Crane as a lens. There is, however, a hidden affinity between the two precisely in the way that both pursue the task of literary invention.

Here is a "story" by Crane, one of a series of little blurbs he worked on but never published, under the title "In Brief." I insist that it *is* a story, though it is only one sentence long: "As Peter Peterson, 32, of 963 East 67th St. was viewing a base ball game he was mistaken for the umpire and killed."[2] Poor Mr. Peterson is the victim less of mob violence than of metaphor. The joke depends on the traditional and even in Crane's day clichéd baseball fan's cry of "Kill the umpire!" Now, no matter how often this sentiment has been expressed, and no matter how deep the feelings giving rise to its utterance, we would actually be shocked to learn of a case in which the words used to express it were taken literally. In fact, no outraged baseball fans have, as far as I know, taken the life of any umpire as an expression of their disagreement with his judgment. Crane's little story, however, assumes that the linguistic form, not the intention behind it, should govern our understanding of this hallowed cry. It assumes, in short, that baseball fans actually *kill* umpires and that anyone unfortunate enough somehow to resemble an umpire would be in mortal danger. The fact that sports officials—in other places and other sports—have suffered grievous physical violence at the hands of angry fans might seem to make Crane into something of a prophet here, but he clearly did not intend to be one. He was unquestionably making a joke out of the literal reading of a figure.

It is easy, I think, to see why we should regard this little tale as an exercise in rhetorical construction, for Crane has developed in narrative form the implications of the language of a common figure of speech. I say that he pays attention to language here because he does not pay attention to the "thought" or "intention"; on the contrary, the thought or intention behind the phrase "Kill the umpire!" is well known though pointedly ignored by this text. Crane has taken the verbal form out of context, as it were, and has mounted it in a narra-

---

2. *The Works of Stephen Crane*, ed. Fredson Bowers (Charlottesville: University Press of Virginia, 1975), vol. 10, *Poems and Literary Remains*, p. 107. All subsequent references to Crane's works will be to the various volumes of the Virginia edition.

tive context at once silly and grim. We laugh at it only because we recognize the trope that has prompted it; if the story were translated into the language of another culture in which this cliché is never heard, it would be transformed from a joke into the report of random and savage violence.

Although the story of Mr. Peterson is only a minor jotting taken from Crane's literary remains, it is by no means the only text in which we can see Crane working in this special fashion. We can find exactly the same verbal imagination operating in works that are widely considered more central to the Crane canon. This is particularly the case with Crane's poetry, which depends to a remarkable degree upon just such attention to language as language. One of the more moving poems from the collection *The Black Riders and Other Lines* is the following:[3]

> In the desert
> I saw a creature, naked, bestial,
> Who, squatting upon the ground,
> Held his heart in his hands,
> And ate of it.
> I said, "Is it good, friend?"
> "It is bitter—bitter," he answered;
> "But I like it
> "Because it is bitter,
> "And because it is my heart."

Here again the evident basis for the poem is the everyday figure of speech "to eat your heart out," taken at its linguistic face value and made the basis of a miniature narrative.

But something different happens here from what we found in the story of Peter Peterson: this is no joke, and we find not the slightest cause for laughter. Why not? After all, this is no more grim a tale than the other, in which a person was wantonly murdered. But here, we notice, Crane's imaginative gloss on the literal linguistic surface does not fail to take into account the figurative "intention" of the trope: Crane's naked and bestial creature is eating his heart out *both* literally and figuratively. Crane develops this double strategy neatly with another verbal device, by playing on both the literal, sensory, and figurative, emotional meanings of the word "bitter." The heart as organ is bitter to the taste, and the heart as emotional center is filled with the

3. Crane, vol. 10, p. 4.

emotion of bitterness. The poem refuses to decide between the "surface" and "intention" of the trope upon which it is based, always allowing the reader to apprehend the figurative meaning that still shadows the fantasy narrative generated from the linguistic form of the locution. We are familiar with this rhetorical mode from Kafka's fictions.

The literal "mis"-reading of the figure still holds the foreground, and it deepens and complicates the concept of "eating your heart out." Crane's character is doing something both conscious and deliberate, something he has evidently chosen to do. The act of choice is made the center of attention both by the poem's form and by the literal acting out of the metaphor. Here is someone who has made a decision to eat his heart out and who finds some benefit in doing so. The possibility of such a deliberate action is implied by the form, but not the import, of the locution. "To eat" is an active verb and one with a great variety of possible objects: the character in the poem could just as well be eating a banana or a mutton chop. Such a choice is not implied by the *meaning* of the metaphor, however: we do not expect a person to eat his heart out because he prefers doing so to other possible activities. We assume, on the contrary, that he would rather not do so, all things considered.

The poem's effectiveness, then, depends on a realignment of the figurative and literal meanings of the locution. The poem proposes a new perspective on the figurative meaning by presenting the emotional pain of eating your heart out as a deliberately chosen alternative. But this new perspective is made possible by the poem's rigorous attention to the verbal surface, in other words precisely by ignoring or "misreading" the intention of the trope and focusing attention on the everyday import of the words "eat" and "heart." By forcing the confrontation, Crane provokes a widening of the figurative import, which must now include the possibility of deliberate choice that is suggested by the literal meaning of the metaphor. This result is very different from what happens in the story of Peter Peterson, which calls attention to the literal meaning of "kill the umpire" only to reduce this meaning, as it were, to the absurd.

Crane's poem displays realism of two distinct kinds. One is the emotional realism of the situation presented. Although we cannot imagine how a man could actually eat his own heart, we can understand the peculiar combination of misery and self-reliant pride in the man's attitude. No matter how we read the man's proclamation that

he likes eating his heart, we see it as the analog of a complex sentiment with which we are familiar. But we may also see a "linguistic
realism" at work here. To the degree that we can identify the literal
level of tropes such as "eat your heart out" with things in the real
world (*res*), Crane's use of the locution can be understood as unex-
pectedly "realistic." In this context, "realistic" would not mean "true to
everyday experience," as much as "radically concrete"—and it certainly would not mean "pertaining to objects." The latter would imply
that the abstract, figurative meaning is somehow transformed into a
pure literal object. My argument hinges on the contention that the
figurative meaning remains a functioning alternative at every moment in the reading of the text. But the concrete reality of the literal
object does indeed achieve greater prominence here than in "ordinary" uses of the trope. This kind of "realism" is most characteristic of
Crane and of Kafka.[4]

Of course, there are times when the verbal imagination does work
in an especially radical way and moves a considerable distance away
from the figurative intent of the language it imitates. Consider this,
one of the most suggestive and at the same time one of the most
elusive of the *Black Riders* poems:[5]

> On the horizon the peaks assembled;
> And as I looked,
> The march of the mountains began.
> As they marched, they sang,
> "Aye! We come! We come!"

One can imagine a writer describing a mountain range on the horizon
as, say, "assembled in a row like soldiers preparing to march." Indeed,
one can imagine Stephen Crane writing in just this way. It would be
"colorful," if not particularly original, prose. Here, however, we have
something very different: the poem quite overlooks the fact that the
reason for comparing the mountain peaks to soldiers is simply that
they are lined up in a row. Instead, it equates the mountains with
soldiers in ways that we no longer find justified in nature: they march,

4. I am aware that this use of the term "realism" is highly unorthodox and in
an important sense flouts established critical practice. I mean not to quarrel with
other uses of the term or with those who view Kafka as more of a "naturalist" than
a realist but only to suggest a different dimension to the relation between language
and ordinary experience in Kafka's writing.

5. Crane, vol. 10, p. 21.

they sing, and indeed they threaten to advance upon us. If mountains could in fact do these things, it would be almost desperately terrifying, and the poem convincingly creates such an atmosphere of dread. That dread, however, is the kind properly kindled by looking at an army assembled, by hearing the soldiers sing their marching songs, by fearing that the army is coming to overwhelm you.

Of course, the sight of a mountain range can be overwhelming, too, but not in this way, not because of any expectation that the mountains are on the move. We would not, except in a nightmare, expect a mountain range to advance upon us and we would certainly not expect mountains to announce that they were doing so. This poem takes the metaphor equating mountains and soldiers and runs with it far beyond the limits of the figurative meaning. Here the figurative meaning seems to be less effaced than left behind: Crane shows us how a mountain range could indeed become an army assembled to advance. This development of the literal meaning of the trope suggests a new range of figurative readings, of course, but these new figurations are enlargements of the "original" figurative import (the mountains are arranged in a row) less than they are departures from it.

The image of the mountains advancing like soldiers reminds us that Crane is most famous for describing the progress of actual armies, not metaphorical ones. His brief novel *The Red Badge of Courage* remains the classic standard by which modern war literature is judged. This is Crane the realist, we feel, and here we would expect to find little employment for his verbal imagination. The surprising fact is, however, that this acknowleged masterpiece of "realistic" prose depends for its most telling effects far more on the manipulation of figurative language than on the accurate perception and representation of the world.

We have good reason to want to explore this possiblity. It is well known that Crane knew nothing of actual warfare when he wrote *Red Badge*, and it remains one of the perennial paradoxes of American literature that one of the most moving depictions of the experience of battle came from the pen of someone totally lacking in such experience. Critics have been on the whole satisfied to assume that in the novel Crane depicted an extraordinarily vividly imagined experience and have been notably less willing to suppose, as I do here, that the basis for the story's power is not experience—either real or imagined—but language.

I will try to make my case, necessarily briefly, on the example of one central metaphor that dominates and focuses much of the story. In the opening paragraph, the narrator gives a justly famous description of the opposing armies that includes the following: "one could see, across, the red, eye-like gleam of hostile camp-fires set in the low brows of distant hills" (*RBC* 3). Here we have figurative language used in the way we would expect a realistic writer to use it, with just a hint at the metaphor implicit in the combination of "eye-like" fires and the "brows" of the hills. No specific reference is made to the creature possessing such eyes and such brows, but its implied presence is enough to add an additional dimension to the threatening atmosphere. The figure seems to belong securely in the matrix of the narrative diction as part of the way the story is told.

In the second chapter, though, the figurative language moves in another, centrally important direction. Here the narrator is describing what his hero, the young soldier Henry Fleming, sees in the opposing army: "Staring, once, at the red eyes across the river, he conceived them to be growing larger, as the orbs of a row of dragons, advancing" (*RBC* 15). A number of things have happened here. (1) The figure has been elaborated and made explicit as a red-eyed dragon. (2) The first half—the "meaning" half—of the trope has been suppressed entirely in the verbal surface of the narrative: Henry does not see fires that are like the eyes of a dragon; he sees "eyes" and imagines the dragons that possess them. (3) The figure is no longer part of the narrative matrix but belongs to the structure of the hero's mind. It thus belongs no longer as much to the telling of the story as to the story itself. The novel is, in a very real sense, about the figure.

The image of the red-eyed dragons governs Henry's experience through the bulk of the narrative. When in chapter 3 he imagines that the enemy is close by, he is described as "certain that in this vista there lurked fierce-eyed hosts. . . . The enemy would presently swallow the whole command" (*RBC* 24–25). And in chapter 12, when the real enemy and real battle burst upon him, he supposes that the "battle was lost. The dragons were coming with invincible strides. The army . . . was going to be swallowed" (*RBC* 69). Later, after he has experienced and survived real fighting, he congratulates himself: "He had been out among the dragons, he said, and he assured himself that they were not so hideous as he had imagined them" (*RBC* 86). Not so hideous, perhaps, but still dragons all the same. The youth's understanding of his own experience is structured by the figure of the dragon that was introduced, just barely, in the opening paragraph.

The actual comparison that initiated the simile—the campfires like red eyes in the dark—has been long since forgotten. The campfires themselves (the "meaning" of the figure) are no longer of any consequence. The language of the comparison, however, proceeds, now forming the explanatory myth for all Henry's most important feelings about the war.

The narrative device has now become an essential element in the story, part of the furniture of the hero's mind. But the power of the figure is such that it cannot be contained even here. It spills over and seems to infect other characters as well. At the end of a later chapter, Henry and his friend are convinced that, once again, disaster is about to befall them: "they nodded in a mute and unprotesting assent when a shaggy man near them said in a meek voice: 'We'll git swallered'" (*RBC* 103). The red-eyed, man-eating dragon belongs not just to the narrator or to his hero's imagination but to the whole narrative universe, even to a nameless minor character with essentially no role to play in the story save to announce the ubiquity of the metaphor.

The story of Henry's ultimate mastery of himself and his fears is in essence the mastery of this figure. Quite late in the novel, in chapter 20, he still thinks in the basic terms of the dragon trope but now with a bit of distance and a touch of humor: "As he noted the vicious, wolf-like temper of his comrades, he had a sweet thought that if the enemy was about to swallow the regimental broom as a large prisoner, it could at least have the consolation of going down with bristles forward" (*RBC* 114). By the time the narration closes, though, Henry is ready to fill his mind with other sorts of figures: "He turned now, with a lover's thirst, to images of tranquil skies, fresh meadows, cool brooks" (*RBC* 135). The dragons are gone.

My brief consideration of one of the linguistic devices in the *Red Badge* should make clear how close this kind of "realistic" prose is to the verbal fantasies of the *Black Riders* poems or even to a narrative jest such as the story of Peter Peterson. J. C. Levenson was more correct than he perhaps knew when he wrote in his introduction to the novel that Crane "could work his reader from . . . almost commonplace figures of speech to a heightened awareness of what war feels like when it penetrates the depths of a mind."[6] I would depart from Levenson's opinion only insofar as to suggest that there is, in Crane's practice, no distance at all between commonplace figures of

6. Crane, vol. 2, xv.

speech and "heightened awareness" of what something feels like. What the reader becomes more aware of, in the end, is not an experience in another's mind but his own experience of language.

Crane's strength as a realistic writer comes from the same source that generates his very unrealistic poetry and humor. The case is very much the same with Kafka except that Kafka's usual practice is to mix realistic and fantastic elements in the same text. Even in those works that contain nothing even faintly marvelous, however, we can see Kafka's verbal imagination at work. The story "A Little Woman" ("Eine kleine Frau"), published by Kafka in his last collection of fiction, inscribes itself precisely between the literal and figurative usages of the word *klein*. The woman designated by the title is described at the outset as "naturally quite slim," but it soon becomes clear that her physical size is perhaps not the central issue. The problem, according to the narrator, is that "she always finds something objectionable in me, I am always doing the wrong thing to her, I annoy her at every step." She thus appears to be *klein* in the figurative sense of "petty, mean, narrow-minded." Kafka draws the reader's attention to the possibility of slippage between the literal and figurative meanings of this adjective when he calls the strained relations between himself and the woman a "small affair." We can only assume that he means that the matter is insignificant or petty. But he immediately performs a logomimetic transformation upon this locution by asserting that he will "keep my hand over it, even quite lightly," and thereby be able to live his life in peace. The fact that he is able to "cover" the affair over with his hand shows that it is physically as well as psychologically small. The story thus discloses itself as, in part, a meditation on smallness, on the relation between the literal and figurative meanings of *klein*.[7]

A significant number of these few fictions totally lacking in fantastic elements can be shown to arise from a rhetorical moment. One of the clearest examples is the little story from the *Nachlaß* that Brod titled "The Top" ("Der Kreisel"). It concerns a philosopher who likes to linger near where children play and to chase their spinning tops in an attempt to catch them while they are still spinning. He does so, the

7. The quotations from "A Little Woman": "Von Natur aus recht schlank" (*CS* 317; *SE* 157) ". . . ist mit mir sehr unzufrieden, immer hat sie etwas an mir auszusetzen, immer geschieht ihr Unrecht von mir, ich ärgere sie auf Schritt und Tritt" (*CS* 317; *SE* 157) ". . . mit der Hand auch nur ganz leicht diese kleine Sache verdeckt" (*CS* 323–324; *SE* 163).

narrator explains, as a consequence of his method of philosophical understanding:

> For he believed that the understanding of any detail, that of a spinning top, for instance, was sufficient for the understanding of all things. . . . Once the smallest detail was understood, then, everything was understood, which was why he busied himself only with the spinning top. And whenever preparations were being made for the spinning of the top, he hoped that this time it would succeed: as soon as the top began to spin and he was running breathlessly after it, the hope would turn to certainty, but when he held the silly piece of wood in his hand, he felt nauseated. The screaming of the children, which hitherto he had not heard and which now suddenly pierced his ears, chased him away, and he tottered like a top under a clumsy whip.[8]

The philosopher's effort appears to stem from an impulse to act out literally the word that, in a conventional figurative usage, describes his calling: *begreifen* ("grasp"). His epistemological goal is to grasp or form a concept (*Begriff*) of the spinning top and thereby to obtain secure knowledge (*Erkenntnis*) about it. The paradox of his situation, which ultimately turns his hope into nauseated despair, is that the act of grasping the spinning top cannot give him a grasp of it: *begreifen* (in the literal sense) positively excludes *begreifen* (in the figurative sense) because of course the act of grasping the top causes it to stop spinning, to become nothing more than a "silly piece of wood" of no philosophical interest.

A second paradox declares itself at the story's end, when we learn that the philosopher's lack of success in grasping the spinning top converts him into a metaphorical top, but one that wobbles as if it had been set in motion by an inexpert spinner. This transformation in turn forces a rhetorical shift in the meaning of "whip" (*Peitsche*) away from its figurative sense as the device used to set a top in motion and back to its literal meaning of "lash." The philosopher is revealed as

8. *CS* 444; *SE* 320: "Er glaubte nämlich, die Erkenntnis jeder Kleinigkeit, also zum Beispiel auch eines sich drehenden Kreisels, genüge zur Erkenntnis des Allgemeinen. . . . War die kleinste Kleinigkeit wirklich erkannt, dann war alles erkannt, deshalb beschäftigte er sich nur mit dem sich drehenden Kreisel. Und immer wenn die Vorbereitungen zum Drehen des Kreisels gemacht wurden, hatte er Hoffnung, nun werde es gelingen, und drehte sich der Kreisel, wurde ihm im atemlosen Laufen nach ihm die Hoffnung zur Gewißheit, hielt er aber dann das dumme Holzstück in der Hand, wurde ihm übel und das Geschrei der Kinder, das er bisher nicht gehört hatte und das ihm jetzt plötzlich in die Ohren fuhr, jagte ihn fort, er taumelte wie ein Kreisel unter einer ungeschickten Peitsche."

one who goes around in circles ("sich im Kreise bewegen"), never coming any nearer to his goal. In fact, he has been going in circles all along: the locution used at the very beginning of the story to describe his "hanging about" the children at play ("Ein Philosoph trieb sich immer dort herum") employs *treiben,* the very verb that is ordinarily used together with *Kreisel* to mean "spin a top." Part of the philosopher's problem is evidently that he does not realize he himself is participating in the phenomenon he wants to study.

The story takes the laws of physics and incorporates them into an economy that is primarily verbal. By this statement I mean that the parable's central point could be taken as illustrating one aspect of Heisenberg's indeterminacy principle but also that the logic follows the laws of the conservation of angular momentum. Spinning continues throughout the story, but it is transferred back and forth. The philosopher is spinning himself about ("treibt sich herum") even at the beginning of the story. He pauses ("lauerte") only when the top starts spinning. But at soon as he grabs the top and stops its turning, it is as if the motion had again been transferred to him: he becomes a top and wobbles away. The story, like its subject, proceeds in circles.

This story, then, seems to render in an image a scientifically correct insight into the problematic of our knowledge of the physical world. At the same time, however, the narrative is clearly at least as much driven by rhetoric as by epistemological subtlety. Here the old witticism "ontology recapitulates philology" rings particularly true, for it is ultimately impossible to disentangle Kafka's remarkably accurate perception of the structure of the physical world from his manipulation of purely verbal structures. The story's depiction of reality has the same beginning in a rhetorical moment that we find in Kafka's most fantastic tales. Kafka's readers regularly discover that in these stories the distinction between fantasy and reality becomes blurred, but for the most part they ascribe this effect to the commingling of marvelous and "ordinary" elements in a single narrative. Kafka's mode of writing (which is also a mode of reading) actually proposes a more subtle and more startling reason for this effect: both fantasy and reality are presented in the fictions as rhetorically structured.

At times we can see how even the most ordinary and unremarkable details in these fictions are related to rhetorical structures. In "A Hunger Artist" ("Ein Hungerkünstler"), for example, the protagonist's final words constitute a startling revelation of the fundamental issue in his fasting: he confesses that he could not help starving because he could never find any food he liked. "If I had found it, believe me, I should have made no fuss and stuffed myself like you or anyone else."[9] The allegation that he would not have "made any fuss" ("Aufsehen gemacht") if he could have found food to his taste is particularly striking because one of the story's central issues concerns the way in which hunger artists were formerly able to attract attention ("Aufsehen erregen") but now can no longer do so. Aufsehen is a concept of considerable importance to both the hunger artist and the narrator. It is all the more noteworthy, then, that the addressee of these final words is none other than an *Aufseher* ("overseer" or "supervisor") whose professional duty is to engage in aufsehen.

The existence of this supervisor in the story is determined therefore by the requirements of both the what we might call the "realistic matrix" and (by way of the verbal hinge) its deepest thematic concerns. Certainly this supervisor functions as a commonplace detail on the margins of the narrative center, but the signifier that serves as his label belongs to a sign system of central importance. The supervisor therefore performs a kind of double duty both as a bit player and as a star in the drama of the hunger artist.

Again and again we find that elements in the realistic matrix in which are embedded the amazing events typical of Kafka's fictions relate verbally to the fundamental, and usually disquieting, issues at stake. The opening sentence of "The Judgment," for example, seems to function comfortably as a traditional setting of the scene familiar in nineteenth-century fiction: "It was a Sunday morning in the very height of spring."[10] It is followed by additional information about the surroundings in which the young merchant Georg Bendemann finds himself, and for several pages the reader is able to proceed on the assumption that the story is going to depict a little slice of bourgeois domestic life in the manner of Balzac. The story does not take its uncanny turn until the reader is very deep into it, and even then nothing occurs that is anywhere near as outrageous as Gregor Samsa's transformation. Still, when we reach the tale's end, we know that we are dealing with something other than a straightforward exercise in realism.

In the new context established by the story's conclusion, though, we might wonder what relevance the time of year, the day of the week,

9. *CS* 277; *SE* 171: "Hätte ich sie gefunden, glaube mir, ich hätte kein Aufsehen gemacht und mich vollgegessen wie du und alle."
10. *CS* 77; *SE* 23: "Es war an einem Sonntagvormittag im schönsten Frühjahr."

and so on, really have. There seems to be little or no connection between the grim and markedly odd events of the conclusion and the reassuring details of the opening lines. But there is a fundamentally verbal connection. Georg's precipitate action in response to his father's startling "sentence" of death is extraordinary. It is distressing to the degree that it might make one shout "Jesus!" as the charwoman does when Georg runs into her on the stairs. Indeed, this shout of "Jesus!" would seem to be a more appropriate context for these events than the narrator's calm setting forth of the time, day, and season of their occurrence. If we look twice at the time, day, and season, however, we discover that the narrator, too, is shouting "Jesus!" at us even as the story opens. The "Sunday morning at the very height of spring" cannot escape association with Easter and its story of death and renewal. My point is not that such Christian symbolism is appropriate to the story's theme (though it obviously is in its ironic way) but rather that the utterance "Jesus!" functions as a rhetorical hinge connecting the commonplace details of the opening sentence with the startling events of the conclusion.

Even the commonplace detail of Georg's surname is connected rhetorically to the complex issues lying at the heart of the narrative. Kafka himself realized that the name had significance, if only in the resemblance between the element "Bende-" and "Kafka."[11] Critics have also noted that this element is a homophone for *Bände*, a word suggesting both writing ("volumes") and, by paronomasia, bonds (*Bande*). The man is named Bendemann at least in part because he is involved in a difficult structure of connections (*Verbindungen*) that is causing him considerable trouble. The very word *Verbindung* appears several times in the opening pages of the story in the context of Georg's musings on his friend in Russia. The friend maintains that he has no connection (*Verbindung*) with his countrymen in Russia, and Georg wonders about keeping up their correspondence ("briefliche Verbindung") in the future. These two uses of *Verbindung* establish the poles between which the story moves: connectedness—as in the bonds with the friend in Russia, the newly formed bond with Frieda, the familial bond that Georg reasserts in his final words—and the lack thereof. The name Bendemann participates in this central issue by way of paronomasia, but at the same time it retains its principal func-

11. "But Bende has exactly the same number of letters as Kafka, and the vowel *e* occurs in the same places as does the vowel *a* in Kafka" (*DI1* 279).

tion on the narrative margin, as part of the realistic matrix. The hero's first name, Georg, functions similarly, alluding on the one hand to a broken family bond (Franz's brother Georg, who died in infancy)[12] and on the other to a newly forming bond with Felice Bauer (Greek *georgos* = German *Bauer*, as Kafka learned in his first Greek lessons), but in this case the allusions are paratextual or extratextual.

Many of the names of Kafka's characters serve this double function, both contributing to the realistic matrix and participating verbally in the thematic structure. This is, of course, hardly a technical innovation on Kafka's part: so-called onomastic imagery is a stock literary device used regularly by many of the authors Kafka knew well, including Goethe ("Werther," "Meister," and so forth). But the fact that Kafka makes such frequent, though subtle, use of the device only reinforces the larger point I am making; that is, that the relationships among narrative elements in Kafka's fiction are intimately linked to relationships at the level of the verbal signifier. Heinz Politzer drew attention to exactly this sort of intimate link when he noted that the physical and psychological relation between Karl Rossmann and Johanna Brummer in *The Missing Person* cannot be separated from a relation that exists between their names. Because *Brummer* and *Roß* are both common nouns in German, the names are subject to the same autonomasia that affects "Kafka." *Brummer* denotes a bluebottle or horsefly, and *Roß* is an elevated term for "horse." Politzer supposes that the figure proposes an analogy between the behavior of the characters and the behavior of the animals embedded in their names: "As a horsefly molests a horse . . . [Johanna] has circled round Karl, has followed and irritated him, and finally thrust herself on him in the manner of a parasite."[13] Politzer apparently wanted to use this behavior as evidence regarding the relative culpability of the two parties for the ill-fated sexual liaison between them, but I suspect the more important issue lies elsewhere. Although the associations that accompany the word *Roß* have positive value and those that accompany *Brummer* negative ones, more fundamentally both words refer to animals. Karl and Johanna are people, but by participating in what to

12. Ernst Pawel, *The Nightmare of Reason: A Life of Franz Kafka* (New York: Farrar, Straus, & Giroux, 1984), 16, notes how important this death must have been for the young Kafka.

13. Heinz Politzer, *Franz Kafka: Parable and Paradox* (Ithaca: Cornell University Press, 1962), 126.

Kafka's mind were sordid acts of copulation, they behave like animals. The story actualizes the troubled moral status of the people like Rossmann, Brummer, and Kafka who have the names, and perhaps also the nature, of animals.

Kafka operates less radically in *The Missing Person* than he does in his more characteristic fantastic fictions. These people do not have the bodies or feeding habits of horses and flies. The story stops short of transforming Karl into a beast of burden, leaving him at the end perhaps just one remove from that status as a manual laborer bearing the alias of "Negro." *The Missing Person* is, in outward form, at any rate, a realistic novel. Its central issue, however—the problem of the social and moral status that Karl has, deserves, or can expect—is inseparable from the rhetorical problematic of names such as Kafka and Rossmann. The story of Bucephalus, "The New Advocate," is after all only a slightly more daring meditation on the difficulties of being a "Roß-mann." In his first sustained novelistic effort, Kafka chooses to leave the rhetorical slide before the ride has taken him as far as he knows it can. Indeed, none of the novel fragments thrusts the action very far past the boundaries of probability—at least not with the arresting force of a "Metamorphosis" or "Country Doctor." There are no talking animals, no living corpses, no machines that run by themselves.

But the *Trial* and *Castle* manuscripts linger, like *The Missing Person*, close to the rhetorical cusp that links the everyday and the uncanny. Kafka surely wanted his readers to notice that the warders (*Wächter*) who inform K. about his ostensible arrest at the opening of *The Trial* act out two substantially different significations of their title. The word *Wächter* can mean both "one who watches" and "one who awakens," and the two warders in fact perform both functions. It is more important in this context, however, that they can be understood to be "awakeners" in both a literal and a figurative sense: in terms of what I am calling the realistic matrix, they awaken K. in the sense that they provoke him to get out of bed, but in terms of the novel's principal theme, they initiate a process that "awakens" K. to his uncertain standing before the law. In that sense numerous other characters in the novel—perhaps all of them apart from K. himself—are metaphoric Wächter also. The entire novel is nothing but the unfolding of this process (*Prozeß*) of awakening. The warders, who are unquestionably marginal figures in terms of the realistic matrix, slip suddenly to the center by virtue of the word that names their office.

A more dramatic example, perhaps, of the metamorphic power of rhetoric even in the context of the ordinary occurs in *The Castle*. In the third chapter, we are introduced to a group of uniformly dressed peasants who turn out to be Klamm's servants. Although at first they are extremely quiet, sitting about the bar "with hardly a movement," they eventually start a kind of dance around Olga that becomes increasingly boisterous and even threatening: "the pace grew faster and faster, the yells more hungry, more raucous, until they were insensibly blended into one continuous howl."[14] Frieda explains that Klamm insists on bringing these people with him in spite of their being "the most contemptible and objectionable creatures" ("das Verächtlichste und Widerlichste") in her acquaintance. No matter how often she complains to Klamm, the same thing always happens:

> "It's all of no use, an hour before his arrival they always come bursting in like cattle into their stalls. But now they've really got to get into the stall, where they belong. If you weren't here, I'd fling open this door and Klamm would be forced to drive them out himself. . . . But now I'll have to turn them out myself." She took a whip from the corner and sprang among the dancers with a single bound, a little uncertainly, as a young lamb might spring. At first they faced her as if she were merely a new partner, and actually for a moment Frieda seemed inclined to let the whip fall, but she soon raised it again, crying, "In the name of Klamm, into the stall with you! Into the stall, all of you!" When they saw that she was in earnest, they began to press toward the back wall in a kind of panic incomprehensible to K., and under the impact of the first few a door shot open, letting in a current of night air, through which they all vanished, with Frieda behind them openly driving them across the couryard into the stalls.[15]

The figure of cattle and stalls, introduced simply as a particularly vivid description of the obnoxious behavior of Klamm's servants, starts to control the action. The metaphorical cattle almost become real cattle—at least Frieda treats them that way, driving them with her whip as Circe does with her wand. The metaphorical stalls do, how-

14. *CA* 51; *RO* 514: "Der Reigen wurde immer schneller, die Schreie hungrig, röchelnd, wurden allmählich fast ein einziger."

15. *CA* 51–52; *RO* 515: "'Alles Bitten ist umsonst, eine Stunde vor seiner Ankunft stürmen sie immer schon herein, wie das Vieh in den Stall. Aber nun sollen sie wirklich in den Stall, in dem sie gehören. Wären Sie nicht da, würde ich die Tür hier aufreißen, und Klamm selbst müßte sie hinaustreiben. . . . Nun werde ich sie aber selbst hinaustreiben müssen.' Sie nahm eine Peitsche aus der Ecke und sprang mit einem einzigen hohen, nicht ganz sicheren Sprung, so wie etwa ein Lämmchen springt, auf die Tanzenden zu. Zuerst wandten sie sich gegen sie, als sei eine neue Tänzerin angekommen, und tatsächlich sah es einen Augenblick

ever, become real ones, and the servants are forced to take refuge
across the courtyard in the stalls usually reserved for literal animals.
Although this passage does not utterly depart from plausible reality, it moves strongly in the direction of the uncanny. Even here, in a
context that calls for something akin to recognizable reality, Kafka
seems sorely tempted to let his verbal imagination run with the metaphor his character has introduced, to let the transformatory power of
the figure change the servants of Klamm from persons into beasts.
But in this case the narrative maintains the integrity of its realistic
surface by limiting the transformation to the actions of one character.
Although Frieda, brandishing her whip, treats the servants like the
cattle with which she compares them, the narrative does not take up
the metaphor itself. It allows us to suppose that the servants remain
human beings after Frieda has driven them into the stall. After all
she, who has been compared to an animal herself (a "young lamb"),
remains manifestly a person.

This is not the only time the *Castle* text teeters on the brink of
outright fantasy driven by rhetoric. Details of a more commonplace
nature than Frieda's treatment of the servants can be shown to derive
from a rhetorical power that can scarcely be contained by the con-
straints of the genre that Kafka has chosen. An example appears in
the ninth chapter, when the landlady criticizes K. for in effect wanting
everything served up to him on a silver platter. When K. balks at
answering a number of questions for a protocol that the secretary
Momus is drawing up for Klamm, the landlady tries to persuade him
that he ought to cooperate. In spite of the lack of assurance that the
protocol will help K. elicit the assurances he wants from the Castle,
the protocol will put him in contact with Klamm: "'Haven't you admitted yourself that you would be content if you only got the chance of
speaking to Klamm, even if he never looked at you and never listened
to you? And won't you achieve that at least through the protocol,
perhaps much more?' 'Much more?' asked K. 'In what way?' 'If you
wouldn't always talk about things like a child, as if they should be
offered up to you in edible form!'"[16] The landlady's metaphor,

---

lang so aus, als wolle Frieda die Peitsche fallen lassen, aber dann hob sie sie wieder.
'Im Namen Klamms,' rief sie, 'in den Stall! Alle in den Stall!' Nun sahen sie, daß es
ernst war; in einer für K. unverständlichen Angst begannen sie, in den Hin-
tergrund zu drängen, unter dem Stoß der ersten ging dort eine Tür auf,
Nachtluft wehte herein, alle verschwanden mit Frieda, die sie offenbar über den
Hof in den Stall trieb."
16. *CA* 150; *RO* 583: "'Haben Sie nicht selbst erklärt, daß Sie zufrieden sein

though appropriate enough in its figurative import, would seem to have nothing at all to do with the story in its literal signification; that is, no one would seem to want actually to *eat* the document in question. Indeed, nobody does eat it. But the narration does set the protocol in the context of eating. After a meditation on the ways in which Klamm resembles an eagle, the narrative returns to the issue at hand: "But assuredly these [similarities to an eagle] had nothing to do with the protocol, over which just now Momus was crumbling a roll dusted with salt, which he was eating with beer to help it out, in the process all the papers becoming covered with salt and caraway seeds."[17] The documents are connected metonymically with the roll Momus is eating, and at the same time they acquire a certain amount of seasoning. If one had to eat a protocol, perhaps a little salt and a few caraway seeds would help. At the close of the scene, then, the papers are very nearly in the "edible form" the landlady says K. wants them in.

I do not mean to argue that the salt and caraway seeds Momus inadvertently spreads over the protocol have any great significance in the story. On the contrary, these are clearly simply little realistic touches that add to the texture of the narrative. But their source is less in the observed behavior of officials trying to eat and work at the same time than in the logomimetic potential of figurative language. Or we might perhaps better say that it is as much in the one as in the other, for indeed the reader is in no position to decide for certain to what degree this little moment arises from imagination or observation. By stressing the importance of rhetoric as I do here, I do not mean to imply that Kafka was not a sensitive and accurate observer; evidence of many kinds indicates that he was. I want to make clear, however, that the verbal imagination plays at least as important a role as observation in producing those very details that make his fictions so convincing.

The case of the edible documents shows how one rhetorical moment turns into another in a chain of hermeneutic ambiguities. The language that describes K. as wanting everything delivered to him "in

---

würden, wenn Sie nur Gelegenheit hätten, vor Klamm zu sprechen, auch wenn er Sie nicht ansehen und Ihnen nicht zuhören würde? Und erreichen Sie durch dieses Protokoll nicht zumindest dieses, vielleicht aber viel mehr?'—'Viel mehr?' fragte K. 'Auf welche Weise?'—'Wenn Sie nur nicht immer,' rief die Wirtin, 'wie ein Kind alles gleich in eßbarer Form dargeboten haben wollten!'"

17. *CA* 151; *RO* 583–584: "Gewiß aber hatte damit dieses Protokoll nichts zu tun, über dem jetzt gerade Momus eine Salzbrezel auseinanderbrach, die er sich zum Bier schmecken ließ und mit der er alle Papiere mit Salz und Kümmel überstreute."

edible form" can be read either figuratively or literally, and only context or what de Man calls an "extratextual intention" can clarify the matter. In this case there is little question that the landlady means the utterance to function figuratively, and indeed we read it in this way. But Kafka takes the language and displaces it to a slightly different context, one related to the matter at hand by metonymy, and there it can be read literally: by accident, as it were, the documents being discussed are associated with eating and are even made slightly more acceptable as food. Kafka, then, makes the landlady's trope into a rhetorical moment by letting it function both literally and figuratively at the same time. The reader is then confronted with an analogous rhetorical moment in reading the description of Momus eating the roll over the protocol. If we read it literally, as presented, it is simply an observed detail appended to the account of the discussion between K. and the landlady. But by reading it figuratively, as suggesting the edible nature of the document, we connect it with Kafka's literal reading of the landlady's trope and thus with an imaginative extension of purely linguistic associations.

The reader really has no alternative but to read the passage both ways, to follow the same rhetorical path that Kafka has opened up by writing as he does. There are no reliable means by which we can decide whether imagination or observation is the more important principle at work in these fictions. This situation undoubtedly results from a deliberate act of rhetorical complication on Kafka's part. The hesitation between faith in observation and an equally powerful certainty that observation cannot penetrate to the truth of things characterizes Kafka's writing from beginning to end. The story "The Top" criticizes—even burlesques—the philosopher's desire for immediate observation of the spinning top. The sensory "grasping" of the phenomenon he wants to observe is not possible. Although the story offers no alternative to which the philosopher may turn, imagination would obviously be one possiblity. Substantial evidence leads one to suppose that Kafka believed in the existence of truths that are unavailable for direct observation. The parable "An Imperial Message" illustrates the need for imagination in the face of overwhelming obstacles to direct apprehension. There is no doubt that the message from the emperor exists, that it is meant for "you," and that it is on its way; there is also no doubt that it will fail to arrive. The only means available to "you" is to sit at your window when evening falls and dream it to yourself. Observation, important as it may be, can only take "you" so far.

Chapter 6

READING THE CLASSICS

Although Kafka is surely one of the most original writers of this century, he is also one very much concerned with the interpretation of important texts of the tradition. Some of his fictions are based on readings of well-known books (such as *Don Quixote*), myths (those of Prometheus and Poseidon), or historical figures (Alexander, Bucephalus, and so on). Of course the one text with which he comes to grips again and again is the Bible, references to which are frequent in both the stories and the notebooks. The question of how to read these authoritative texts concerned him throughout his life, and often this question served as the impetus for his own writing.

The very issue of reading an authoritative text becomes the matter of Kafka's fiction on a number of occasions. "In the Penal Colony" is only the most extreme example. Everyone remembers the extensive scene of reading that stands at the center of the "Cathedral" chapter of *The Trial*. Here the parable "Before the Law" is treated as a "scripture" (*Schrift*) that is "unalterable" and deserves a certain reverence. But although the structure of words (*Wortlaut*) is certain—unchangeable and unchanging—its meaning is not, and Joseph. K. can only puzzle over its implications for his own situation. Similarly, Landsurveyor K. must puzzle over the letter from Klamm that ostensibly admits him to castle service. The words of the letter are clear, but their import remains unfathomed, in spite of or because of considerable advice from various villagers. The analogy between these never completed acts of reading and the ongoing process of biblical exegesis is as clear as can be, but the question raised by the analogy is never explicitly answered. The question is: can one read such authoritative texts both correctly *and* productively?

Kafka's own engagement with the reading of canonical texts suggests an implicit answer, that productive readings are practically never "correct" in the sense of being true to the author's assumed intention. An examination of some of Kafka's readings shows the writer's creative imagination at work in one of its most basic and characteristic modes.

Significantly one of Kafka's earliest uses of material from a recognized classic (in this case the Bible) appears in the context of a discussion of figurative language. In the "Description of a Struggle," the narrator (at this point the fat man) accuses his interlocutor, the supplicant, of resorting to metaphor from a kind of diseased impatience with ordinary reality:

> Don't you feel it's this very feverishness that is preventing you from being properly satisfied with the real names of things, and that now, in your frantic haste, you're just pelting them with any old names? You can't do it fast enough. But hardly have you run away from them when you've forgotten the names you gave them. The poplar in the fields, which you've called the "Tower of Babel" because you didn't want to know it was a poplar, sways again without a name, so you have to call it "Noah in his cups."[1]

The fat man thus accuses the supplicant of an illegitimate use of the biblical figures, to which he allegedly resorts only because of his sickness, his dissatisfaction with proper names. If the fat man is right, calling the poplar "The Tower of Babel" or "Noah in his cups" is a misuse of scripture as well as a falsification of reality. A rhetorical joke embedded in the fat man's discourse, however, radically undercuts his argument. The German word *Pappel* ("poplar") is not an entirely innocent example here; the verb *pappeln*, an apparent variant of *Pap-*

1. *CS* 33; *BK* 89: "Ist es Euch nicht so, dass Ihr vor lauter Hitze mit den wahrhaftigen Namen der Dinge Euch nicht begnügen könnt, davon nicht satt werdet und über sie jetzt in einer einzigen Eile zufällige Namen schüttet. Nur schnell, nur schnell! Aber kaum seid Ihr von ihnen weggelaufen, habt Ihr wieder ihre Namen vergessen. Die Pappel in den Feldern, die Ihr den 'Turm von Babel' genannt habt, schaukelt wieder namenlos und Ihr müsst sie nennen 'Noah, wie er betrunken war.'" (Note that the transcription of the "B" version in *BK* uses "ss" for "ß.")

pel, means "to chatter" or "talk nonsense." By suggesting that his interlocutor would be talking nonsense in calling the *Pappel* by a "wrong"
name, he is in effect accusing him of "pappeln," a paronomastic citation of the "right" name. But the joke goes further: *pappeln*, which
resembles a relative of *Pappel*, is in fact a variant of *babblen* ("To
chatter, babble"), a verb of course derived from the name of the
tower. To call the tree "Babel" is phonologically very like calling it
Pappel after all.

The structure of language, in other words, contradicts the structure
of the argument. Although the fat man says that these biblical images
are inappropriate, an evasion of the "genuine" names, the complex
relation between the words *Pappel, pappeln, babblen,* and *Babel* argues
silently in favor of their appropriateness. The Bible (German *Bibel*)
with its *Babel* has already occupied the heart of the sign system before
the act of exclusion can make itself heard. The fat man's discourse is
self-deconstructing in the most basic way, and this self-deconstruction
calls into question the opposition between "real" (*wahrhaftig*) and "acci-
dental" (*zufällig*) upon which the fat man's contention is based.

The discovery of a textual propriety for associating the tree called
Pappel with the story of the tower of Babel also justifies the substitution of "Tower of Babel" by "Noah in his cups." The tower, after all,
was built at Babylon in the land of Shinar, the territory belonging to
the descendants of Ham. It was Ham who had the misfortune of
seeing his father, drunk and naked, lying in his tent and thereby
received his father's curse. From the standpoint of the biblical narrative, then, the existence of *Babel/Pappel* directly results from Noah's
being in his cups. This is arguably a better motivation for the figure
than the one suggested by the fat man, who would lead us to believe
that the drunken Noah is metaphorically analogous to the swaying
poplar. The biblical Noah does not sway, however: he does not even
stand upright in the episode in question. If we were to accept the fat
man's implication that the figure of Noah is such a metaphor, it would
indeed support his argument that such a "name" is inappropriate. But
if instead the trope is not metaphor but metonymy, a pure figure of
contiguity based on the structure of the Genesis narrative, the fat
man's position is weaker.

The fat man's discourse thus supports both the view that the appearance of elements from the Bible in this context is an unjustified
intrusion by an external and irrelevant text and the belief that these
figures from the Torah are somehow already inside the text at issue

(that is, Pappel) that is merely brought out into the open by employment of the tropes. The relation between text and intertext might be either antagonistic, alienated, and unseemly or friendly, intimate, and entirely proper. Perhaps it is all of these at once, in a fusion of opposites akin to the fusion of Prometheus and the rock in Kafka's fragment "Prometheus."[2] This fragment, too, both asserts and denies the unity of text and intertext. On the one hand, it asserts that there are "four legends" regarding Prometheus:

> According to the first, he was clamped to a rock in the Caucasus for betraying the secrets of the gods to men, and the gods set eagles to feed on his liver, which was perpetually renewed.
> According to the second Prometheus, goaded by the pain of the tearing beaks, pressed himself deeper and deeper into the rock until he became one with it.
> According to the third his treachery was forgotten in the course of thousands of years, forgotten by the gods, the eagles, forgotten by himself.
> According to the fourth everyone grew weary of the meaningless affair. The gods grew weary, the eagles grew weary, the wound closed wearily.[3]

But are these really four separate stories? Actually, these four paragraphs seem to relate four different stages in the same story, although one rather different from that handed down from antiquity: Prometheus betrays the gods and is fastened to the rock, where eagles feed on his liver. Attempting to retreat from the pain, Prometheus presses himself against the rock so forcefully that he actually makes himself part of the stone. When his alleged treachery is finally forgotten by all concerned, they become tired of the whole business. The narration thus takes a single simple—and indeed very short—story and tries to

2. Other approaches to "Prometheus" can be found in Roman Karst, "Kafkas Prometheussage oder das Ende des Mythos," *Germanic Review* 20 (Spring 1985), 42–47; and Gerhard Schepers, "The Dissolution of Myth in Kafka's 'Prometheus' and 'The Silence of the Sirens,'" *Humanities: Christianity and Culture* 18 (May 1984), 97–119.

3. *CS* 432; *SE* 306: "Nach der ersten wurde er, weil er die Götter an die Menschen verraten hatte, am Kaukasus festgeschmiedet, und die Götter schickten Adler, die von seiner immer wachsenden Leber fraßen. Nach der zweiten drückte sich Prometheus im Schmerz vor den zuhackenden Schnäbeln immer tiefer in den Felsen, bis er mit ihm eins wurde. Nach der dritten wurde in den Jahrtausenden sein Verrat vergessen, die Götter vergaßen, die Adler, er selbst. Nach der vierten wurde man des grundlos Gewordenen müde. Die Götter wurden müde, die Adler wurden müde, die Wunde schloß sich müde."

divide it into four separate entities. The narrative itself, however, seems not to accept the division. The final paragraph refers to "the legend" in the singular: "There remained the inexplicable mass of rock. The legend tried to explain the inexplicable. As it came out of a substratum of truth it had in turn to end in the inexplicable."[4] The text itself thus seems unable to decide whether it is recounting one story or several.

More radically, the tale opens the question of the significance of the very "legend" it is retelling. If the subject of the Prometheus legend is indeed a "meaningless affair" ("das grundlos Gewordene"), one is compelled to wonder why recounting it should be worthwhile. The story apparently seeks to enforce a distinction between the material in the "four legends" and the explanatory frame in which it is embedded. Although one of the legends claims that it deals with something that has become *grundlos* ("groundless"), the frame maintains that the legend (as a whole) has emerged from something possessing a *Grund*, a "substratum of truth" (*Wahrheitsgrund*). Perhaps we are to understand that the material originally had a Grund but lost it in the course of time. If so, it is remarkable for the embedded narrative to recount a process that moves, on the literal level at least, in just the opposite direction. Prometheus, at one time unattached to the earth (*Grund*), is at first fastened to it by the gods, then by his own efforts unites with it, so that there is no longer any distinction between Prometheus and the Grund itself. The only remaining thing to suggest that any of these events took place is in fact Grund, a piece of earth, "the inexplicable mass of rock." Far from becoming grundlos, the legend seems to have been transformed into nothing but Grund.

Here again, the structure of the story's language comes into conflict with the argument it seems to be making. Because the conflict centers upon the value (or lack of value) of a classical text or set of texts being recounted, the story raises the issue of how a preexisting text relates to a new one derived somehow from it. This relation is associated with an interplay between groundlessness and groundedness mediated by rhetoric. Not only is the problematic of Grund established by rhetorical play, but the story's central event, the merging of Prometheus with the rock, comes into being when a trope is read rhetorically. The

---

4. *CS* 432; *SE* 306. "Blieb das unerklärliche Felsgebirge.—Die Sage versucht das Unerklärliche zu erklären. Da sie aus einem Wahrheitsgrund kommt, muß sie wieder im Unerklärlichen enden."

narrative delivers an apparent hyperbole: the pain caused by the eagles tearing his flesh was so great, and Prometheus shrank back from it so hard, that he practically pushed himself right into the rock. But of course this figure is also not a figure; it is a sober description of the "facts" of the legend. If we have any doubts, the final paragraph dispels them by citing the inexplicable mass of rock as the only reminder of Prometheus. In this way a piece of language that might under other circumstances have remained a decorative flourish on the margins of the discourse (a "colorful" way of describing the intensity of Prometheus's pain) becomes embedded in the center.

The story both describes and enacts a paradoxical movement of joining and sundering. It describes a Prometheus who is on the one hand torn apart (*zugehackt*) by one element in the apparatus of his torture, the eagles, and on the other becomes fused with an another element in that apparatus, the mountain to which he is chained. As the "second" legend makes clear, the joining directly results from the sundering. The tale also enacts an analogous movement by both dismembering an apparently simple story into four different legends and fusing them together by embedding them in the new narrative in which they are now presented. The relation of the Prometheus story to Kafka's story is therefore almost identical to the relation of the Prometheus character to the environment in which the gods place him. The symmetry is too neat to ignore. By embedding within the frame of his story another allegedly preexisting story about a hero who becomes embedded in the means of his destruction, Kafka greatly complicates and broadens the scope of his subject. As the opening sentence hints, if we read it carefully, the topic under examination here is as much discourse (*Sagen*) as it is Prometheus.

"Prometheus," like many of Kafka's fictions, is ruthlessly self-referential. It is a reading of a classic that presents an image of reading the classics. It answers the implicit question of how one can make a new story out of old material, suggesting that the old story must first be subjected to a certain abuse—it is torn apart and its meaning is forgotten—before it can take part in a new tale. Kafka, with deliberate zeal, abuses the classical Prometheus story in just this way, dismembering it into tiny pieces and reformulating it in such a way as to ignore its original meaning utterly. He introduces a set of new elements (essentially all of the second, third, and fourth legends) that are completely foreign to any intention we could presume the ancient legend to have had. This Prometheus is certainly a far cry from the figure most familiar to Kafka's German-speaking audience, the hero of Goethe's poem "Prometheus." The Prometheus of Goethe's poem is characterized by high energy and ambition, a self-assurance that does not shrink from hardship. Kafka calmly inverts these qualities: instead of energy we have fatigue, instead of self-assured striving a definitive retreat. Nothing remains of the original story but the name "Prometheus" itself, now transformed into an "inexplicable mass of rock."

But if Prometheus has become a bare signifier no longer securely attached to any particular signified, the story would not have us lament the fact. On the contrary, the final paragraph insists on the propriety of the return of this discourse to the ground of inexplicability. That, surprisingly, is the guarantee of its connection to the "substratum of truth." Because truth is here associated with the Grund and therefore with the process of embedding and effacement that Prometheus undergoes, the story leads us to suppose that a certain concealment is characteristic of all truth. My language may sound Heideggerian, but the sentiment is pure Kafka. Story after story drives home the point that unavailability (for *us*) is one of the essential qualities of truth. When the story is seen in this light, it is not so surprising after all that Kafka insists on stripping his central image of all its conventional significance before pronouncing it to be in contact with the ground of truth.

The return of a classical text to a ground of truth is effected by a process precisely comparable to the rhetorical reading of tropes. When Kafka reads the figure "drückte sich . . . immer tiefer in den Felsen, bis er eins mit ihm wurde" ("pressed himself deeper and deeper into the cliff until he became one with it"), he temporarily ignores its obvious figurative import in favor of a literal reading capable of generating a narrative twist. In the same way, Kafka ignores the classical meaning of the Prometheus legend (whatever we suppose that to be) in favor of a new reading that preserves the original only as a naked signifier. He characteristically takes this approach to classical texts: like all other pre-existing discourse, they can be exploited as convenient storehouses of signifiers.

Sometimes there is no observable difference between Kafka's revision of a classical text and the rhetorical reading of a particular text associated with it. A good example can be found in the fragment "Poseidon." In Kafka's description of the Greek god of the sea, Poseidon spends much of his time engaged in bureaucratic tasks. He sits at a desk and "goes over accounts" (*rechnete*). Because he takes his job seriously, he does not find it proper to delegate these time-consuming details to assistants; on the contrary, he zealously attends to them all himself, in spite of the fact that they keep him from pursuing other, perhaps more enjoyable employment. Because he is so taken up with this routine administration, he has not time to do what others imagine him doing: "cruising through the waves with his trident."[5] It makes him angry to hear these rumors going about when the reality is that "he had hardly seen the oceans, save fleetingly during his hasty ascent to Olympus, and had never really sailed upon them. He used to say that he was postponing this until the end of the world, for then there might come a quiet moment when, just before the end and having gone through the last account, he could still make a quick little tour."[6] The story's central conceit is evidently the paradox that the divinity with absolute authority over the seas has no experience of them.

Because the fragment explains the situation in terms of the crushing burden of Poseidon's bureaucratic duties, one is understandably tempted to see as the basis of the story Kafka's own experience as a bureaucrat in the Workers Accident Insurance Company of Bohemia. Kafka undoubtedly felt from time to time that his office supervised a vast sea of human activity with which he had only infrequent and superficial contact, and this feeling probably did have an effect on shaping the story. The basis for the narrative, however, is probably at least as much a matter of verbal invention as of observed experience. The story seems to be generated in part from the German language, from a sentence that one can view (in a highly metaphorical fashion) as the "deep structure" of the narrative. That generating sentence is, "Poseidon übersieht die Meere."

The word *übersehen* is an antithetical sign, similar to words like the English *cleave*, the Latin *sacer*, or the Greek *pharmakon*. Such signs are capable of indicating two opposed semantic fields: *cleave* can mean either "stick together" or "hew apart"; *sacer* can mean both "holy" and "unholy"; *pharmakon*, as is now well known by way of Derrida's de-

5. *CS* 435; *SE* 308. "Wie er etwa immerfort mit dem Dreizack durch die Fluten kutschiere."

6. *CS* 435; *SE* 308: "So hatte er die Meere kaum gesehen, nur flüchtig beim eiligen Aufstieg zum Olymp, und niemals wirklich durchfahren. Er pflegte zu sagen, er warte damit bis zum Weltuntergang, dann werde sich wohl noch ein stiller Augenblick ergeben, wo er knapp vor dem Ende nach Durchsicht der letzten Rechnung noch schnell eine kleine Rundfahrt werde machen können."

construction of Plato's *Phaedrus*, can mean both "remedy" and "poison"; and *übersehen* can mean both "oversee," "take in at a glance," or "perceive" on the one hand and "overlook," "fail to see," or "take no notice of" on the other. Depending on context, *übersehen* can imply either seeing excellently or not seeing at all. Kafka's story presents a situation in which the two opposed notions are both correct at the same time.

Indeed, one results from the other. Poseidon's work in supervising, taking things in at a glance, requires him to take no notice of the oceans he administers. Kafka has devised a way to produce a narrative necessity for the semantic duplicity of *übersehen*: if the god were not obliged to sit at his desk overseeing the administration of the oceans, he would then have the opportunity to pay attention to and experience his domain. This narrative connection between Poseidon's divine duties and the problematic of perception is further reinforced by the homophonic relation between one of the German words for "oceans," *Seen*, and the word for "seeing," *sehen*. The story explores a not altogether harmless interplay between the two words. It is as if Kafka had taken a silly verbal joke ("Poseidon konnte die Seen nicht sehen, aber er sollte und wollte die Seen sehen," that is, "Poseidon could not see the seas, but he was supposed to and wanted to see the seas") and discovered a darker side beneath it. The joking quality of the text, however, is not lost altogether.

Part of the joke is that we are not exactly sure what Poseidon is doing while he sits at his desk. The text reports that he was engaged in some activity properly designated by the verb *rechnen*: "Poseidon . . . rechnete." The English translation is forced to be more specific than the German and therefore covers only a portion of the semantic field of *rechnen* with "going over the accounts." But this verb can also mean simply "to consider" or "think things through," and nothing in the text prevents our supposing that Poseidon's main duty is "considering" things. Indeed, the material that the story seems to report is precisely Poseidon's (implicit) consideration of the difficulty of his position. The "erlebte Rede" style, with its unannounced but pervasive first-person perspective, allows us to suppose that Poseidon's own thoughts are reflected in the narrative. When we are told that the sea god remains at the bottom of the sea and "rechnete ununterbrochen" ("calculated/considered uninterruptedly"), we might very well assume that his entire employment is brooding over the unceasing demands of his employment. If so—and the rhetorical richness of the text allows it to be so—then the joking paradox becomes even greater. The great work that prevents Poseidon from seeing the sea is his endless worry about the endlessness of his worry. In this construction, the story's second sentence ("The administration of all the waters gave him endless work") could be read in an unexpected way, for not the *carrying out* of this administration but the *thought* of it would be the source of the labor. We could also readily understand why he would consider other work—any other work—"more cheerful" (*fröhlicher*).

Still, the translator's choice of "going over accounts" as the better translation of *rechnen* here seems correct, even though the text gives no explicit reason in the immediate context for preferring it.[7] The preference is justified by a detail that we might not notice consciously on first reading: another half-submerged verbal joke turns the god of the sea, the "Gott der Meere," into a god of accounts, a "Gott der Mehre." There is no phonetic difference at all between the word for "seas" and that for "surpluses" or "increases." Kafka's German-speaking audience would thus find a certain justice in Kafka's picture of the sea god doing calculations and reviewing balance sheets. Although Kafka never actually writes *Mehre* instead of *Meere,* the narrative proceeds on the assumption that the homophones are semantically as well as phonologically interchangeable. After all, the identification of the oceanic with the numerical is built into the structure of the language. Instead of trying to escape this semantic surplus, Kafka here does something typical: he exploits that surplus, makes out of it a space in which a story can be inscribed. Rather than trying to correct or restrain an inconvenient and seemingly uninformative paronomasia, he finds in it the occasion for transforming traditional material into something distinctly his own. He imagines the traditional material first as a text describing Poseidon's duties: "Poseidon übersieht die Meere." He might have seen a sentence like this in a book on Greek mythology, or he might have invented it. It does not matter; in either case it is a correct statement of the tradition about Poseidon. But because the tradition is or can be a text, it can be read rhetorically, thereby producing a new and surprisingly original text. The relation of Kafka's story to its classical intertext is once again both intimate and antagonistic. On the one hand it embraces the ancient tradition about Poseidon's authority over the oceans, but on the other it rejects most

---

7. The very end of the story, with its mention of a "Rechnung," clarifies matters only retrospectively in the German text.

of the associations that cluster around the tradition. Kafka's Poseidon is in fact nothing like the Olympian divinity we tend to imagine, in spite of the story's scrupulous adherence to the (imaginary) text of the tradition.

Another well-known figure from the classical past, Bucephalus, receives similar treatment, but here the results are even more dramatic. This old war-horse (*Streitroß*) participates in a rhetorical transformation from the literal to the figurative, from a genuine war-horse to a forensic "war-horse." Bucephalus's old profession is presented more or less as tradition has handed it down. As in the case of Poseidon, Bucephalus's classical grandeur is more than a little tarnished by the bureaucratic role the fiction gives him, but again that bureaucratic role is justified, as it were, by the language proper to the tradition. Poseidon's and Bucephalus's administrative roles may be unexpected and even shocking, but they are not external impositions upon the classical material. They are on the contrary founded upon the very signifiers that preserve and communicate the cultural heritage.

In general we find in Kafka's reading of the classics that double movement I identified earlier in the discussion of "The Silence of the Sirens," where Odysseus seems to act out both the lethetic and alethetic modes of reading. Such works as "Prometheus" and "Poseidon" seem to want both to preserve and to destroy their intertexts in the same gesture. This double movement, essential to all acts of reading,[8] tends to be more often repressed than explicitly played out in the canonical texts of the Western tradition. Kafka distinguishes himself as an exception in this regard not because he was one of the first or the few to experience an ambivalence about reading but because he was one of the very few who chose to make it the stuff of his fictions.

The double impulse toward preservation and destruction that characterizes Kafka's reading of the classics also typifies his attitude toward the self, at least to the degree that the self could be conceived as a text. For a man who could tell his fiancée that he consisted of nothing but literature, this degree must have been very high indeed. Kafka evidently considered the central and essential part of himself to be text, some combination of his own textual production and the pre-existing language that played such an important role in his life. Reading the classical texts was for him a way to both investigate and

---

8. Susan Noakes, *Timely Reading: Between Exegesis and Interpretation* (Ithaca: Cornell University Press, 1988), argues to this effect.

produce himself. Because the very notion of a self, particularly the literary self, had already been formulated in a well-known set of classical texts, Kafka could in fact discover and produce himself by reading these classics in his characteristic way. The texts with which he needed to come to grips were those that had become for his culture the locus of a powerful definition of the artistic self: the works of Goethe.

Kafka admired Goethe greatly, of course, and the diaries testify that in 1911–1912 the young writer engaged in a sustained immersion in Goethe's works. He mentions his reading of *Dichtung und Wahrheit* in late 1911, and in early 1912 (on February 4) he cites the "zeal, permeating every part of me, with which I read about Goethe (Goethe's conversations, student days, hours with Goethe, a visit of Goethe's to Frankfurt) and which keeps me from all writing."[9] This almost paralyzing interest in Goethe continues well into the summer, when he makes the pilgrimage to Weimar to visit the Goethehaus, the Goethe-Schiller Archives, and so on. The Goethe obsession abated in the fall, along with the literary paralysis, but the impression that this period of immersion left was unquestionably a lasting one.[10]

One text in particular must have made a special impression on Kafka, as it did on many of his contemporaries. It is the description in *Dichtung und Wahrheit* of the "domestic situation" of the very young Goethe:

> a father certainly affectionate and well-meaning, but grave, who, because he cherished within a very tender heart, externally, with incredible consistency, maintained a brazen sternness, that he might attain the end of giving his children the best education, and of building up, regulating, and preserving his well-founded house; a mother, on the other hand, as yet almost a child, who first grew up to consciousness with and in her two eldest children; these three, as they looked at the world with healthy eyes, capable of life, and desiring present enjoyment. This contradiction floating in the family increased with years. My father fol-

9. *DI1* 228; *TB* 244–245. "Der mich ganz durchgehende Eifer, mit dem ich über Goethe lese (Goethes Gespräche, Studentenjahre, Stunden mit Goethe; ein Aufenthalt Goethes in Frankfurt) und der mich von jedem Schreiben abhält."

10. Another possible connection between Kafka's works and Goethe's is explored in Gerhard Neumann, "Der Wanderer und der Verschollene: Zum Problem der Identität in Goethes *Wilhelm Meister* und Kafkas Amerika-Roman," in J. P. Stern and J. J. White, eds., *Paths and Labyrinths: Nine Papers Read at the Franz Kafka Symposium Held at the Institute of Germanic Studies on 20 and 21 October 1983* (London: Institute of Germanic Studies, 1985), 43–65.

lowed out his views unshaken and uninterrupted; the mother and children could not give up their feelings, their claims, their wishes.[11]

The contradiction between paternal discipline and maternal spontaneity that Goethe describes in this passage is not simply something
that "floats in the family," as he puts it. It is in fact one of the fundamental conditions of his youth, the formative years of his personality.
As we are all well aware, in other works by Goethe, such as *Faust* and
Wilhelm Meister, for example, he frequently presents such a distinction
between discipline, restraint, sternness, "building up, regulating, and
preserving" on the one hand and spontaneity, sensuality, a desire to
experience the world directly, and "capacity for life" (as he expresses
it) on the other. This distinction, it can be argued, becomes a central
structure in Goethe's understanding of the world and his place in it.
At least some important part of his conception of "das ewig-
Weibliche" derives from that experience of his mother, and that
which is "drawn onward" by this power is precisely the masculine
principle derived from the father: the concept of duty, restraint to the
point of renunciation, and so on.

Indeed, Goethe's concept of the self as an amalgam of traits inherited from his forebears is so strong that he is even ready to suggest
that he himself may have contributed nothing to his own character.
Kafka very likely read or heard quoted these famous and charming
verses from Goethe's old age, which propose just such a view:

> Vom Vater hab' ich die Statur,
> Des Lebens ernstes Führen,
> Von Mütterchen die Frohnatur
> Und Lust zu fabulieren.
> Urahnherr war der Schönsten hold,
> Das spukt so hin und wieder,
> Urahnfrau liebte Schmuck und Gold,
> Das zuckt wohl durch die Glieder.
> Sind nun die Elemente nicht
> Aus dem Komplex zu trennen,
> Was ist denn an dem ganzen Wicht
> Original zu nennen?[12]

11. *The Autobiography of Johann Wolfgang von Goethe*, trans. John Oxenford
(Chicago: University of Chicago Press, 1974), 242–243 (book 6).

12. *Goethes Werke*, ed. Erich Trunz et al. (Hamburg: C. Wegner, 1955–60), I,
320. My prose translation: "I have my stature from Father, as well as his earnest
conduct of life, but from Mommy I have my happy disposition and love of story-

Even here, the maternal side is still associated with poetry and with liveliness, whereas the paternal heritage connotes the discipline of the serious conduct of life.

Just as important as these founding texts is the tradition they found. By Kafka's time this conception of the Goethean self as an amalgam of maternal and paternal qualities had become the standard and accepted way of understanding Goethe's character and work. Even scholarship comes to see him as the combination of opposing qualities, and indeed the very opposing qualities Goethe ascribes to his maternal and paternal heritages. An example of the assimilation of this conception by scholarship can be found in Albert Bielschowsky's influential biography of Goethe. Although this work may no longer be considered reliable by today's Goethe scholars, it nevertheless reflects accurately enough how Goethe was perceived in the early decades of this century. Bielschowsky characterized Goethe in this way:

> Seldom has the physical aspect of an intellectually highly developed person been so independently active and so intimately suffused the spiritual aspect. This marvelous, perfect mixture of his nature gives to it an extraordinary character and at the same time causes it to manifest itself in contradictory ways. . . . One could say that the entire first half of Goethe's life was over before he succeeded in bringing body and spirit, and his intellectual powers, into enough balance both in themselves and with respect to each other that substantial disturbances, both internal and external, could be avoided.[13]

Bielschowsky's dichotomy of "body and spirit" does not come from his own imagination, of course: it is merely another version of the opposition between "capacity for (the sensuous enjoyment of) life" and order, discipline, restraint posited by Goethe in his autobiographical writings.

This model of the self as a joining of paternal discipline and maternal ebullience is familiar to us now not only because Goethe and those who study him have made it so but because it was taken over and

telling. Grandfather was gracious to the Lovelies, and a touch of that lingers here and there; Grandmother loved jewelry and gold, which sends a thrill though my limbs, too. So if the elements can't be sorted out of the mixture, what is there in any of this fellow that can be called original?"

13. Albert Bielschowsky, *Goethe: Sein Leben und seine Werke* (München: C. H. Beck'sche Buchhandlung, 1911), I, 2–4 (translation mine).

reused by many who followed and participated in the classical nineteenth-century central European education. One of those who reused
it was Kafka. Here, for example, in a passage from the "Letter to His
Father," Kafka attempts to explain the special ambivalence of his
nature by recourse to the Goethean formula: "I, to put it in a very
much abbreviated form, a Löwy with a certain basis of Kafka, which,
however, is not set in motion by the Kafka will to life, business, and
conquest, but by a Löwyish spur that impels more secretly, more
diffidently, and in another direction, and which often fails to work
entirely."14 The writer sees himself, then, in Goethean terms—that is,
as a combination of the maternal (Löwy) and paternal (Kafka) sides of
his family. He also understands his sister Ottla's character to be such a
mixture, but with an interesting difference:

> I don't, of course, quite see to the bottom of this very complicated case,
> but at any rate here was something like a kind of Löwy, equipped with
> the best Kafka weapons. Between us [that is, Herrmann and Franz]
> there was no real struggle; I was soon finished off; what remained was
> flight, embitterment, melancholy, and inner struggle. But you two
> [Herrmann and Ottla] were always in a fighting position, always fresh,
> always energetic. A sight as magnificent as it was desperate. At the very
> beginning you were, I am sure, very close to each other, because of the
> four of us [children] Ottla is even today perhaps the purest representa-
> tion of the marriage between you and Mother and of the forces it
> combined. I don't know what it was that deprived you both of the
> happiness of the harmony between father and child, but I can't help
> believing that the development in this case was similar to that in mine.
> On your side there was the tyranny of your own nature, on her side the
> Löwy defiance, touchiness, sense of justice, restlessness, and all that
> backed up by the consciousness of the Kafka vigor.15

Kafka's description of Ottla suggests a model along the lines of the
fusion that Goethe envisioned in himself, wherein the child combines

14. *LF* 10–11: "Ich, um es sehr abgekürzt auszudrücken, ein Löwy mit einem
gewissen Kafkaschen Fond, der aber eben nicht durch den Kafkaschen Lebens-,
Geschäfts-, Eroberungswillen in Bewegung gesetzt wird, sondern durch einen
Löwischen Stachel, der geheimer, scheuer, in anderer Richtung wirkt und oft
überhaupt aussetzt."
15. *LF* 64–67: "Ich durchschaue ja den komplizierten Fall nicht ganz, aber
jedenfalls war hier etwas wie eine Art Löwy, ausgestattet mit den besten Kafkaschen Waffen. Zwischen uns [Herrmann und Franz] war es kein eigentlicher
Kampf; ich war bald erledigt; was übrig blieb war Flucht, Verbitterung, Trauer,
innerer Kampf. Ihr zwei [Herrmann und Ottla] waret aber immer in Kampf-
stellung, immer frisch, immer bei Kräften. Ein ebenso großartiger wie trostloser

the best of father and mother, creating a personality superior to either parent. We ought to note also that the qualities Kafka ascribes to the Löwy side of his family—sensitivity, restlessness, a sense of justice—correspond quite well with the characteristics of the mother-world of the Goethean tradition.[16] And on the paternal side we have the familiar qualities of power, duty, and discipline but here in the case of Herrmann Kafka somehow divorced from reason. In any case, Franz also sees himself as a combination, but in him, unlike Goethe and unlike even his own sister Ottla, the parts fail to fuse and combine into a successful whole. Franz's maternal, Löwy part drives him "in another direction" from that "basis of Kafka" he inherited from his father. The whole thing never seems to operate correctly, as it did for Goethe and for the horde of his literary descendants in the works of such writers as Hermann Hesse and Thomas Mann.

Kafka's picture of himself problematizes the Goethean model even further than it was already problematized in one of Kafka's favorite stories, "Tonio Kröger." Mann used the paradigm in self-confessed emulation of Goethe, not only because it fit so well with many of Mann's particular artistic concerns, but also because it had attained by the turn of the century the currency and authority of myth. Although Kafka had direct access to this myth through his own reading of Goethe, it came to him yet again in the mediation of "Tonio," a story Kafka loved particularly because it was "enamored of the contradictory."[17] The master trope that governs all the oppositions with which the story is in love is the contrast between the bourgeois, Teutonic discipline of the father and the artistic exoticism of the mother. This is the Goethean paradigm but with a substantial variation. Whereas

---

Anblick. Zu allererst seid ihr Euch ja gewiß sehr nahe gewesen, denn noch heute ist von uns vier [Kindern] Ottla vielleicht die reinste Darstellung der Ehe zwischen Dir und der Mutter und der Kräfte, die sich da verbanden. Ich weiß nicht was Euch um das Glück der Eintracht zwischen Vater und Kind gebracht hat, es liegt mir nur nahe zu glauben, daß die Entwicklung ähnlich war wie bei mir. Auf Deiner Seite die Tyrannei Deines Wesens, auf ihrer Seite Löwyscher Trotz, Empfindlichkeit, Gerechtigkeitsgefühl, Unruhe, und alles das gestützt durch das Bewußtsein Kafka'scher Kraft."

16. Bielschowsky's description of Goethe's parents (cited here once again simply as a reflection of widely held views) fits Kafka's situation almost exactly—a fact that could not have failed to strike Franz: "Stammte Goethe mütterlicherseits aus einer Gelehrten- und Beamtenfamilie, so gingen väterlicherseits die Wurzeln seines Geschlechts in den Handwerkerstand zurück" (Bielschowsky, *Goethe*, 20).

17. "Verliebtsein in das Gegensätzliche." From a letter to Brod in 1904 (*BR* 31).

Goethe understood himself to complete the fusing of the maternal and paternal sides in him, Mann presents Tonio as an incomplete fusion at best.

In the case of Goethe, two principles that had created a "contradiction floating in the family" came together in one single self. In their coming together, the contradiction ceased—not immediately and not without adventure, but finally nonetheless, the two forces were formed into a single personality. What had caused a division in the family created not a contradictory self but a more complex self, one in which the natural love of life was tempered by discipline. The happy and productive individual—and Goethe surely had reason to consider himself one—balanced maternal and paternal qualities. Such a balanced personality is the final product of a process of *Bildung* presented fictionally in *Wilhelm Meister* and biographically in *Dichtung und Wahrheit*. Mann, too, used the model to describe in Tonio a successful personality, but the fusion implied by Goethe's case is never fully achieved. Tonio never ceases to feel the stresses in himself that come from the conflicting values of the paternal and maternal sides. What was for Goethe a thorough alloy of the two metals is for Mann more problematic; one can still easily discern in Tonio the strains of maternal copper and paternal tin in the bronze of his character.

Kafka's case as he describes it in the "Letter" participates in this tradition while at the same time pulling it apart. A crucial element that makes the fusion of mother and father possible seems to be missing. For Goethe and for Mann the model of marriage that operates at the heart of this myth of the self is one that is driven by an essentially erotic desire for union: the two entities that combine in a marriage really *want* to combine physically and in fact succeed in doing so, not only or most importantly in the sexual act, but more essentially and permanently in the offspring that arise from that act. But this erotic element is absent in Kafka's conception of marriage, and the absence is surely connected with the permanent antagonism he repeatedly represents as being at work within the elements of his personality. Kafka characteristically purges everything erotic from his conception of his parents' marriage even as he praises it: "In your marriage I had before me what was, in many ways, a model marriage, a model in constancy, mutual help, number of children; and even when the children grew up and increasingly disturbed the peace, the marriage as such remained undisturbed."[18] The Kafka-Löwy mar-

18. *LF* 114–115: "Ich hatte in Euerer Ehe eine in vielem mustergültige Ehe vor mir, mustergültig in Treue, gegenseitiger Hilfe, Kinderzahl, und selbst als dann

riage is an alliance of two separate, independent powers, and though one of them seems always to dominate and efface the other, no genuine union of the two ever takes place—not, at any rate, in the son's rhetoric. This rhetoric is of course the issue here. The actual facts of the relationship between Kafka's parents may have been otherwise.

The notion of a sexless marriage appears over and over again in Kafka's diaries and nowhere more decisively than in the famous entry where he speaks of "Coitus as punishment for the happiness of being together." He expresses the desire to live ascetically, "more ascetically than a bachelor," even within marriage, even saying that marriage could only be possible for him only on such terms.[19] The anxiety voiced here is not just the distaste for the sexual act that appears time and again in Kafka's writings but a fear of any kind of union. Another diary entry cites the "fear of the connection, of passing into the other" as an argument against marriage. Any kind of connection would be dangerous: "Then I'll never be alone again."[20] The self is pictured here as an entity mortally endangered by intimate contact with another.

But the Goethean model of the self as read by the "Letter to His Father" proposes a self already composed of two such entities living in ascetic, even hostile separation within the same psyche. The failure of Kafka's self to become an integrated whole thus reflects and repeats the inability of Kafka the individual to enter into any connection with another person. This anxiety becomes entangled with another, the fear of failing to produce connected discourse in his writing. As I have suggested in an earlier chapter, some of Kafka's most powerful fiction proposes a metaphorical relation between sexual and literary activity. This relation again becomes evident when Kafka pursues a similar metaphor in a diary entry about his writing. He tries to console himself that a story, if it is worth anything, resembles an organism and carries its "complete organization" ("fertige Organisation") within itself. Therefore, he argues, just as it is pointless for parents to despair about the viability of the infant, so is it pointless for the author to worry about his story. The story, like the child, will succeed or not, depending on whether or not it has the requisite "complete organiza-

---

die Kinder groß wurden und immer mehr den Frieden störten, blieb die Ehe als solche davon unberührt."

19. *DI1* 296; *TB* 315: "Coitus als Bestrafung des Glückes des Beisammenseins . . . asketischer als ein Junggeselle."

20. *DI1* 292; *TB* 311: "Die Angst vor der Verbindung, dem Hinüberfließen. Dann bin ich nie mehr allein."

tion," and one can simply never be sure at the outset whether despair is warranted. Kafka concludes that "reflecting on it can give one a certain support," but whatever support it gave him must have been transitory.[21] Although he knew of people like his sister Ottla who were born with the psychic integration necessary to succeed, the case he knew best was his own, the model of failure. That Kafka destroyed or wanted destroyed most of what he had written in his lifetime shows that he felt that most of his stories, like his own divided self, lacked the inner unity he thought necessary.

Herrmann and Julie Kafka did evidently successfully enter into a union, both in their marriage and in the fusion of maternal and paternal qualities in Ottla, but their success does not figure in the story Franz tells about his own case. This story gives us an inversion of the classical model of the self that Kafka inherited, both directly and through Thomas Mann, from Goethe: the traditional elements associated with a maternal and paternal half remain unchanged, but the paradigm of successful renewal and union is transformed into an explanatory myth of failure. A Kafka and a Löwy may have temporarily joined to engender Franz, but the jackdaw (*kavka*) and the lion (*Löwe*) cannot truly unite, in this mythology at any rate, to form any viable creature, nor could such a creature expect to produce viable offspring, human or literary. Kafka presents himself as the locus of a nearly absolute inability to form unions, whether externally, with another person, or internally, either in his writing or in his personality.

And yet—the very terms in which this inability to form unions is presented result from a very effective union between the preexisting classical text (Goethe's model of himself) and Kafka's unique style. The rhetoric with which he laments the failure of the two impulses within himself to fuse exhibits a fusion of old and new materials that is as nearly complete as Prometheus's fusion with the rock. This fusion is accomplished by the characteristic method of taking the classic at its word, by reading it more rigorously (and in this case more literally) than it was probably meant to be read. Kafka is in a way truer to the letter of Goethe's myth than Goethe is because Kafka's version carries forward into the tenor of the metaphor qualities that for Goethe belong only to the vehicle. Because two human beings cannot actually become one, as Goethe's figure presumes they do, the two metaphori-

---

21. *DI*2 104; *TB* 450: "Einen gewissen Halt kann diese Überlegung geben."

cal people within Kafka cannot ever successfully unite. They remain true to the conditions of their literal being, unique and alone, in some form of conflict with other individuals with whom they must live in close association. Kafka's text merges with Goethe's by taking its terms more "seriously" than Goethe takes them and thereby insisting upon the impossibility of human merger.

Kafka presents himself as the failed and infertile combination of hostile forces within his personality, and his writings, his literary children, represent a similar situation on the textual level. The offspring of his pen often result from a combination of two systems of signs, one a classical text or some other preexisting discourse and the other Kafka's peculiar and personal structure of meaning. Although Kafka evidently believed that many of these offspring were failures, they were so only in his own eyes. The world sees and continues to marvel at a dazzlingly successful effort that fuses individual vision with the body of an inherited cultural discourse. And in spite of his deep and abiding doubts about the viability of his fictional children, Kafka never restrained his ambitions for them. For all his anxiety, he continued to create his own stories by reading the classics, even and especially those that have been the most powerful in shaping our heritage. Not only does he take on the classics of antiquity and of German culture; he returns again and again to his effort at rereading the Old Testament.

Much of Kafka's literary activity was devoted to various efforts to recapture for his own purpose the material of the Book of Genesis. These efforts are perhaps most clearly visible in the numerous notebook entries, many in aphoristic form, offering interpretations of the Tree of Knowledge, the expulsion from the Garden of Eden, and so forth. Less clear, but perhaps of greater importance for Kafka's artistic production, is his long-term fascination with the Joseph story. The name "Josef" figures importantly in both *The Trial* and *The Castle* (where Landsurveyor K.'s given name may or may not be Joseph), in the fragment from the *Trial* material published as "A Dream" ("Ein Traum"), and of course in "Josephine the Singer" ("Josefine, die Sängerin; oder, das Volk der Mäuse"). The juxtaposition of "Joseph" with the initial K. in so much of this material suggests strongly that Kafka identified himself with the biblical Joseph—understandably, given Kafka's sense of being threatened by the seduction of women and of being spiritually exiled from his family, not to mention his abiding concern with dreams.

What is probably Kafka's closest adaptation of the Joseph story, however, does not contain the name "Joseph" at all. The novel fragment that Kafka tentatively titled *The Missing Person (Der Verschollene)*, which Brod published as *Amerika*, follows the biblical narrative in a number of key respects not the least of which is the very fact that it concerns a missing person. The central fact of Joseph's adventures is that he is *verschollen* (that is, "missing and presumed dead") as far as his family is concerned. He is forced to take up residence in a foreign land and to try to adapt to alien norms. Joseph is exiled from the comfort and familiarity of his homeland, expelled, as it were, from his father's garden. Kafka's novel invokes the biblical expulsion from Eden in the opening paragraph, where he describes the Statue of Libery ("Statue der Freiheitsgöttin") as holding not a torch but a sword.[22] The statue thus represents not so much "Liberty" as the angel guarding the entrance to a lost paradise. The language of the description suggests that the weapon is being brandished especially for Karl, as if he were the reason for its being there: "The arm with the sword rose up as if newly stretched aloft."[23]

If Karl is a transformation of Joseph, it follows that the principal paternal figure in the novel should be called Jacob. He is an uncle and not Karl's actual father, but he takes on a parental role in the opening chapters. In a very Jacob-like way, he bestows his favor on his nephew and offers the advantages his great wealth and position can supply. As Uncle Jacob describes it, Karl's parents have played the role that Joseph's brothers do in the Bible: at their instigation he is "turned out . . . just as you turn a cat out of the house when it annoys you."[24] Uncle Jacob works to remedy what he understands as an injustice by taking Karl in, but eventually he repeats the fundamental gesture that marks the narrative: he, too, sends the boy into exile.

Karl's exile is in Amerika and not in Egypt, but as it is presented in the novel, this America might as well be Egypt. There are even indications that at least parts of it really are Egypt. A town called Ramses figures prominently in the action, a name surely more fitting for the land of the pharaohs than for even a legendary America. Joseph's life in Egypt is marked by his relation to a seducing woman, Potiphar's wife, whose vengeful denunciation leads to what is in effect Joseph's

22. See Heinz Politzer, *Franz Kafka: Parable and Paradox* (Ithaca: Cornell University Press, 1962), 122.
23. *AM* 3; *RO* 7: "Ihr Arm mit dem Schwert ragte wie neuerdings empor."
24. *AM* 26; *RO* 25: "Einfach beiseitegeschafft worden, wie man eine Katze vor die Tür wirft, wenn sie ärgert."

second exile. There are numerous seductresses in Karl's life, the most important being the first, Johanna Brummer. For Kafka, whose life was filled with frequently vain struggles to maintain his physical and emotional chastity against a variety of tempting females, the episode of Potiphar's wife was perhaps the most highly charged of the biblical story. In *The Missing Person*, it is repeated, transformed in various ways, but also displaced from the center to the beginning of the tale. This Joseph is exiled precisely because of an assault on his chastity, one that in Karl's case seems to be successful.

Kafka's America novel is unquestionably a version of the story he read in the Bible, though its genealogy is never made public. Its link with the Joseph-romance is so greatly suppressed that we must work to recover it. It is in a way an inverted image of what Kafka does in such stories as "Poseidon," in which a classical theme is announced and then at least partly effaced. Here Kafka retains many of the key elements in the intertext but refrains from naming the object of his reading. There is probably more of the Bible in *The Missing Person* than there is of the *Odyssey* in "The Silence of the Sirens," but here the author chooses to remain silent about his source. We might compare this suppressed but faithful retelling of the Joseph story to another fiction based on the book of Genesis, "The City Coat of Arms" ("Das Stadtwappen"). The very first sentence of this posthumously published fragment both names the intertext and marks a radical swerve away from it: "At first all the arrangements for building the Tower of Babel were characterized by fairly good order; indeed the order was perhaps too perfect, too much thought was given to guides, interpreters, accommodations for the workmen, and roads of communication, as if there were centuries before one to do the work in."[25] The first few words, with their reference to the "building of the Tower of Babel" (in the origninal, "babylonischen Turmbau," that is, "Babylonian tower-construction") conjure up the biblical story with which we are so familiar. And lest the reader suspect that this "babylonischer Turmbau" might refer to some other construction project undertaken by the Babylonians, Kafka later clarifies the matter definitively: "The essential thing in the whole business is the idea of building a tower that will reach to heaven."[26]

25. *CS* 433; *SE* 306: "Anfangs war beim babylonischen Turmbau alles in leidlicher Ordnung; ja, die Ordnung war vielleicht zu groß, man dachte zu sehr an Wegweiser, Dolmetscher, Arbeiterunterkünfte und Verbindungswege, so als habe man Jahrhunderte vor sich."

26. *CS* 433; *SE* 306: "Das Wesentliche des ganzen Unternehmens ist der Gedanke, einen bis in den Himmel reichenden Turm zu bauen."

We hardly need to glance back at Genesis 11 to recall the central issue of that story of the Tower of Babel, announced in the introductory phrases: "Once upon a time all the world spoke a single language and used the same words."[27] The Genesis narrative presents the building of the tower to heaven as the origin of the many mutually incomprehensible human languages. Whatever else it is doing, it is unquestionably explaining why, if Adam gave the proper names to all things in the Garden of Eden (Genesis 2) and thus created the perfect language, there are now so many different languages in the world. This is the fundamental meaning of the story, the one that orders all the other elements.

Although Kafka explicitly proclaims that he is writing about the Tower of Babel we know, he shows in his first sentence that he is not interested at all in the meaning of the biblical narrative. We cannot assume that he has failed to understand this meaning—how could one miss it? He has rather ignored it by acting as if it were not there. If one were to take the story in Genesis seriously, one would suppose that there was one profession that did not and could not exist prior to the building of the Tower: interpreter (*Dolmetscher*). By introducing interpreters into the work force of the tower builders, Kafka demonstrates that his story is not simply a different version of the biblical narrative but a different story altogether. His story takes place in a different world from the one presented in Genesis: this world is already fallen, already thoroughly secularized, and already so full of division and disagreement that no divine intervention is necessary to bring about confusion. But of course these issues of fallenness, division, and confusion belong properly to the Book of Genesis.

For all its obliviousness to the intention of the story from the Old Testament, "The City Coat of Arms" is still recognizably built with various elements taken from the old tale and reordered into a new structure. Kafka has not merely taken the notion of building a tower to heaven and pasted it on a story that bears no relation to the biblical one; on the contrary, he has taken many important features from the Old Testament and fit them together in a surprising way. One of the key features of Genesis 11, for example, is the opposition between order and disorder: the project begins with order but, because of divine intervention, ends in confusion. Kafka takes this fundamental

27. I quote from *The New English Bible* (Oxford and Cambridge: Oxford and Cambridge University presses, 1970).

opposition and, in typical Kafka fashion, makes it into a paradoxical unity. The order that exists at the commencement of the construction is *already* disorder; it is an order so complex as to be indistinguishable from chaos. The planners are so concerned with thoroughness in all their preparations that they never actually begin work on the tower, whereas the preparations become chaotically complex. The chaos manifests itself quickly in the rivalries that develop among the various groups engaged, not in building the tower itself, but in the preliminary work, building the construction workers' city: "Every nationality wanted the finest quarter for itself, and this gave rise to disputes, which developed into bloody conflicts. These conflicts never came to an end."[28] Kafka suggests the paradox in the very language of the opening sentence, where he refers to the order as "tolerable" ("in leidlicher Ordnung"). The word *leidlich* contains the morpheme *leid*, which carries a lengthy burden of negative meanings: "painful, disagreeable, unpleasant, bad," and so on. Thus the word Kafka has selected to inform us that the order was, as the Muir translation puts it, "fairly good," tells us at the same time that this order was fairly bad, painful, disagreeable, and unpleasant.

Divine intervention, another element of central importance to the Genesis narrative, plays a vital role in Kafka's story as well. But Kafka has completely transformed the role this element plays in his story, moving it from the center of the reported action to a kind of appendix placed at the end of the description of the city, where it is cited as part of an apocalyptic prophecy: "All the legends and songs that came to birth in that city are filled with longing for a prophesied day when the city would be destroyed by five successive blows from a gigantic fist. It is for that reason too that the city has a closed fist on its coat of arms."[29] The role of divine intervention in "The City Coat of Arms" is thus radically different from that in the Old Testament story of the Tower of Babel. In the Bible, God intervenes by introducing disorder for the purpose of halting a project that has, from the divine point of view, all too great prospects for success: "Here they are, one people

28. *CS* 433; *SE* 307: "Jede Landsmannschaft wollte das schönste Quartier haben, dadurch ergaben sich Streitigkeiten, die sich bis zu blutigen Kämpfen steigerten. Diese Kämpfe hörten nicht mehr auf."
29. *CS* 434; *SE* 307: "Alles was in dieser Stadt an Sagen und Liedern entstanden ist, ist erfüllt von der Sehnsucht nach einem prophezeiten Tag, an welchem die Stadt von einer Riesenfaust in fünf kurz aufeinanderfolgenden Schlägen zerschmettert werden wird. Deshalb hat auch die Stadt die Faust im Wappen."

with a single language, and now they have started to do this; hence-forward nothing they have a mind to do will be beyond their reach" (Genesis 11, v. 6). In Kafka's story, the project to build the tower has absolutely no prospect for success because "the second or third generation had already recognized the senselessness of building a heaven-reaching tower."[30] Divine intervention, if it were to come, would not halt a dangerous effort to achieve something like equal status with divinity; it would on the contrary bring to a merciful end a sick organism that is unable to put itself out of its own misery.

"The City Coat of Arms" is unquestionably a text that derives from Kafka's reading of the Old Testament, but his reading has been quite untouched by the meaning discoverable by any "serious" reader. His reading passes "through the midst of the book . . . as once the Jews passed through the Red Sea," to use Kafka's own metaphor of reading derived from the Old Testament. Just as the Jews following Moses were able to go through the very center of the Red Sea without being flooded by it, "through the sea on dry ground," as it is reported in Exodus 14, so does Kafka pass through this and other monumental texts of the tradition without being "influenced" (that is, "flooded") by them. Although he suffers from anxiety about his writing, it is not in these cases the anxiety of influence.

The classics that Kafka read and reworked in the course of making his fictions were most often those canonical texts regularly subjected to hermeneutic attention: the Bible, materials from Greek and Roman antiquity, and the literary classics of the German tradition. But Kafka could apply his particular mode of rhetorical reading to other kinds of classics as well, even to nonbelletristic or scientific texts ordinarily exempt from creative acts of interpretation. The most striking example of Kafka's interest in this second class of "classics" is the story "A Report to an Academy" ("Ein Bericht für eine Akademie"), which presents the account of the transformation of an ape into a human being.[31] Although the subject of such transformations held a

30. *CS* 434; *SE* 307: "Schon die zweite oder dritte Generation die Sinnlosigkeit des Himmelsturmbaues erkannte."
31. The critical studies devoted to this text include Patrick Bridgwater, "Rotpeters Ahnherren: oder, Der gelehrte Affe in der deutschen Dichtung," *DVLG* 56 (September 1982), 447–462; Gerhard Neumann, "Werk oder Schrift? Vorüberlegungen zur Edition von Kafkas 'Bericht von einer Akademie,' *Acta Germanica* 14 (1981), 1–21; Ralf R. Nicolai, "Nietzschean Thought in Kafka's 'A Report to an Academy,'" *Literary Review* 26:4 (1983), 551–564; and Dabney Stuart, "Kafka's 'A Report to an Academy': An Exercise in Method," *Studies in Short Fiction* 6 (1969), 413–420.

permanent fascination for Kafka because of the human-animal combination already present in his name, this particular tale seems to have
its beginning in a somewhat whimsical confrontation with Darwin's
The Descent of Man.

It would be nearly impossible for any educated reader to miss the
allusion to Darwin in the story's opening paragraphs: "You have done
me the honor of inviting me to give your Academy an account of the
life I formerly led as an ape."[32] But we realize instantly that Kafka is
not going to give us anything like "natural history" as Darwin would
have understood it. The distinguished speaker notes that at the time
of his report it is "nearly five years" have passed since he was an ape
and that those five years were so eventful that he can no longer say
much about what it was like to be an ape: "To put it plainly, much as I
like expressing myself in images, to put it plainly: your life as apes,
gentlemen, insofar as something of that kind lies behind you, cannot
be further removed from you than mine is from me."[33] We will hear
not the story of mankind's evolution but rather the personal history of
an individual who happens to be—to have been—an ape.

Kafka plays several games with Darwin's theory here. The first and
most obvious is that he reads it lethetically, performing a logomimesis
on a vulgar metaphor of its central thesis. The theory says that mankind evolved from earlier primates possibly resembling modern apes
more than modern humans. The popular metaphor of the theory
expresses this statement as "people used to be apes" or "long ago we
were all monkeys." This metaphor is the basis for Red Peter's citation
of "your own life as apes, gentlemen," though his instant qualification
("insofar as something of that kind lies behind you") suggests that,
unlike many people, he is well aware of the figure's limited adequacy
to Darwin's hypothesis. The story, then, begins with a literal reading
of this metaphor, giving us a protagonist whose personal development comprises both the ape state and the human along with the very
interesting transitional period. It is no wonder that Red Peter likes to
express himself in images: he is himself the expression of an image.

But Kafka extends the central logomimetic reading of the meta-

---

32. *CS* 250; *SE* 147: "Sie erweisen mir die Ehre, mich aufzufordern, der
Akademie einen Bericht über mein äffisches Vorleben einzureichen." Kafka's
interest in Darwin was intense at one point in his life, according to Klaus Wagenbach, *Franz Kafka: Eine Biographie seiner Jugend* (Bern: Francke, 1958), 60.

33. *CS* 250; *SE* 148: "Offen gesprochen, so gerne ich auch Bilder wähle für
diese Dinge, offen gesprochen: Ihr Affentum, meine Herren, soferne Sie etwas
Derartiges hinter sich haben, kann Ihnen nicht ferner sein als mir das meine."

phor almost as soon as he presents it. If Red Peter "used to be an ape" in a more literal way than the rest of us, it does not necessarily bring him any closer to apehood than his audience. The "used to be" is as important an element in the figure as the "ape." The members of the academy, thinking that five years will make a much smaller gap than many millions, expect Peter to tell them about life as an ape, but he cannot do so. In fact, he knows less about his own life as an ape than certain humans: "For the story of my capture I must depend on the evidence of others."[34] It was only after he was shot and placed in a cage that Peter "came to himself" (*erwachte*) and began to develop memories. What there was of the ape in him is now essentially gone, and indeed he refers to himself pointedly as "ein gewesener Affe," a *former* ape. Just as the reader is coming to learn that the author of the narrative being read is an ape, it is being made clear that this ape is indeed an ape no more. He may be covered from head to foot with "well-groomed fur," but that is only an apish appearance. The very fur serves in fact as evidence in favor of Red Peter's human nature; that he takes off his pants in public to show his scar is no great scandal (no *Affenschande,* as the Germans say) precisely because his fur preserves modesty. Those who regard his public disrobing as a sign that "my ape nature is not yet quite under control"[35] fail to reckon with this fact, he claims.

In the meantime, a figurative inversion is taking place. Although the "literal" ape is demonstrating his high level of human culture to the academy, human beings are shown to be metaphorical apes. Red Peter complains about his name, declaring it to be a "horrible name, utterly inappropriate, which only some ape could have thought of."[36] By claiming that his name was "förmlich von einem Affen erfunden," he presumably does not mean that a member of his erstwhile species thought up the name. *Affe* is more likely used here in the sense of "stupid, ridiculous person." In typical fashion, though, Kafka makes us hesitate over the choice between the literal and the figurative, using the slippery adverb *förmlich* (which can mean either "really" or "as it were") to underscore the ambiguity. This same figurative inversion is repeated near the end of the story, when Red Peter reports on

34. *CS* 251; *SE* 148: "Darüber, wie ich eingefangen wurde, bin ich auf fremde Berichte angewiesen."
35. *CS* 251; *SE* 148: "Meine Affennatur sei noch nicht ganz unterdrückt."
36. *CS* 251; *SE* 148: "Den widerlichen, ganz und gar unzutreffenden, förmlich von einem Affen erfundenen Namen."

the speed of his transformation into a human being: "My ape nature fled out of me, head over heels and away, so that my first teacher was almost himself turned into an ape by it, had soon to give up teaching and was taken away to a mental hospital."[37] The translation, though correct, misses the subtle point of the original, for the phrase "fast äffisch wurde" ("almost turned into an ape") can be read to mean "became almost silly" or, to put it in the contemporary American idiom, "went ape." The end of the sentence actually confirms the figurative reading; the teacher winds up in a mental hospital and not in a zoo. Still, the force of the literal reading cannot be ignored, and we must recognize the symmetry of the set of transformations described by the story. As the ape becomes a human, a number of humans go ape, a possibility that Darwin did not foresee.

Although this "erstwhile ape" can say nothing about what life is like for an ape, he can tell much about the process of his humanization. This process is the core of the story, which describes it in detail. The experience is not at all as we might have expected, for it is far more demeaning than ennobling for Red Peter. The essential skills to be learned for a move into the human realm are not intellectual or spiritual ones but rather matters of ingestion and expectoration: "I learned to spit in the very first days."[38] His next lesson is pipe smoking, which he also masters relatively quickly. The hardest and most essential thing of all, though, is drinking liquor: "My worst trouble came from the schnaps bottle. The smell of it revolted me; I forced myself to it as best I could; but it took weeks for me to master my repulsion."[39] Smoking, drinking, and other human vices hardly seem central and defining characteristics of our species, but Red Peter so presents them. Kafka's decision to focus on these matters appears to have been motivated in part by the passage in *The Descent of Man* where Darwin adduces as evidence in favor of the close biological relationship between man and apes exactly this kind of material:

Many kinds of monkeys have a strong taste for tea, coffee, and spirituous liquors: they will also, as I have myself seen, smoke tobacco with

37. CS 258; SE 154: "Die Affennatur raste, sich überkugelnd, aus mir hinaus und weg, so daß mein erster Lehrer selbst davon fast äffisch wurde, bald den Unterricht aufgeben und in eine Heilanstalt gebracht werden mußte."
38. CS 255; SE 152: "Spucken konnte ich schon in den ersten Tagen."
39. CS 256; SE 152: "Die meiste Mühe machte mir die Schnapsflasche. Der Geruch peinigte mich; ich zwang mich mit allen Kräften; aber es vergingen Wochen, ehe ich mich überwand."

pleasure. Brehm asserts that the natives of north-eastern Africa catch the wild baboons by exposing vessels with strong beer, by which they are made drunk. He has seen some of these animals, which he kept in confinement, in this state, and he gives a laughable account of their behaviour and strange grimaces. On the following morning they were very cross and dismal; they held their aching heads with both hands, and wore a most pitable expression: when beer or wine was offered them, they turned away with disgust, but relished the juices of lemons. An American monkey, and Ateles, after getting drunk on brandy, would never touch it again, and thus was wiser than most men.[40]

Because some of this account comes from Brehm's famous *Tierleben*, Kafka may have seen it there as well. Darwin's argument, however, must have seized Kafka's imagination because the argument is precisely inverted by the story. Darwin is attempting to dismantle the boundary between human and animal by showing that monkeys and apes easily acquire a taste for tobacco and alcohol. "These trifling facts," Darwin says, "prove how similar the nerves of taste must be in monkeys and man, and how similarly their whole nervous system is affected."[41] But it is by no means easy for Red Peter to acquire a taste for schnaps; on the contrary he must battle his "aversion for the schnaps bottle" ("Widerwille gegen die Schnapsflasche") again and again before he can finally overcome it and thus become human. The boundary between the animal and the human is crossable—as Red Peter has proven—but the effort required is extreme.

Even more important, though, is the obvious fact that Darwin does not regard "these trifling facts" as having any relevance to the question of the intellectual gap between monkeys and people. He is talking only about matters of physiology. Darwin assumes that the intellectual difference between animals and humans remains very great in spite of the "similarity of the tissues and blood." Kafka, on the other hand, virtually equates intellectual accomplishment with the "trifling" ability to drink alcohol:

> What a triumph it was then both for him [my teacher] and for me, when one evening . . . I took hold of a schnaps bottle that had been carelessly left standing before my cage, uncorked it in the best style, . . . set it to my lips without hesitation, with no grimace, like a professional drinker, with rolling eyes and full throat, actually and truly drank it empty; then

40. Charles Darwin, *The Descent of Man and Selection in Relation to Sex* (New York: Collier, 1911), I, 23–24.
41. Ibid., 24.

threw the bottle away, not this time in despair but as an artistic performer; forgot, indeed, to rub my belly; but instead of that, because I could not help it, because my senses were reeling, called a brief and unmistakable "Hallo!" breaking into human speech, and with this outburst broke into the human community, and felt its echo: "Listen, he's talking!" like a caress over the whole of my sweat-drenched body.[42]

Learning to speak is not a problem: it is not even a task that Red Peter ever takes on. His intellectual abilities simply spring into being along with his mastery of the schnaps bottle. Nothing could be further from the central hypothesis of *The Descent of Man*.

Kafka takes Darwin's material and plays with it, deliberately oblivious to its original intention. Instead of a genealogical "descent" over many millions of years, we have an intellectual "ascent" that takes place in a matter of days, weeks, and months, until the former ape achieves nothing less than "the cultural level of an average European."[43] It is an astounding and unique achievement for Red Peter but one that his report also calls into question. His goal all along is not intellectual or cultural enrichment but merely "a way out" of his cage. Becoming a human being is not Red Peter's aim; he becomes one only because doing so allows him to avoid life in a cage. Once captured and confined by the Hagenbeck firm, the poor ape can foresee no future for himself save behind bars; it is clear to him that Hagenbeck thinks no other place proper for an ape. The one alternative is clear: "I had to stop being an ape."[44]

Red Peter's great achievement in becoming human casts considerable doubt on the value of human status. Rather than seeing humanity as the pinnacle of an enormously complex and lengthy process of biological adaptation, Red Peter sees it merely as a kind of dodge. Again and again he insists that all his efforts were bent toward finding

42. *CS* 257; *SE* 153: "Was für ein Sieg dann allerdings für ihn wie für mich, als ich eines Abends . . . eine vor meinem Käfig versehentlich stehen gelassene Schnapsflasche ergriff, . . . sie schulgerecht entkorkte, an den Mund setzte und ohne Zögern, ohne Mundverziehen, als Trinker von Fach, mit rund gewälzten Augen, schwappender Kehle, wirklich und wahrhaftig leer trank; nicht mehr als Verzweifelter, sondern als Künstler die Flasche hinwarf; zwar vergaß den Bauch zu streicheln; dafür aber, weil ich nicht anders konnte, weil es mich drängte, weil mir die Sinne rauschten, kurz und gut 'Hallo!' ausrief, in Menschenlaut ausbrach, mit diesem Ruf in die Menschengemeinschaft sprang und ihr Echo: 'Hört nur, er spricht!' wie einen Kuß auf meinem ganzen schweißtriefenden Körper fühlte."
43. *CS* 258; *SE* 154: "Die Durchschnittsbildung eines Europäers."
44. *CS* 253; *SE* 150: "Nun, so hörte ich auf, Affe zu sein."

the *Ausweg* (both "way out" and "expedient" or "shift, dodge") that will help him out of his confinement. He insists that his choice of this term is particularly important:

> I fear that perhaps you do not quite understand what I mean by "way out." I use the expression in its fullest and most popular sense. I deliberately do not use the word "freedom." I do not mean the spacious feeling of freedom on all sides. As an ape, perhaps, I knew that, and I have met men who yearn for it. But for my part I desired such freedom neither then nor now.[45]

By stressing that the "way out" (*Ausweg*) is to be understood in its "most ordinary and fullest" sense, Red Peter is reminding his audience of the negative value that can be placed on it and is assuring them that this negative quality is intended. And by stressing the great difference he finds between *Ausweg* and *Freiheit*, the freedom he "perhaps" knew as an ape, he further questions the moral superiority of human beings over apes.

Although Darwin admits that the monkey who refused to touch brandy after becoming drunk on it behaved more wisely than many men, his purpose is not to suggest the moral inferiority of the human condition. This is Kafka's purpose, however, and the material supplied by Darwin suits it very well. Red Peter's transformation into a man might properly be called a "descent," a paradoxical loss of something highly desirable for which men can only yearn. The "freedom" of this story is a powerful, unspecified value akin to the "grace" of Kleist's essay on the marionette theater. Both Kleist and Kafka contrast man's fallen state with some earlier, perhaps better condition known to animals. Red Peter's spiritual metamorphosis, a process that took him out of the literal jungles of Africa, returns to a figurative jungle: when he says that he has "fought through the thick of things" (*CS* 258) in order to achieve his high level of civilization, the German idiom he uses is "sich in die Büsche schlagen" (*SE* 154), that is, to throw oneself into the bushes or "go into the brushwood," as a (now possibly obsolete) British expression puts it. He cites this expression as

---

45. *CS* 245; *SE* 150: "Ich habe Angst, daß man nicht genau versteht, was ich unter Ausweg verstehe. Ich gebrauche das Wort in seinem gewöhnlichsten und vollsten Sinn. Ich sage absichtlich nicht Freiheit. Ich meine nicht dieses große Gefühl der Freiheit nach allen Seiten. Als Affe kannte ich es vielleicht und ich habe Menschen kennen gelernt, die sich danach sehnen. Was mich aber anlangt, verlangte ich Freiheit weder damals noch heute."

"an excellent German locution" ("eine ausgezeichnete deutsche Redensart"), thus drawing the reader's attention to its unexpected implication.

Red Peter fights his way out of the wilderness (of life as an animal) less than he precipitates himself into the wilderness (of life as a person). It is a movement into a kind of confinement, though one less severe than the imprisonment in Hagenbeck's cage. He speaks of his becoming human as a process of submitting himself to a "yoke" (*CS* 250), the obligation precisely to rid himself of the memory of his animal freedom. The very ability to engage in human thought seems to be conditioned by the imposition of unaccustomed constraint. In a melancholy reading of the commonplace expression "Not macht erfinderisch" ("necessity is the mother of invention"), Peter's report chronicles the onset of "thinking" in response to dire exigency. Faced with the alternative of drowning in the deep blue sea, Peter begins to engage in an activity that might not have been human thought but was in many ways indistinguishable from thought: "I did not think it out in this human way, but under the influence of my surroundings I acted as if I had thought it out."[46] The environmental pressure that is so central to Darwin's evolutionary hypothesis appears here in literal form, and the organism responds not at the species level but as an individual and not through slow evolution but in an instant transformation.

Darwin's text has served Kafka well but not in any way congruent with Darwin's intention. Kafka reads this classic as he does others, obliviously.[47] Indeed, his reading of the classics tends on the whole more toward the lethetic pole than the alethetic one. Both the parable about Prometheus and his use of the Goethean paradigm of the self, as well as the response to Darwin in "A Report to an Academy," suggest that the mode of "good" reading that he otherwise prized so highly would not often be appropriate. The self-effacement required by this "good" reading could lead all too easily to the disappearance of the new text under the crushing weight of the old. Even in his treatment of the biblical Joseph story in *The Missing Person*—the closest Kafka comes to an alethetic reading in any of this material—he is

46. *CS* 255; *SE* 151: "Ich rechnete nicht so menschlich, aber unter dem Einfluß meiner Umgebung verhielt ich mich so, wie wenn ich gerechnet hätte."
47. The notion of "oblivious reading" is defined and discussed in detail in my *The Incredulous Reader* (Ithaca: Cornell University Press, 1984), 143–157.

careful to submerge the classical text in the flood of his own invention. The partial effacement of the classic appears to be necessary, in his practice, to give the new text a chance to establish its own identity. The classic is too powerful to be allowed to enter this new union at full strength. Kafka's acts of mutilation performed on these textual monuments are gestures of respect.

Chapter 7

THE RHETORIC OF PARABLE

Kafka typically casts many of his fictions as parables. Parabolic discourse is in fact so characteristic of Kafka's fictions that Heinz Politzer proposed the paradoxical parable as *the* Kafkan genre. Politzer argued that Kafka's fictions both participated in the familiar, mainly biblical, tradition of explanatory fictions and deviated from that tradition in important ways: "His parables are as multilayered as their Biblical models. But, unlike them, they are also multifaceted, ambiguous, and capable of so many interpretations that, in the final analysis, they defy any and all."[1] Like traditional parables, Kafka's fictions seem to draw the reader in at first, to invite him or her to hear a narrative illustration of some principle or moral, but in the end they exclude the reader definitively by allowing no clue as to what this principle or moral might be or by offering the principle that principles are not to be found. "Franz Kafka's importance," Politzer claims,

---

1. Heinz Politzer, *Franz Kafka: Parable and Paradox* (Ithaca: Cornell University Press, 1962), 21. Page numbers cited below in the text refer to this edition. Other discussions of Kafka's use of parable include: Ulrich Füllerborn, "Zum Verhältnis von Perspektivismus und Parabolik in der Dichtung Franz Kafkas," in Renate von Heydebrand and Klaus G. Just, eds., *Wissenschaft als Dialog* (Stuttgart: Metzler, 1969), 289–313; Heinz Hillmann, "Fabel und Parabel im 20. Jahrhundert: Kafka und Brecht," in Peter Hasubek, ed., *Die Fabel: Theorie, Geschichte, und Rezeption einer Gattung* (Berlin: Schmidt, 1982), 215–235; and Klaus-Peter Philippi, "Parabolisches Erzählen: Anmerkungen zu Form und möglicher Geschichte," *DVLG* 43 (1969), 297–332.

"derives from the fact that he was probably the first and certainly the most radical writer to pronounce the insoluble paradox of human existence by using this paradox as the message of his parables." Politzer concludes that these stories somewhat resemble "literary Rorschach tests" that "reveal the character of the interpreters rather than their own" (21) and that "any interpretation of his work will have to return to the text itself" (22), that is, to a simple repetition of the text's words.

Politzer's rhetoric seems to deny the appropriateness of what Politzer in fact does, which is to provide an interpretation. The words "insoluble paradox of human existence" are evidence enough, I think, that Politzer has not failed to take the Rorschach and reveal himself as committed to a certain moral/philosophical position. I raise this point not to take Politzer to task for such a commitment or even for apparently denying its relevance; both the commitment and its denial serve an important purpose in his very fruitful approach to Kafka. I mention it rather to show how powerful the mechanism is to which Politzer alludes. The critic himself becomes caught up in, implicated in, the paradoxical hermeneutic knot he finds represented in the parable. He recognizes and responds to both the invitation to interpret offered by the parabolic form and the ban on interpretation imposed by the absence of any clearly defensible principle by which one might interpret.

I will explore this topic further, not because Politzer's treatment is inadequate, but because it takes a different direction from the one I want to pursue. Politzer wanted to reveal Kafka to the world as the great poet of "the insoluble paradox of human existence" and argue thereby for Kafka's rightful place in the canon of literary giants. Thanks to Politzer and others, this argument need no longer be made. Kafka's place in the canon seems assured, for now and for some time to come, and the relevance of his stories to the eternal problems of the human condition is now readily—perhaps all too readily—granted. I will instead explore the still perplexing matter of how and why Kafka's fictions function as parables and how that parabolic function relates to the question of reading that remains central to my inquiry.

It is best to begin (as Politzer did) with a specific text before us. A good one for my purpose here is a story that Kafka himself never titled but that Max Brod called "A Little Fable" ("Kleine Fabel"). Indeed, Kafka appears to present in it a fable in the manner of La Fontaine:

> "Alas," said the mouse, "the world is growing smaller every day. At the beginning it was so big that I was afraid. I kept running and running, and I was glad when I saw walls far away to the right and left, but these long walls have narrowed so quickly that I am in the last chamber already, and there in the corner stands the trap that I must run into."
> "You only need to change your direction," said the cat, and ate it up.[2]

Here the tradition Kafka calls upon is less the biblical parable than the animal apologue, a rich heritage with many examples in both folklore and belles lettres.[3] In keeping with that tradition, Kafka's story appears to invite efforts at a sort of moral/philosophical allegorizing but at a level of generality that might place the topic in the realm of Politzer's "insoluble paradox of human existence." Such a reading would try to see in the cat and the mouse as representatives of two human types or two ethical or philosophical positions. This is the model of the traditional fable. We could compare Kafka's text, for example, with La Fontaine's fable of cat and mouse, to which Kafka's story indeed bears certain resemblances. The central character in the French text is also a philosophical mouse who tries to confront a desperate situation by means of rhetoric:

> A young mouse of little experience
> Imagined that he could argue in his defense
> And that hard old Rominagrab would set him free.
>   "Why not grant me liberty—
>   Too minute to be an expense
>   Amid such prodigality?
>   Say by what possibility
>   I could hurt you, your lady, or friends?
>   A grain of wheat's enough for me,
>   A mere nut makes a mouse immense.

---

2. *CS* 445; *SE* 320: "'Ach,' sagte die Maus, 'die Welt wird enger mit jedem Tag. Zuerst war sie so breit, daß ich Angst hatte, ich lief weiter und war glücklich, daß ich endlich rechts und links in der Ferne Mauern sah, aber diese langen Mauern eilen so schnell aufeinander zu, daß ich schon im lezten Zimmer bin, und dort im Winkel steht die Falle, in die ich laufe.' — 'Du mußt nur die Laufrichtung ändern,' sagte die Katze und fraß sie."

3. For an examination of Kafka's relation to this heritage, see Egon Schwartz, "Kafka's Animal Tales and the Tradition of the European Fable," *CT*, 75–100.

Since I am thin at present, wait till I expand.
Your offspring will need food, as any mouse would understand."
When in straits, that is what a poor mouse found to say
    And was told, "Your logic is astray.
Who am I to listen to your unseasoned fears?
Your logic is wasted on one of my years.
A cat, an old cat pardon? Never anywhere.
    Realize, mouse, that you will go
    Where dead mice congregate below.
    Logic is not a thing about which the Three Fates care.
My young heirs must find other mice on which to grow."
    And that was all.
                As for my fable, well,
This is the moral that seems applicable here:
Fond youth flatters itself that all must heed its prayer;
    Old age is inexorable.[4]

La Fontaine's cat and mouse represent moral/philosophical attitudes alleged to be typical of broad segments of the human community. The mouse's position reflects the way in which young people are understood to view the world, whereas that of the cat represents—what? Not exactly the way the old characteristically behave, surely, for the more mature among us are not necessarily grimmer or more unforgiving. No, the cat seems to represent more the unforgiving advance of time itself, associating itself with the Three Fates and the inevitability of death. In any case, the poem offers its own gloss, and so the reader does not have to grope about for principles by which to interpret the story. Even if we do not find the poet's interpretation correct (or crystal clear), it at least suggests the lines along which an interpretation can be developed. From the standpoint of hermeneutic method, then, it does not matter whether we regard the cat as representing the unforgiving nature of old people in general or the unforgiving nature of time. The poem, together with its gloss, shows us the way toward a reasonable, if not definitive, interpretation.

But, one might ask, why do we need to interpret either story at all? In both cases, the invitation to allegorical interpretations emerges largely from the nature of the narrative material: it presents events that superficially appear to be incredible nonsense. Any reader likely to take the trouble to read these fictions would not likely believe that a

4. *The Fables of La Fontaine*, trans. Marianne Moore (New York: Viking Press, 1964), 284–285.

mouse and a cat hold conversations of this kind or any other. Indeed, with the very opening words, " 'Alas,' said the mouse," Kafka invokes a convention of alethic fiction in which the reader is encouraged to disregard the nonsense of the surface, to convert disbelief in the literal meaning into belief in the figurative import. We know that mice do not say "alas," and because we know that the author knows this, too, we suppose he must mean something else. The "mouse" that speaks must be not a "real" mouse, the small furry creature that occasionally shares our dwellings, but a figurative "mouse," a person, perhaps, with some mouselike characteristic such as timidity. Once we suspect the presence of this convention, we immediately become sensitive to the figurative potential of all the fictive elements in the parable: the "corner" is transformed from a physical place into a psychological state, the "trap" quickly metamorphoses into an existential bind, and so on. The reader ceases to be interested primarily in the story of the literal mouse who fears running into a literal corner where she (mice are feminine in German) might encounter a literal trap, instead searching for the human situation that fits the figurative meanings of the words. The classical apologue rewards this hermeneutic activity by disclosing a pertinent observation about human values, for example about the relative worth of prudence as opposed to rashness. When we begin reading "A Little Fable," it seems altogether likely that such an interpretive strategy will be successful.

As Politzer would have told us, however, the strategy does not work. Although it apparently cries out for interpretation, the story at the same time frustrates our expectations by offering no hint of a principle by which it could possibly be interpreted. On the contrary, the traditional methods of interpretation present the reader with awful difficulties. If we accept the invitation to allegory, we must see the story's ending—the philosophical mouse made into a meal by the equally philosophical cat—as proposing a caution of some sort. After all, we know that little piggies who are eaten by the wolf come to this sorry pass by their improvident behavior. The question then arises, what mistake cost the mouse so dearly? What is this fable cautioning us metaphorical mice against? At first, the answer seems simple: mice, metaphorical or otherwise, should not take advice from cats. La Fontaine could have written a pointed couplet along such lines. But half a moment's consideration leaves us dissatisfied with this reading because it fails to account completely for anything but the last few words of the story. How are we to interpret the mouse's concern about the world's shrinking every day, which after all occupies most of the little tale? In fact, if we take seriously the thrust of the mouse's concern, the cat's advice is just right. Moreover, it is just the right sort of advice for one fable creature to give another: if your current direction seems to be taking you away from where you want to go, turn around and go the other way. This is indeed a moral and one you might well expect from a traditional fable.

My interpretation presents a problem, however, in that it directly conflicts with the other moral to be drawn: do not take advice from cats. The uncomfortable fact seems to be that the cat's advice is both exactly right and exactly wrong for the mouse. The mouse must take it in order to avoid what we must understand as a (metaphorically) deadly trap, but if she does take it (as she apparently does), she ends up in the jaws of the cat. She is damned if she does and damned if she doesn't, and so is the reader. Is there no way out of this hermeneutic bind?

Perhaps we need to follow Politzer's advice, if not his example, and completely abandon allegorical or symbolic interpretation. Perhaps we should just return to the text's words and assume that they mean exactly what they say: a cat and mouse engage in a philosophical discussion. On this assumption, the piece is pure nonsense, something closer to Lewis Carroll than to La Fontaine. Carroll's talking animals are not allegories of human traits or ethical positions but more often purely verbal flights of fancy deriving from a kind of literal reading of ordinary language—a procedure entirely congenial to Kafka, after all. Carroll's Mock Turtle is less a kind of turtle than an imaginative gloss on the phrase "mock turtle soup." He does not expect us to believe in the reality, on any level, of his Mock Turtle or to engage in complex hermeneutic acts to extract a "deeper" stratum of meaning. Kafka, we must admit, might be doing the same thing, pulling the leg of language by putting philosophical words into a mundane, trivial, and brutal context of cat-catches-mouse.

In one sense "A Little Fable" does indeed work as a species of nonsense. It begins by snaring the reader into accepting the fairy-tale assumption of a talking mouse, then elaborates that assumption in an unexpected way by letting the mouse discuss matters of considerable psychological complexity. In a very few words, the tale carries us away from its announced animal context into a realm of existential concerns that, if we thought about it, we would suppose very far removed from anything that might occur to an actual mouse. Even at the most literal level, the mouse's speech is psychologically subtle, disclosing an apparent ambivalence between agoraphobia ("[the world] was so big I was afraid") and claustrophobia ("there in the corner stands the trap I must run into"). We do not believe that mice have such concerns, though we allow the story to proceed as if they do. We assume that our acceptance of such an incredible premise will pay off somehow, that in the end the story will do something for us in return for our accepting this nonsense. But the story ends by pulling the rug out from under the reader, brutally reimposing the literal, animal level from which the narrative had drawn us away. The cat eats the mouse. Regarded in this way, the story thumbs its nose at the reader who had accepted the story's own invitation to forget for a moment that what was at issue here was a *mouse*, that little creature which is pursued and devoured by cats. It would be something like the children's trick of "Look up. Look down. See my thumb? You're dumb!" The victim is invited to participate in what is seemingly a game in good faith only to discover that the game's sole purpose is to deride his willingness to perform what he supposes is the behavior required by the game— that without which the game could not function.

If my analysis is correct, then Kafka's parable of the mouse does not call upon us to consider the "insoluble paradox of human existence" but rather forces the question of reading. The story absolutely re-quires from the reader the very thing its conclusion proposes to ex-clude: that is, the reader's willingness to "grant the author his subject." Regarded as a single signifying unit, the text suggests the absurdity of its own process of signification. It begins by inviting us to read it but ends by making us feel stupid for trying to do so.

But is this analysis correct? Is the reader really required to under-stand the text as a high-level species of nonsense? Is there really no way to follow through on the story's apparent invitation to an allegori-cal reading? Indeed there is, if only because allegorical reading can never definitively be excluded by any text reflecting upon itself.[5] One cannot absolutely preclude, for example, an interpretation of the fable as a straightforward allegory of despair. In this view, the mouse's comments are simply accurate: all options lead to disaster. The cat's remark, on the other hand, must be read as self-servingly ironical: the cat in fact *agrees* with the mouse but is happy to let the mouse's misfortune turn to the cat's own good.

Although this interpretation of the story would seem perfectly rea-

5. See my *The Incredulous Reader: Reading and the Function of Disbelief* (Ithaca: Cornell University Press, 1984), pp. 37–38.

sonable, its apparent simplicity masks a substantial difficulty. Actually, this reading forces us to read allegorically *and* literally at the same time. To call the cat's comment "self-serving irony" is to posit a realistic motivation for the cat *as cat* (that is, a creature who wants to eat mice). But such a realistic motivation is inconsistent with the rest of the interpretation, which cannot account for the motivation of the mouse as mouse; the mouse of this reading is the spokesman for a position of existential despair. If a proper "realistic" fictional cat is motivated by a desire to eat mice, a proper realistic fictional mouse should want nothing more than to eat cheese or the like. Such a mouse would not be concerned about such issues as whether or not "the world" was growing smaller.

The reader attempting to construct a consistent interpretation discovers after a while that it cannot be done. There is no plausible allegorical reading that does not harbor a contradiction. If the usual allegorical approaches fail, however, may we not become meta-allegorical and understand the difficulties that the tale presents as themselves metaphors? Taken in this way, the story becomes an allegory on the unreliability of allegories. Instead of telling mice (metaphorical or otherwise) not to take advice from cats, the parable tells readers not to take advice from writers of parables. But of course as a result the story becomes a version of the liar's paradox, for we are then reading it as saying something like "Never take my advice." If we obey it, we disobey it. Kafka was certainly fond of paradox, but this one would undermine the very foundation on which fables are constructed. Stanley Corngold has recently argued that Kafka might very well have wanted to do exactly this, to expose the lie of his own fictions and thereby in a sense "save" the authorial self.[6] My argument here is not centrally concerned with the question of the self, but it takes a similar direction: part of the purpose of the fiction is to discredit fiction. Kafka, author of parables, seems to tell us not to pay attention to parables.

Such reading, in other words, discloses a sign structure that is just as contradictory as the other. The most likely allegorical meaning is one that actually denies the efficacy of allegory, so that the reader is sent back chasing his logical tale in a hopeless attempt to do what the

---

6. Stanley Corngold, "The Author Survives on the Margin of His Breaks: Kafka's Narrative Perspective," in Corngold, *The Fate of the Self: German Writers and French Theory* (New York: Columbia University Press, 1986), 161–179.

story wants him to do. The fiction makes an antithetical gesture that I would call "rhetorical" because it actualizes in a particularly dramatic way the coexistence of two opposed systems of meaning in a single signifying structure. Kafka's fable places the reader in the position of the condemned prisoner of the penal colony: one is obliged to read a text that is in a fundamental way undecipherable. The text, the more we look at it, resembles less and less Politzer's allegory of the human condition and more and more what Paul de Man called an allegory of reading. But to the extent that reading may be understood as the most basic and important human activity (and only to that extent), we can still consider Politzer to be correct.

The Kafkan parable characteristically problematizes the act of reading by setting up fictions that are themselves images and as images essentially rhetorical. It is important to keep in mind that the German words for "parable" and "image" are the same: *Gleichnis*. Kafka's frequently cited fragment "On Parables" ("Von den Gleichnissen") could just as correctly be called in English "On Metaphors." The "parable" that is cited in this story consists of just two words, "Gehe hinüber" ("Go over") and is in fact a straightforward metaphor. The text explains that the sage who utters these words "does not mean that we should cross to some actual place, which we could do anyhow if the labor were worth it; he means some fabulous yonder, something unknown to us, something he cannot designate more precisely either, and therefore cannot help us here in the very least."[7] The problem of this metaphor/parable lies in the complex relation between literal and figurative meaning. In the case of "Go over," just as in the case of "A Little Fable," the literal meaning is perfectly comprehensible but trivial, whereas the (apparently intended) figurative meaning is unknown and undefinable. The injunction to "go over," as presented in this context, is pure rhetoric: it forces an unending oscillation between two incompatible meanings, in this case a knowable but unimportant literal one and an unknowable but potentially priceless figurative one.

Kafka exploits the rhetorical potential that has long existed in the parable genre. It seems clear that this exploitation involved an acquaintance not only with the tradition of the apologue as practiced by

7. *CS* 457; *SE* 359: "Wenn der Weise sagt: 'Gehe hinüber,' so meint er nicht, daß man auf die andere Seite hinübergehen solle, was man immerhin noch leisten könnte, wenn das Ergebnis des Weges wert wäre, sondern er meint irgendein sagenhaftes Drüben, etwas, das wir nicht kennen, das auch von ihm nicht näher zu bezeichnen ist, und das uns also hier gar nichts helfen kann."

La Fontaine and the Old Testament but also with that of the New Testament. If we may take Ezekiel as standing for the practice of the Old Testament, we find that the parable (Hebrew *mashal*) is used there much as it was by La Fontaine. Ezekiel reports (Ezekiel 17:1–24) that the Lord told him to "propound an allegory" to the people of Israel, the text of which the voice of the Lord then delivers. It is the parable of the eagles and the vine, telling how a great eagle took "the tip of a cedar" from Lebanon and set it growing as a vine in another land in order that its "tendrils might turn toward him, / And its roots be under him." But the vine inclines its roots and tendrils in the direction of another eagle, much to God's displeasure. The voice of the Lord then instructs Ezekiel to interpret the parable to the "rebellious" people as a warning to the Jewish nobility held captive by the king of Babylon not to attempt to seek aid against the Babylonians from the Egyptian pharaoh. The purpose of Ezekiel's parable is apparently also similar to that of La Fontaine: to provide a concrete and memorable means of making a more abstract moral point. The Hebrew prophet and the French fable writer have as their chief goal an unmistakable moral clarity.

But clarity is not always the goal of parables. Kafka had as an alternative model the practice of another prophet, who explicitly used the parable as a means to both facilitate and prevent understanding. This tradition, admittedly Christian, has been powerful enough in our culture that it could not fail to attract the attention of a person of Kafka's officially "classical" (that is, Christian-humanist) education. Both possibilities are proposed by passages in the New Testament. In Mark 4:2ff., for example, Jesus tells the famous parable of the sower, some of whose seed fell on rocky ground and failed to prosper, whereas other seed fell on fertile soil, where it grew and bore fruit. Explaining the parable to his disciples, he says, "To you the secret of the kingdom of God has been given; but to those who are outside everything comes by way of parables, so that (as Scripture says) they may look and look, but see nothing; they may hear and hear, but understand nothing" (Mark 4:10–12). In Matthew's expanded version of the same material, Jesus explains that he does not want the secrets of the Kingdom to reach those whose "ears are dulled" and whose "eyes are closed" (Matthew 13:15). As the parable of the sower makes clear, Jesus expects that his parabolic form of teaching to work in two opposite ways: it will make understanding easier for those who are initiated, where the teaching will take root and bear fruit, but it will prevent understanding altogether for those who are not spiritually prepared for it.

In the New Testament tradition, then, the antithetical nature of the parable depends not upon the inherently contradictory quality of the text's interpretants but on the assumption of two fundamentally different sorts of audiences. In the parables of Jesus, two groups of listeners are envisioned, one that has "ears to hear" and is thus invited to participate in understanding the parable, and another (unbelievers) that is excluded. Unlike La Fontaine and Ezekiel, Jesus frequently declines to offer his own (or the Lord's) magisterial and thus also definitive interpretation of the parables. He offers only a general context: "The Kingdom of Heaven is like," expecting the initiated to know what to make of it. And they apparently do. "Do you understand all of this?" he asks his audience. "They said to him, 'Yes'" (Matthew 13:51). For them—as indeed for the uninitiated as well—the parable is not problematic at all: those invited in are supposed to find it crystal clear, whereas those who are excluded will find nothing in it to provoke curiosity, not to mention frustration.

This double structure of the parable has been well understood by many writers who are now part of the tradition. Few have expressed it better or in a way more pertinent to this discussion than did Nietzsche in aphorism 381 of *The Gay Science*:

> *On the question of being understandable.*—One does not only wish to be understood when one writes; one wishes just as surely *not* to be understood. It is not by any means necessarily an objection to a book when anyone finds it impossible to understand: perhaps that was part of the author's intention—he did not want to be understood by just "anybody." All the nobler spirits and tastes select their audience when they wish to communicate; and choosing that, one at the same time erects barriers against "the others." All the more subtle laws of any style have their origin at this point: they at the same time keep away, create a distance, forbid "entrance," understanding, as said above—while they open the ears of those whose ears are related to ours.[8]

This paragraph opens a section that is chiefly concerned with the advantages and difficulties of Nietzsche's own style, but the reference to "opening the ears" makes it clear on which tradition he is drawing. Nietzsche slyly and ironically compares himself to the parable-telling

8. Friedrich Nietzsche, *The Gay Science*, trans. Walter Kaufmann (New York: Vintage Books, 1974), 343.

Jesus depicted in the synoptic gospels, all the while aware that those most likely to suppose themselves equipped with open ears for the New Testament are precisely those whom his *Gay Science* will tend to exclude. In spite of this irony, however, Nietzsche holds firmly to the orthodox tradition that envisions two audiences, initiated and uninitiated, for every parable.

Nietzsche's assertion here that a writer might not necessarily always want to be understood reminds us, too, that Kafka also occasionally hinted at a preference for misunderstanding. In the passage from the letter to Felice of February 1, 1913 (quoted above), he cites Stoessl's "complete lack of understanding" for his book *Meditation* as evidence "that the book must really be good." Kafka proposes that the level of misunderstanding shown by Stoessl is far greater than what one expects in the case of books and is "possible only with living, hence complex, human beings." It is worthwhile to consider the possibility that Kafka's use of parable was motivated in part by a desire to achieve, in a regular and predictable way, this "living" and "complex" incomprehensibility.

In the case of Kafka's parables, there seems to be a difference between the expectations tacitly assumed by the formal properties of the text and the actual situation. These stories do not have an audience readily divisible into initiated and uninitiated groups. No cadre of insiders has special "ears to hear." This point cannot be sufficiently stressed, for it discloses both the affinity with and difference from the New Testament practice characteristic of Kafka's fables. In a sense they are a kind of amalgam of the animal apologue such as we find in La Fontaine or Ezekiel and the moral/theological parables of Jesus. In "A Little Fable," for example, the reader has good reason to suppose that the text will conclude with an explanation of the moral, as La Fontaine's fables do. Instead, it simply ends, leaving us wondering how to become initiated into the group possessing the interpretive key. But there is no such group. All of Kafka's readers are in this respect created equal, for none has a special knowledge that would make clear the allegorical meaning toward which we seem to be directed. Everyone is invited in, and everyone is ultimately excluded.

The practice of Jesus as reported in the gospels assumes that a certain group of hearers knows for certain the topic of Jesus' discourse: he always talks about the Kingdom of God. Knowing this, the appearance in his discourse of a story about a man and his prodigal son presents only a momentary difficulty, solvable as soon as the listener applies a straightforward hermeneutic process. The listener in effect says to himself, "This is Jesus talking, whose business is not to divert us with tales of domestic dissension but to enlighten us about the Kingdom of God. This material must, somehow, do just that; it is my business to work out the method of proper understanding." But Kafka's reader is not in a position to make any analogous assumption about what Kafka might want to talk to us about, not with any certainty at any rate. To be sure, readers have tried various hypotheses: Kafka always talks about Judaism, Kafka always talks about God and man, Kafka always talks about himself, Kafka always talks about the dehumanizing effects of modern society, and so on. None of these assumptions has proven reliable as a key to the apparent allegory of Kafka's parables. The effort to apply any of them to the fable of the mouse, for example, leads only to frustration.

We cannot rely on Kafka to speak obliquely about any particular topic, even a topic as broad as the paradox of human existence. We can rely on him, however, to stage a scene of reading that foregrounds the pathos of interpretation, insisting on its necessity while demonstrating its impossibility. As Theodor Adorno remarked of Kafka's fiction, "Each sentence says 'interpret me,' and none will permit it."[9] This formula would appear to arise from despair, but despair is not—not quite—its source. The source is passion. Kafka's passion of reading is both a drama of desire, an erotic yearning to "go over" and bathe in the fullness of immediate truth, and a drama of suffering in the knowledge that the yearning is never to be satisfied. The suffering may be extreme, but it never kills the desire.

Perhaps nowhere in Kafka's work is the drama of desire and suffering offered with such tantalizing, lapidary opacity as in the parable "Before the Law," the only section of the novel fragment *The Trial* that Kafka saw fit to publish. This scene of reading, or, more accurately, this scene of the desire to read, enacts the frustrated yearning of a man from the country who seeks access to the "Law." In front of the building housing the Law is a doorkeeper who tells the man that he may not have access "at the moment," though in fact "the gate stands open, as usual, and the doorkeeper steps to one side" to let the man see in. The doorkeeper even invites the man to try "to go in despite

9. Theodor W. Adorno, "Notes on Kafka," in Adorno, *Prisms*, trans. Samuel Weber and Shierry Weber (Cambridge, Mass.: MIT Press, 1982), 246.

my veto. But take note: I am powerful. And I am only the least of the doorkeepers." The man from the country is daunted and decides to wait. "The doorkeeper gives him a stool and lets him sit down at one side of the door. There he sits for days and years. He makes many attempts to be admitted," but he is always told that he cannot yet get in. He grows old waiting. Finally, just before this poor seeker after the Law dies, the doorkeeper tells him that the door before which he stands is meant *only for him* and at that same moment closes the door forever. Like the reader of Kafka's parables, the man from the country has been both invited in, as evidenced by the fact that there is a special door just for him, and definitively excluded by the door-keeper's refusal of permission to enter.[10]

The similarities between the "Law" to which the story alludes only vaguely and The Torah, the Law most familiar to Kafka, cannot be ignored. Like the Torah, this Law is kept in a kind of sanctuary, and it is described as something that "everyone strives to reach." Further-more, Politzer's suggestion that "Mann vom Lande" is a translation of the Yiddish "Amhoretz" or Hebrew "Am ha-aretz" must be given credence, in view of the context. Kafka's "man from the country" would then be a religious and hermeneutic *naif*, a "babe in the woods" seeking access to a text that he is not equipped to understand. These allusions to a holy scripture are, moreover, quite characteristic of Kafka's scenes of reading: we need only remember the illegible "scrip-ture" of the old Commandant that the officer in the penal colony treated with such reverence. All these allusions to the Old Testament, uncertain as each of them may be, combine to indicate that the read-ing of a difficult but incredibly valuable text is at stake here. After all, what would the man from the country do with the Law if he were permitted access to it? He could not simply take possession of it; he would have to *read* it. But of course the act of reading is, according to innumerable repetitions of a powerful topos, the opening of a door, the finding of a way, the penetration of a tough exterior "shell" or "husk" in order to reach the meaning protected within.

10. *CS* 3–4; *SE* 131–132: "Da das Tor zum Gesetz offensteht wie immer und der Türhüter beiseite tritt, bückt sich der Mann, um durch das Tor in das Innere zu sehn. . . . 'Wenn es dich so lockt, versuche es doch, trotz meines Verbotes hin-einzugehen. Mèrke aber: Ich bin mächtig. Und ich bin nur der unterste Türhü-ter.' . . . Der Türhüter gibt ihm einen Stuhl und läßt ihn seitwärts von der Tür sich niedersetzen. Dort sitzt er Tage und Jahre. Er macht viele Versuche, eingelassen zu werden, und ermüdet den Türhüter durch seine Bitten."

If the Law kept safe inside the structure of doors and doorkeepers presented in Kafka's parable is some kind of holy text, the structure itself is one, too. It is the structure precisely of Gleichnis, of parable, image, fable—the *fabula* described by Boccaccio as the essential form of both scripture and secular poetry. The crucial feature of such texts, as Boccaccio and the tradition he represents describe them, is that they deny easy access. Each is surrounded by shells, veils, doors, and doorkeepers that drive off the impatient, the uncaring, the unimaginative reader. Only the most persistent can penetrate the *cortex* surrounding a poetic fable. "You must read," Boccaccio tells those who seek entry to such texts, "you must persevere, you must sit up nights, you must inquire, and exert the utmost power of your mind." Boccaccio has faith that such persistence will be rewarded, though he displays an awareness of the great demands it makes on the reader: "If one way does not lead to the desired meaning, take another; if obstacles arise, then still another; until, if your strength holds out, you will find that clear which at first looked dark."[11]

Kafka's tale of the man from the country closely follows the traditional model of hermeneutic activity. The poor man does indeed "sit up nights" keeping watch (*vigilandum* is Boccaccio's term), making many attempts to be admitted, wearying the doorkeeper with his demands. He sacrifices all he possesses in bribes for the doorkeeper, to no avail. He even finds light where at first he saw only darkness: "At length his eyesight begins to fail, and he does not know whether the world is really darker or whether his eyes are only deceiving him. Yet in his darkness he is now aware of a radiance that streams inextinguishably from the gateway to the Law."[12] This radiance is not quite the light of understanding implied by Boccaccio's figure, but it serves as assurance that the clarity to which the man from the country aspires does indeed exist, even if he cannot reach it.

The only way in which Kafka's image of entering the inner sanctum of the text differs from Boccaccio's presentation of hermeneutic orthodoxy is that the would-be interpreter fails utterly. His strength

---

11. Vincenzo Romano, ed., *Genealogie deorum gentilium libri* (Bari: Gius. Laterza Figli, 1951), II, 717; Charles C. Osgood, trans., *Boccaccio on Poetry* (Indianapolis: Bobbs-Merrill, 1956), 62.

12. *CS* 4; *SE* 132: "Schließlich wird sein Augenlicht schwach, und er weiß nicht, ob es um ihn wirklich dunkler wird, oder ob ihn nur seine Augen täuschen. Wohl aber erkennt er jetzt im Dunkel einen Glanz, der unverlöschlich aus der Türe des Gesetzes bricht."

does not hold out, and it is implied that human strength could never be sufficient. Kafka sets up his fictional world as if one of the traditional justifications of parable were all too correct: the meanings hidden by a parabolic cortex are simply too important to be cast forth in the world like pearls before swine. Augustine and other church fathers valued figural utterance in the Bible as a means by which the holy text could ward off the contaminating gaze of the unworthy. This apotropaic power of the parable is perfected in the parable "Before the Law," where the ability of the one who would penetrate the text falls far short of the text's ability to resist penetration. Its resistance is perfect, even at those points where it appears to invite entrance. The man from the country believes that the Law "should be accessible at all times and to everyone," and in a certain sense it is. The gate is always open, and the doorkeeper does not block it. He even invites the man to go in without permission. But he will not give the man permission to enter, and that refusal is sufficient to ward off a man who, after all, is characterized mainly by his devotion to the Law. He, least of all, would wish to take matters into his own hands and disregard the doorkeeper's refusal.

This scene of frustrated (and figural) reading is embedded in another, as it appears in the novel fragment, but here reading itself and not its allegory is displayed, and its object is the parable just recited. K. responds to an invitation to interpret the story offered by the priest by the very act of telling the story as an illustration of K.'s situation: "'You are deluding yourself about the court,' said the priest. 'In the writings which preface the Law that particular delusion is described thus: . . .'"[13] The priest suggests that the parable is somehow about delusion (*Täuschung*), and K.'s reading of it attempts to enter into the discourse by way of this opening: "So the doorkeeper deceived [*getäuscht*] the man" is his reaction. But the priest immediately warns K. away from this interpretation by insisting that the "very words of the scriptures" that he has repeated to K. contain "no mention of deception."[14] This statement is perfectly true, but it contradicts the very point that the priest was apparently trying to make by telling the story, that is, that the parable illustrates a certain kind of delusion.

13. *TR* 276; *RO* 432: "'In dem Gericht täuschst du dich,' sagte der Geistliche, 'in den einleitenden Schriften zum Gesetz heißt es von dieser Täuschung: . . .'"
14. *TR* 269; *RO* 434: "'Der Türhüter hat also den Mann getäuscht.' . . . 'Ich habe dir die Geschichte im Wortlaut der Schrift erzählt. Von Täuschung seht darin nichts.'"

When K. asserts in reply that the priest's "first interpretation of it was quite right," he means that the priest was correct in presenting it as a story about deception, and he betrays a certain impatience, not unjustified, with the priest's sudden unwillingness to accept anything but the "very words of the scriptures."

The relationship between the priest and K. obviously doubles that of the doorkeeper and the man from the country, as Politzer has suggested (179). The priest marks an opening into the text that he suggests is specifically relevant to K. and is therefore, like the door to which the man from the country comes, intended precisely for him, but at the same time he steadfastly refuses to allow K. to pass through the opening. Like the man in the parable, K. sticks doggedly to this way in and "forgets the other doorkeepers," though the priest makes every effort to point out alternatives. All of these opinions, however, lead nowhere. The priest even suggests that the various readings of the text do little more than express the "commentators' despair" over the "scripture" itself, or possibly over its inalterability. Eventually all of the fruitless effort exhausts K.: "He was too tired to survey all the conclusions arising from the story, and the trains of thought into which it was leading him were unfamiliar."[15] Like the man from the country, K. finds himself finally worn out by his attempts to go in by the opening offered to him and unable to continue. He stands in the dark, unable to be sure what it is he has seen.

The parable introduced to K. as a means to facilitate his understanding appears instead to have prevented it. Politzer reads the scene in the cathedral as a "nihilistic turn" and as "Kafka's bill of particulars in which he indicts the Court for having summoned K. and then abandoned him to misery" (184), for inviting K. in and then excluding him. We may wonder, though, whether K. has really been excluded. If the lesson K. was to learn from the parable of the Law was indeed, as the priest indicated, something about deception, we might suspect that the lesson has been driven home all too well. The very pattern of summoning and abandoning that the parable both narrates and provokes precipitates K. into a vivid experience of the varieties of Täuschung and Enttäuschung that one can suffer in the passion of reading. The parable's failure becomes its success, if the priest's "first

15. *TR* 277; *RO* 439: "Er war zu müde, um alle Folgerungen der Geschichte übersehen zu können, es waren auch ungewohnte Gedankengänge, in die sie ihn führte."

interpretation" really was correct, and indeed even if Politzer's reading of *The Trial* is correct. The parable does exactly what its teller
claims for it. It does what parables always do, according to the narrator of "On Parables": "All these parables really set out to say merely
that the incomprehensible is incomprehensible, and we know that
already."[16] But we do not know it "already" in the painful way in
which parables teach us to know it.

An important component in the painful lesson of Kafka's parables
is their confirmation of the importance of an activity that has no
reasonable hope of success. The terrible pathos of a parable like "Before the Law" is precisely that it is *not* nihilistic in its attitude toward
the poor seeker's failure. Kafka goes out of his way to make sure the
reader understands that, as far as the man from the country is concerned, there is no doubt about the existence of the wonderful, powerful force, "the Law," to which he wishes to gain access. Because his
eyesight is failing, the evidence of the "radiance that streams inextinguishably from the gateway of the Law" is possibly not entirely
trustworthy. But there is no hint in the story that the man does not
trust it, nor is there any hint in Kafka's writings that Kafka doubted
the existence of the absolute truth that he himself could never grasp.
K.'s attempt to read the parable the priest tells shares this persistent
faith. K.'s final comment on the priest's exegesis—that "untruth is
made the order of the universe"—is explicitly presented as tentative:
"it was not his final judgment." If he were not so tired he would keep
trying to find the meaning he is still sure resides in the "simple story."

If Kafka the reader believes in an inaccessible truth concealed within texts he is unable to decipher, Kafka the writer produced parables
whose indecipherability is their only hope of authenticity. I mean to
suggest that Kafka would have another reason for composing self-
deconstructing fables in addition to the one proposed by Corngold.
In Corngold's view, Kafka undermines the basis for his own fictions as
a means of reasserting the primacy of an otherwise effaced self. The
fictions' failure is their author's success; his authority over them becomes visible precisely at those points where they cease to cohere,
where they become, like "Before the Law" in the eyes of an exhausted
K., *unförmlich*, shapeless, clumsy, irregular, inexact. But their failure
is also the guarantee of their genuineness, for their lack of a de-

16. CS 457; SE 359: "Alle diese Gleichnisse wollen eigentlich nur sagen, daß das
Unfaßbare unfaßbar ist, und das haben wir gewußt."

monstrable and certain significance shows their kinship to everything Kafka finds valuable. The orthodox tradition of textual truth implies that the value of a text's inner meaning is covered and yet revealed by the toughness of its exterior surface. The structure of summons and abandonment characteristic of Kafka's parables is typical of religious experience and indeed of life when life is understood as a mysterious text demanding interpretation. It is, perhaps more important, the structure of truth, which Kafka understands as something very like a Derridean trace, a combination of the not-there and the not-that. "One cannot express what one is, for that *is* precisely what one is; one can only communicate what one is not, that is, the lie."[17] Being is Being, and not a sign that stands for Being. One can only point in the direction of truth or perhaps merely surround the place where truth might be with a darkness so that the true radiance might be glimpsed, if only by contrast and at a distance. Because this truth is by its very nature transcendent (it has "gone over"), one cannot lay hands on it or even know where it might be. One might therefore reveal the truth, though indirectly and by accident, simply by wrapping up something unknown in a dense enough darkness.

One of the consequences of having a name like Amschel Kafka is that one is compelled, at least from time to time, to understand the self as a text, in this case a text capable of being read in a number of ways that do not necessarily cohere logically. If one were to try to "express what one is" by means of literature, one might attempt to repeat the gesture made by one's name. This attempt would seem in a certain sense appropriate and even reasonable, particularly for a person who believed, occasionally at any rate, that he consisted of nothing but literature. Part of what Kafka's parables do, then, is to present the image of Kafka's self as a text that is both readable and unreadable at the same time. The name "Kafka" is exactly like a Kafkan parable in that it invites interpretation but issues such a broad invitation that too many interpretations are possible. The simple name, like the simple story of the man from the country, loses its clear outline after extensive hermeneutic inquiry; it becomes unförmlich in that it seems to say too much at once, to lead us down too many paths in too many different directions.

17. *WP* 338; *HO* 343: "Das, was man ist, kann man nicht ausdrücken, denn dieses ist man eben; mitteilen kann man nur das, was man nicht ist, also die Lüge."

Such parables as "A Little Fable" and "Before the Law" figure the rhetoricity of Kafka's name and thereby—in a paradoxical way, of course—express with a subtle accuracy the precise nature of the authorial self. If Kafka suggests, in the fragment quoted above, that the truth of the self might be approached by a chorus of lies ("Erst im Chor möchte eine gewisse Wahrheit sein"), the parable, with its expressed or implied chorus of incompatible interpretations, makes the best available image of such truth. The author survives not only "on the margin of his breaks" (to borrow Corngold's phrase) but also in his unreadability that calls for reading. The structure of summons and abandonment that strikes Politzer as an expression of nihilism seems to me an emphatic repetition of a primal "I AM," a way of filling the void of the universe with the stuff of the self. I do not deny that this self is also presented as a kind of negative value, a hindrance to the happy progress of the rest of creation, but it is a big, almost unscalable hindrance. It is not nothing; it is a negative something.

It is also something individual and unique. If Politzer is able to find in Kafka's parables a pronouncement of "the insoluble paradox of human existence," the reason is that he finds it appropriate to do what Kafka himself would never have wished, that is, to see the self projected in Kafka's fiction as a universal human paradigm. The persona represented by Gregor Samsa and Josephine the singer, figured forth in the crystal-clear illegibility of parabolic rhetoric, is not intended to be an Everyman. That they are not so intended does not necessarily make it wrong to read them so, as Politzer does, but it ought to make such a reading more difficult, or at the very least more paradoxical. Kafka always insists on his own isolation from the human community, on his being "as lonely as Franz Kafka," a trope that of course makes a figure of comparison into an expression of incomparability. Kafka thinks of himself as comparable only to himself, trapped inside a circle of armed men, unable even to attempt contact with others without tearing himself apart. He is not nobody, but he is also not everybody. He is an isolated titan fused with a wall of rock, inexplicable in the truth of his being. If he is a poor man from the country, unable to gain access to the Law he yearns for, he is also the radiant Law itself, unreadable though longing to be read.

Chapter 8

THE CLOTHED BODY

As I suggested earlier, one of the principal lessons of Kafka's earliest experience with rhetoric must have been the linguistic divisibility of the self. To the degree that the self is conceived as a text—a text as apparently simple as the single word "Kafka" or as complex as Goethe's *Dichtung und Wahrheit*—it can be understood as composed of several elements, some of which may be incompatible with others. Such a sense of self-division very naturally leads to attempts to recapture the self as a coherent unit in stories that carry their "complete organization" inside themselves, as Kafka put it in a diary entry that I discussed above. But this act of attempted recuperation only complicates the problem, because the act of self-inscription requires that the writer effectively divide the self into a writing subject and a written object, the one who makes the story and the one who is the story.[1]

1. The division of the self in Kafka's fiction, especially as a result of the narrative act, has been treated in depth by Walter Sokel. See, for example, his essays "Zur Sprachauffassung und Poetik Franz Kafkas," *TP*, 26–47; "Kafka's Poetics of the Inner Self," in Reinhold Grimm, Peter Spycher, and Richard A. Zipser, eds., *From Kafka and Dada to Brecht and Beyond* (Madison: University of Wisconsin Press, 1982), 7–21; and "Narzißmus, Magie, und die Funktion des Erzählens in Kafkas *Beschreibung eines Kampfes*: Zur Figurenkonzeption, Geschehenstruktur, und Poetologie in Kafkas Erstlingswerk," *DJK*, 133–153. Other important work in this area includes Charles Bernheimer, "The Splitting of the 'I' and the Dilemma of Narration: Kafka's *Hochzeitsvorbereitungen auf dem Lande*," *CT*, 7–24 (German version in *DJK*); Gilles Deleuze and Félix Guattari, *Kafka: Toward a Minor Literature*,

182 KAFKA'S RHETORIC

And that act of writing the self presupposes another, that of reading the self, of making the self somehow at once both an observer and the object of observation. Once the self has been read, it may be written, and then it can be read again in its alternative textual form. The whole process of self-inscription, including both its motivation and its result, depends on the unrestricted divisibility of the self.

It is little wonder, then, that so much of Kafka's fiction both employs and dramatizes the possibility of self-division, so much so in fact that it is one of the most prominent and stable characteristics of his writing. It begins early, with the first surviving work of fiction in the Kafka oeuvre, the "Description of a Struggle." It is a kind of dream narrative, similar in this respect to one of Kafka's later masterpieces, "A Country Doctor" ("Ein Landarzt"), and it chronicles the adventures of a pair of acquaintances who meet at a party one evening and decide to take a walk together. There is really little more to the plot than that, and even that is introduced in a pointedly arbitrary and almost silly way. The first-person narrator simply rises from his chair and proclaims that he will accede to his new acquaintance's demands and accompany him on a walk up the Laurenziberg, though as matter of fact the friend has not mentioned anything of the kind. What he has mentioned is that he has been closeted with his lady friend: "And I kissed her, I kissed her—her mouth, her ears, her shoulders."[2] But the friend goes along for the walk anyway, as if the narrator had indeed known what he wanted and had reacted to his unspoken wish. This is the first clue that the narrator and his friend are more closely connected than two people normally are. As the narrator says a few pages later, "It certainly wasn't I who had insisted on this walk."[3]

On the way out, a housemaid who helps the men with their coats, a

---

trans. Dana Polan (Minneapolis: University of Minnesota Press, 1986), 30–31; Peter Dettmering, "Aspekte der Spaltung in der Dichtung Kafkas," in *Litteraturpsychologische Studien und Analysen* (Amsterdam: Rodopi, 1983), 205–220; and Anthony Stephens, "Er ist aber zweigeteilt: Gericht und Ich-Struktur bei Kafka," *Text & Kontext* 6 (1978), 215–238.

2. *CS* 10; *BK* 13: "Und ich habe sie geküsst, geküsst—habe—ich—sie auf ihren Mund, ihre Ohren, ihre Schultern." (I quote from the "B" version unless otherwise indicated. Note that the transcription of Kafka's "B" manuscript in *BK* uses "ss" for "ß.")

3. *CS* 11; *BK* 17: The rhetoric of the original hints at the segmentation of the self by using the word *gerissen:* "Ich war es wahrhaftig nicht gewesen, der sich um diesen Spaziergang gerissen hatte."

girl wearing "a black velvet ribbon around her throat," advances upon the acquaintance, "embraced him, kissed him, and remained in the embrace."[4] This may or may not be the lady friend mentioned before. In any case, the friend seems to have a special attraction for the ladies, including the hostess of the evening, whose hand he kisses several times. "I had to drag him away,"[5] the narrator complains. The object of this friend's desire seems to be capable of multiplying with great rapidity, even if the housemaid (or the hostess) is identical with the lady friend of whom he had spoken before. Our suspicion that such a multiplication may already have occurred in the case of the narrating persona is confirmed by a number of textual details, all of which suggest that the narrator and his friend are textual variants of the same self. Only a few pages after the description of the housemaid's embrace of the acquaintance, the narrator ponders to himself the possibility that he might benefit from such behavior: "By all means let them kiss and hug him. . . . After all, when they kiss him they also kiss me a little—with the corners of their mouths, so to speak."[6] This emotional identification with the acquaintance becomes more intense when the narrator consoles himself in his pain—he has injured his knee—with the recollection that "I [that is, the narrator] was loved by a girl with a black velvet ribbon around her neck."[7] If these words are not enough to alert the reader, a little further on the acquaintance falls down, and when the narrator examines him he learns that "he was badly wounded in the knee."[8] The emotional identification is now also physical.

But this substantial identification of the two principal characters in the story as fragments of a single person does not prevent a deadly conflict between them. The narrator supposes from very early on that the acquaintance intends to try to kill him. The topic is introduced in a kind of nonsequitur: "He lifted his right arm, flicked his hand, and listened to the castanetlike sound of his cuff links. Obviously, this is

4. *CS* 10–11; *BK* 15: "Ihr Hals war . . . nur unter dem Kinn von einem schwarzen Sammtband umbunden . . . umarmte ihn und küsste ihn und blieb in der Umarmung."

5. *CS* 10; *BK* 13: "Ich musste ihn fortziehn."

6. *CS* 13; *BK* 23: "Mögen sie ihn küssen und drücken. . . . Wenn sie ihn küssen, küssen sie mich ja auch ein wenig, wenn man will; mit dem Mundwinkel gewissermassen."

7. *CS* 19; *BK* 37: "Dass ich von einem Mädchen mit schwarzem Samtband um den Hals geliebt würde."

8. *CS* 21; *BK* 47: "Dass er am Knie schwer verwundet war."

the time for the murder. I'll stay with him and slowly he'll draw the dagger—the handle of which he is already holding in his pocket—along his coat, and then plunge it into me."⁹ There has not been the slightest indication that the friend intends any violence, but the narrator seems to have good reason for his suspicions. And why should he not, given the peculiar nature of their relationship? It is therefore only to be expected that the friend does indeed do an act of violence with a knife at the story's conclusion, and it is only to be expected who the victim of this violence will be: "Then without further ado, my acquaintance pulled a knife out of his pocket, opened it thoughtfully, and then, as though he were playing, he plunged it into his left upper arm, and didn't withdraw it. Blood promptly began to flow. . . . 'My dear, dear friend,' said I, 'you've wounded yourself for my sake.'"¹⁰ The irony is deep and complex, because the wound would indeed appear to have been inflicted "for my sake" (*meinetwegen*) but not in the charitable spirit that might be supposed. The friend's act of aggression against himself is, given what we know about these characters, directed just as much against the narrator and is thus quite correctly viewed as done "for his sake." The irony is deepened even more by the rhetoricity of the narrator's discourse. It might be a declaration of sympathy ("I feel the wound, too"), but it might just as well be an expression of disdain; *meinetwegen* can also mean "for all I care." His sentence could be read as "For all I care you've wounded yourself (and not me)," thereby stressing the narrator's relief at his separation from his alter ego.

But how does the separation come about? What means does the narrator use to split off fragments of himself and keep them at a safe distance? He does it, as we might have guessed, by rhetoric. The first demonstration of how rhetoric can develop a version of the self that can be understood as belonging to another appears in the first section of the "B" version of the story, when the narrator begins to imagine to himself how his acquaintance will talk about him with his lady friend

9. *CS* 17; *BK* 31: "Er hob den rechten Arm[,] zuckte mit der Hand und horchte auf den Kastanettenklang des Manschettenskettchens[.] Jetzt kam offenbar der Mord. Ich werde bei ihm bleiben und er wird das Messer, dessen Griff er in der Tasche schon hält, an seinem Rock in die Höhe führen und dann gegen mich."

10. *CS* 50–51; *BK* 136–138 ("A" version): "Da zog mein Bekannter ohne Umstände aus seiner Tasche ein Messer, öffnete es nachdenklich und stieß es dann wie im Spiele in seinem linken Oberarm und entfernte es nicht. Gleich rann Blut. . . . 'Du Lieber, du Lieber,' sagte ich, 'meinetwegen hast du dich verletzt.'"

Anna. He quotes this prospective speech word for word (in the "A" version, the speech is set in quotation marks): "Last night, Annie, after the party, you remember, I was with a man the like of which you've certainly never seen," and continues at considerable length.[11] When this quotation is finally concluded, the narrator reports, "I didn't spare my acquaintance—we had just reached the first steps of the Franzensquai—the smallest fraction of the humiliation he must have felt at making such a speech."[12] The reader has two choices when trying to understand this remark: either the narrator actually takes his acquaintance to task for a discourse he never made, in which case the imaginary, proleptic text becomes incorporated into the structure of the "real" events narrated, or the narrator's reported harshness is part of a continuing act of imagination, in which case we have no way of telling where the boundary betweeen the "real" and "imaginary" events in the narrative might be. Carefully embedded in the middle of the sentence about not sparing the acquaintance humiliation is a description of an apparently external "fact" of the story: the narrator and his friend take their first steps on the Franzensquai. If the sentence refers to an imaginary act, the "fact" is to some degree compromised, and along with it all the other "facts" of the narration, including the existence of the acquaintance himself. And the attentive reader will not fail to notice that inside the report of this "fact" is another, external to the fiction and yet in some sense constitutive of it: the name of the author, Franz.

The peculiar position of the author's name, buried inside a text outside which it is supposed to stand (on the title page) reflects the peculiar status of the self when engaged in an act of self-inscription. The text can contain nothing that is not the self, for the text belongs, from one point of view, to the unity of that self. But from another point of view, the text becomes in the moment of its inscription an alien thing of which the self relieves itself like a piece of excrement, the Ka(cke) so often named in Kafka's works as a fictional protagonist. "Franz" is a term readable both as the name of an omnipotent author, master of everything inside this story, and as the label for a thing, a

11. CS 14; BK 23: "Gestern, Annerl, in der Nacht, nach unserer Gesellschaft, weisst du, war ich mit einem Menschen beisammen, wie Du ihn ganz bestimmt noch nie gesehen hast."

12. CS 14; BK 25: "Und ich erliess meinem Bekannten—wir machten gerade die ersten Schritte auf dem Franzensquai—nicht den geringsten Teil der Beschämung, die er bei solcher Rede fühlen musste."

dock, an object of hardly any importance and certainly of no power. "Franz" is thus treated as a rhetorical structure exactly analogous to "Kafka," capable of attaching itself to incompatible meanings and of being at once both powerful and powerless, everything and nothing, everybody and nobody. "Franz" is a text like the friend's proleptic and fictive speech to Anna: it is both a trivial, barren detail and a fruitful generating force. The acquaintance is the offspring of this rhetoric, made up as he is from a piece of discourse cast off by the narrator and yet somehow still a part of him. The narrator and the acquaintance stand together here, their feet resting perhaps precariously on a structure named "Franz."

The acquaintance as we know him from the fictive speech to Anna is the creation of a nonexistent text or at best a text whose existence is only putative. The rhetoricity of this discourse is such that one cannot even decide for certain the ontological status of the words themselves, never mind the person to whom they are ascribed. This dialogue between existence and nonexistence continues later in the story, near the beginning of section 1 of the second part ("B" version). The narrator begins to exercise playfully his power over the world of his narrative, altering its properties by means of his act of writing: "The road on which I was riding was stony and rose considerably, but just this I liked and I let it become still stonier and steeper."[13] A particularly interesting passage brings up the topic of textual creation from a kind of nothingness:

> "I don't know," I cried without a sound, "I really don't know. If nobody comes, then nobody comes. I have done nobody any harm, nobody has done me any harm, but nobody will help me. A pack of nobodies. But it isn't quite like that. It's just that nobody helps me, otherwise a pack of nobodies would be nice, I would rather like (what do you think?) to go on an excursion with a pack of nobodies. Into the mountains, of course, where else? Just look at those nobodies pushing each other, all these arms stretched across or hooked into one another, these feet separated by tiny steps! Everyone in frock coats, needless to say."[14]

13. CS 21; BK 45: "Die Landstrasse, auf der ich ritt, war steinig und stieg bedeutend, aber gerade das gefiel mir und ich liess sie noch steiniger und steiler werden."

14. CS 21; BK 47. "'Ich weiss nicht' rief ich ohne Klang 'ich weiss ja nicht. Wenn niemand kommt, dann kommt eben niemand, Ich habe niemandem etwas Böses getan, niemand hat mir etwas Böses getan, niemand aber will mir helfen, lauter niemand. Aber so ist es doch nicht. Nur dass mir niemand hilft, sonst wäre lauter niemand hübsch, ich würde ganz gerne, (was sagen Sie dazu?) einen Ausflug mit

The phrase translated as "a pack of nobodies" is "lauter niemand," perhaps more prosaically rendered as "nobody at all" or "nothing but nobody." The word *lauter* refers to something pure, unalloyed, untainted by anything else. It suggests not multiplicity and plenitude (as "a pack of" might be understood to do) but rather uniformity and even an absence of difference. But the translation is not inaccurate, because Kafka turns the unprepossessing phrase "lauter niemand" into a rhetorically complex discourse that does indeed generate multiplicity from its simple uniformity: "lauter niemand" is expanded into "eine Gesellschaft von lauter niemand" ("a party composed of nobody at all") and then into an explicit plural, "diese Niemand" ("these nobodies").

At the same time, of course, the place-holding cipher "nobody" undergoes a metamorphosis into a label for certain unspecified persons capable of jostling each other, linking arms, and wearing clothes. An emptiness becomes suddenly a whole crowd of people. The process is reversible, as we discover later when the supplicant inquires of the drunk, "Are there people in Paris who consist only of sumptuous dresses, and are there houses that are only portals, and is it true that on summer days the sky over the city is a fleeting blue embellished only by little white clouds glued into it, all in the shape of hearts?"[15] A person may become a void wrapped up in a glittering surface as easily as a void can become a whole crowd of people. "Nobody" can wear fancy clothes, and fancy clothes can encase nobodies, all at the whim of rhetoric.

This scenario happens at the behest of a discourse that is itself a kind of void, because the quoted speech is introduced by the phrase "I cried without a sound" ("rief ich ohne Klang"). The soundless cry may be a well-known expressionistic theme, familiar to us from the famous painting "The Scream" and, in a later version, from the soundless wail

---

einer Gesellschaft von lauter niemand machen. Natürlich ins Gebirge, wohin denn sonst? Wie sich diese Niemand aneinander drängen, diese vielen quergestreckten oder eingehängten Arme, diese viele Füsse durch winzige Schritte getrennt! Versteht sich, dass alle in Frack sind.' (It is interesting to note that Kafka deleted the words "was für ein Einfall!" ["What a clever idea!"] from the midst of this passage.)

15. *CS* 42; *BK* 110 ("A" version): "Giebt es in Paris Menschen, die nur aus verzierten Kleidern bestehn und giebt es dort Häuser die bloß Portale haben und ist es wahr, daß an Sommertagen der Himmel über der Stadt fliehend blau ist, nur verschönt durch angepreßte weiße Wölkchen, die all die Form von Herzen haben?"

of Brecht's Mother Courage. But this is clearly different. The painting and the stage gesture are visual signifiers in which the lack of a verbal component is part of the meaning. The narrator of the "Description," however, gives us just the opposite, a verbal structure with no visual component. How can this discourse be properly described as at once both a "cry" and "without a sound?" To cry or call (rufen) implies a vigorous dissemination of the utterance; it could not be a kind of "thinking to one's self." But the paradox of the soundless cry does rather nicely fit one form of discourse: writing and especially self-inscription. This writing is a vigorous verbal dissemination of the self that makes no noise at all. Calling one's writing a soundless cry, however, emphasizes the negativity of the situation. When writing is figured as a form of speech, as it is here, the reminder that no sound issues forth is a kind of denial of communicative power; to speak without sound is not to speak at all. This very act of writing, then, is a powerful act of self-dissemination that is also quite impotent. It is a something that is a nothing, like the "pack of nobodies" that constitutes its subject. It is a clothed void.

This observation about the "nobodies" is more than idle chatter. It is specifically relevant to the situation in which the narrator finds himself. His expressed wish to go on an excursion into the mountains with a group of companions merely restates the situation depicted in the story: the narrator climbs the Laurenziberg in the company of an acquaintance who appears to be a purely textual artifact and meets up with a fat man (and, by way of the fat man, with the supplicant and the drunk) who seems to be similarly conjured up in the act of narration. The narrator spends his time in a company of nobodies ("eine Gesellschaft von lauter niemand") in the sense that all of his interlocutors are, or might be, rhetorical constructs. They are secular and ironical examples of the word becoming flesh—in the case of the fat man, a lot of flesh, as befits his great loquacity.

The creative power of the word is an especially prominent motif throughout the "Description." Kafka lets his narrator engage in a melancholy parody of the verbal creativity ascribed to the Lord in the opening lines of Genesis. I have already mentioned the narrator's modification of his environment by letting the road on which he walks "become still stonier and steeper." This kind of thing occurs relatively frequently. A bit later, the narrator tires of climbing the road and "let it become gradually flatter."[16] The fat man has the same kind of

16. CS 22; BK 47: "Liess ich den Weg immer flacher werden."

power: when he asks the mountains to give him more room, "the surrounding mountains began to shift in hasty obedience."[17] And the fat man in turn ascribes a similar act to the supplicant: at the end of their conversation he "blew away a few bruised little clouds, allowing the uninterrupted surface of the stars to emerge."[18] The narrator is even able to conjure up creatures and events seemingly ex nihilo. He says that he "whistled down a few vultures" to guard his friend (there were no vultures there before), and he lets "a squirrel of my whim" share a tree branch with him.[19] Most striking of all is his own enactment of the divine *fiat lux*: he tells himself that he "ought to be content, it's gay here. The sun's shining." The next paragraph opens with the announcement: "Whereupon the sun shone and the rain clouds grew white and light and small in the blue sky."[20]

As is fitting in a text described as a *Beschreibung*, all activity that takes place within it can be understood as verbal, no matter what is supposedly being described. Words have a kind of priority here that runs contrary to the assumption ordinarily presumed to underlie narrative practice. No matter what the case may really be, author and audience generally collude in the fiction that the words of the narrative reproduce actions, persons, and things that existed prior to their utterance. The narrative is thus a "description," in the ordinary sense of the term. But Kafka's story struggles precisely with that relation of priority, insisting at many points that words come first or at least that they have an equal claim to ontological priority. The text often blurs the distinctions between the physical and the verbal:

I felt convinced that every movement and every thought were forced, and that one had to be on one's guard against them. Yet nothing seemed more natural than to lie here in the grass, my arms beside my body, my face hidden. And I tried to persuade myself that I ought to be pleased to be already in this natural position, for otherwise many painful contortions, such as steps or words, would be required to arrive at it.[21]

17. *CS* 27; *BK* 64 ("A" version): "Da entstand ein eilfertiges Verschieben in den umliegenden Bergen."
18. *CS* 46; *BK* 125: "Einige zerstossene Wölkchen blies mein Freund weg, so dass sich jetzt die ununterbrochene Fläche der Sterne uns darbot."
19. *CS* 22, 23; *BK* 47, 51: "Pfiff nur einige Geier aus der Höhe herab . . . ein Eichhörnchen meiner Laune."
20. *CS* 24; *BK* 54 ("A" version): "'Du kannst zufrieden sein, es ist lustig hier. Die Sonne scheint.' Da schien die Sonne und die Regenwolken wurden weiß und leicht und klein im blauen Himmel."
21. *CS* 24; *BK* 56 ("A" version): "Ich war überzeugt, daß jede Bewegung und

The narrator does not attempt to distinguish between thoughts and movements or between steps and words. The passage is disarming in its candor because it reminds the reader that all movements reported in this text are the product of thoughts and that all the steps taken by its characters are indeed precisely words on a page.

This passage helps to establish the connection between this narrative situation and the problem of self-division by means of rhetoric. The narrator is aware of feeling a form of compulsion, but he is unaware of what is compelling him. He describes himself as speaking "as though compelled," and mentions that in the moment of compulsion, "I heard someone sigh terribly near."[22] The nearness of this "someone" is terrible and horrifying: Kafka's adverb *entsetzlich* serves to foreground the horror of the feeling. The narrator does not ever find out who this someone is, but the reader by this point can only suppose that it is the narrator himself or that part of him that is inscribing the narrator as a character in the story. The sigh is horrifyingly close because it is both the narrator's creation and the thing that creates him and indeed compels him to undertake everything he does in the story. The sigh that connects the narrator to this nearby other is also the thing that drives them apart; it stands for the discourse that separates the unitary self into writing subject and written object.

It has also made the self into the reader of his own writing. At this point in the story, there is no audience for the narrator's words other than himself. Even the textual variants of the self are absent here: the narrator has parted company from the acquaintance and has not yet met the fat man. He is alone, but his solitude does not prevent conversation or even struggle. He fights against the sense of being compelled to act out the orders of his narrating self; for like the sun, the landscape, and all the physical elements of the story, he is obliged to do exactly what the words of his narration tell him to do. Within the boundaries of the fiction, he exists only as a figment of discourse.

---

jeder Gedanke erzwungen seien, daß man sich daher vor ihnen hüten solle. Dagegen sei es das natürlichste, hier im Grase zu liegen, die Arme am Körper und das Gesicht verborgen. Und ich redete mir zu, mich eigentlich zu freuen, daß ich in dieser selbstverständlichen Lage mich schon befinde, denn sonst würde ich vieler mühseliger Krämpfe, wie Schritte oder Worte bedürfen, um in sie zu kommen."

22. *CS* 24; *BK* 54 ("A" version): "Da hörte ich jemanden entsetzlich nahe seufzen."

Kafka cleverly lets the narrator turn this logic back on itself, however, in that he presents self-inscription as the homeopathic cure for the ills of self-inscription. The narrator quite simply divides himself again into addresser and addressee and talks himself out of his discomfort: "I persuaded myself ['redete mir zu'] to be pleased." This statement implies that the rhetorical act of self-division can be repeated any number of times, and the implication is borne out by the rest of the story. The narrator produces the fat man, who in turn produces the supplicant, who in turn produces the drunk. These additional characters, however, are developed from the same set of conditions that allowed the narrator to speak to himself and talk himself into something: that is, the possibility that every speaker is also the audience for that same speech. Every act of writing produces a reader (at a minimum the self-reader) who is also potentially a writer. Such acts of textual self-dissemination are theoretically endless and can be stopped in practice only by an arbitrary act. One must "murder" one of the textual selves to terminate the process.

The "Description of a Struggle" displays a highly self-conscious, sometimes embarrassingly frank act of textual self-dissemination that Kafka's later creation, Raban, will call sending the "clothed body" into the world. Kafka seems to have had this metaphor in mind at the time he composed the "A" version of the "Description" because he prefaced it with the following verse epigraph:

> Und die Menschen gehen in Kleidern
> schwankend auf dem Kies spazieren
> unter diesem großen Himmel,
> der von Hügeln in der Ferne
> sich zu fernen Hügeln breitet.[23]

The placement of these lines at the head of the story invites their application to the issues the story raises. In this context, the "people in clothes" are most readily understood as the characters in the narrative, who also take a walk over rocky ground. These characters are all "clothed bodies" sent forth by the entity who resides so horribly close to the narrator, the one who has inscribed him in this text.

These clothed bodies inhabit a landscape that is, like themselves,

23. *BK* 8, *CS* 9: "And people in their Sunday best / Stroll about, swaying over the gravel / Under this enormous sky / Which, from hills in the distance, / Stretches to distant hills."

subject to rhetorical dissemination: they walk about under "this large sky" and not under its implied alternative, *that* one. Compare with the epigraph the description of the night into which the two partygoers emerge: "Over the deserted, evenly lit street stood a large moon in a slightly clouded, and therefore unusually extended, sky."[24] The rhetorical substitution of the indefinite for the definite article ("a moon" for "the moon" and so forth) is a commonplace device, of course. It ordinarily functions to stress the particularity of the observed features, as if to say that the moon, seen tonight as "a large moon," might under other circumstances make itself visible as "a small moon." But Kafka, as is typical of him, reads this rhetoric literally as well as figuratively. In this story, there is no "the" moon, only infinitely shifting varieties of moon:

> Thank God, moon, you are no longer moon, but perhaps it's negligent of me to go on calling you so-called moon, moon. Why do your spirits fall when I call you "forgotten paper lantern of a strange color"? And why do you almost withdraw when I call you "the Virgin's pillar"? As for you, pillar of the Virgin Mary, I hardly recognize your threatening attitude when I call you "moon shedding yellow light."[25]

The moon no longer possesses a unique identity as a certain heavenly body; it is now a set of textual variants. To the degree that the story treats it as a physical phenomenon, it is subject to mutation in the crucible of unfettered metaphor.

Metaphor allows for dissemination not only by way of multiplication but also by way of enlargement. The sky, like the moon, is transferred from a definite to an indefinite category, just as it is in the verse epigraph. And in both cases the sky is described as particularly large. The story proposes that the sky looks "unusually extended" because of the presence of clouds, but it is not entirely clear what this means. The poem provides in this case better information about how such a process of extension comes about: the sky spreads itself out from "hills in the distance" to "distant hills." These two sets of hills

24. I am grateful to James Gussen for calling attention to the complex rhetoric of these lines.
25. *CS* 41; *BK* 106 ("A" version): "Gott sei dank, Mond, du bist nicht mehr Mond, aber vielleicht ist es nachlässig von mir daß ich dich Mondbenannter noch immer Mond nenne. Warum bist du nicht mehr so übermüthig, wenn ich dich nenne 'vergessene Papierlaterne in merkwürdiger Farbe.' Und warum ziehst du dich fast zurück, wenn ich dich 'Mariensäule' nenne und ich erkenne deine drohende Haltung nicht mehr Mariensäule, wenn ich dich nenne 'Mond, der gelbes Licht wirft.'"

might be physically the same, because "distant hills" is a synonymous syntactic variant of "hills in the distance," no more different in substance than Betsy is from Bess. The two textual variants have, however, the effect of enlarging the imaginative space they occupy; we need to accommodate two sets of hills where otherwise only one set resided. The dialeptic multiplication of hills expands the space covered by the sky, now properly described as "this large sky."

The clothed bodies that inhabit this landscape are subject to the same rhetorical deformation. Not only can they be multiplied at will, like the moon and the hills, but also they are subject to monstrous enlargement:

> After all, I was small, almost smaller than usual, and a bush of white hips shaking itself very fast towered over me. This I saw, for a moment ago it had been close to me.
>
> Nevertheless I was mistaken, for my arms were as huge as the clouds of a steady country rain, save that they were more hasty. I don't know why they were trying to crush my poor head. It was no larger than an ant's egg, but slightly damaged, and as a result no longer quite round. I made some beseeching, twisting movements with it, for the expression of my eyes could not have [been] noticed, they were so small.
>
> But my legs, my impossible legs, lay over the wooded mountains and gave shade to the village-studded valleys. They grew and grew! They reached into the space that no longer owned any landscape, for some time their length had gone beyond my field of vision.
>
> But no, it isn't like that—after all, I'm small, small for the time being—I'm rolling—I'm rolling—I'm an avalanche in the mountains! Please, passers-by, be so kind as to tell me how big I am—just measure these arms, these legs.[26]

26. CS 46–47; BK 126–28 ("A" version): "Ich war doch klein, kleiner als gewöhnlich und ein Strauch mit weißen Hagebutten, der sich ganz schnell schüttelte überragte mich. Ich sah das, denn er war von einem Augenblick nahe bei mir. Aber trotzdem hatte ich mich geirrt, denn meine Arme waren so groß, wie die Wolken eines Landregens, nur waren sie hastiger. Ich weiß nicht, warum sie meinen armen Kopf zerdrücken wollten. Der war so klein, wie ein Ameisenei, nur war er ein wenig beschädigt, daher nicht mehr vollkommen rund. Ich führte ihm bittende Drehungen aus, denn der Ausdruck meiner Augen hätte nicht bemerkt werden können, so klein waren sie. Aber meine Beine, doch meine unmöglichen Beine lagen über den bewaldeten Bergen und beschatteten die dörflichen Thäler. Sie wuchsen, sie wuchsen, sie wuchsen! Schon ragten sie in den Raum der keine Landschaft mehr besaß, längst schon reichte ihre Länge aus der Sehschärfe meiner Augen. Aber nein, das ist es nicht—ich bin doch klein, vorläufig klein—ich rolle—ich rolle—ich bin eine Lawine im Gebirge! Bitte, vorübergehende Leute, seid so gut, sagt mir wie groß ich bin, messet mir diese Arme, die Beine."

The narrator's uncertainty about his size reflects the central paradox of rhetorical dissemination and repeats the ambivalence of self-multiplication in "a pack of nobodies." As the narrator is at once both everybody and nobody, he is also at once both tiny and huge. The request addressed to "passersby" ("vorübergehende Leute") at the close of the passage is rhetorical in the way of a "rhetorical" question. On the one hand, it is not a genuine illocutionary act of requesting on the part of the narrator; there do not appear to be any passersby to respond. On the other hand, the phrase "vorübergehende Leute" might not refer to passersby at all: inasmuch as *vorübergehend* means "transitory" as well as "passing by," it might refer to the "transitory people" created by the text, those very clothed bodies invoked in the epigraph. If so, the narrator is calling upon himself to help himself and is thereby continuing the process of textual dissemination.

We must accept the possibility that the request is genuine in another sense, that here the writing self is calling upon those "passing by" his writing to measure the written self. "Tell me, reader," the author might be saying, "how does my textual alter ego measure up? To me it seems sometimes worthless, sometimes the greatest thing in the world, sometimes both at once." Under this construction, the insecure young writer hopes that his act of self-dissemination will provoke a reading that will help him know "wie groß ich bin" in the sense of "how *great* I am." Material from the letters and diaries (to be discussed later) suggests strongly that the young Kafka might have wanted to pose just such a question. But being Kafka, he could not pose it in any but rhetorical form, in a context so complicated by undecidability that the fragile self who is casting all these shadows is insulated from any possible response. The clothed body protects the self from unwanted contact with others, but it also prevents desired contact. The same text that reaches out to an audience keeps that audience at a distance.

The interplay of intimacy and distance characterizes Kafka's writing just as it typifies his relations with friends, family, and fiancées. That Kafka could never decide whether his greater desire was for a close interaction with others or for complete isolation is evident to everyone who has read the letters and diaries. Perhaps less evident is that Kafka endured an almost exactly parallel ambivalence about himself. A fiction like the "Description of a Struggle" makes it possible to explore this ambivalence with considerable economy, because all of the "others" with whom the self enters into relation are also versions of that same self. But the formal economy is overcome in this text by the chinese-box structure of textual doubling: self-dissemination drives the narrative ever onward, stretching it out and enlarging the textual body between two identical but different hills, the Laurenziberg of the opening section and the Laurenziberg of the conclusion. In between is a text grown corpulent and appropriately occupied by a character whose only name is "the fat man."

The cure of such a corpulent landscape could not be effected in this early abandoned fragment, but it does take place in a text rightly considered one of Kafka's mature masterpieces, "Ein Landarzt" ("A Country Doctor").[27] I cite the title first in German here in order to foreground its own rhetoric. The expression *Landarzt* will be universally understood to refer to a doctor who lives and practices in the country, but it need not be so construed. If we were in the habit of providing medical services to landscapes, we would probably interpret *Landarzt* exactly the way we do *Tierarzt* ("veterinarian")—that is, with the first element considered as the object of the second. In this connection we might want to compare the hero of this story with the hero of *The Castle*, who styles himself a *Landvermesser* ("surveyor" or "land measurer"). He also is a kind of physician, in his younger days known as "the bitter herb," who aspires to act as a cure of the ground.[28] K.'s alleged profession—and the title that designates him through most of the novel—alerts us to Kafka's interest in the "Land" as the object of improvement. Kafka's fictional universe is such that the notion of "doctoring the country" lies well within the bounds of plausibility. Certainly the environment described in the "Description"

27. The reader interested in other approaches to this story might consult the following: Peter M. Canning, "Kafka's Hierogram: The Trauma of the *Landarzt*," *German Quarterly* 57:2 (1984), 197–212; Lawrence O. Frye, "Reconstructions: Kafka's *Ein Landarzt*," *Colloquia Germanica* 16:4 (1983), 321–336; Paul Konrad Kurz, "Verhängte Existenz: Franz Kafkas Erzählung 'Ein Landarzt,'" *Stimmen der Zeit* 177 (1966), 432–450; Joachim Müller, "Erwägungen an dem Kafka-Text: 'Ein Landarzt,'" *Orbis Litterarum* 23 (1968), 35–54; Susan Ray, "The Metaphysics of the Doppelgänger Motif in Kafka's 'Ein Landarzt,'" *Seminar* 21 (May 1985), 123–138; J. D. Thomas, "The Dark at the End of the Tunnel: Kafka's 'In the Penal Colony,'" *Studies in Short Fiction* 4 (1966), 12–18; and Edward Timms, "Kafka's Expanded Metaphors: A Freudian Approach to *Ein Landarzt*," in J. P. Stern and J. J. White, eds., *Paths and Labyrinths: Nine Papers Read at the Franz Kafka Symposium Held at the Institute of Germanic Studies on 20 and 21 October 1983* (London: Institute of Germanic Studies, 1985), 66–79.

28. I deliberately echo here the phrase used by J. Hillis Miller in "Stevens' Rock and Criticism as Cure," *Georgia Review* 30:1 and 2 (1976).

is so subject to distortion and sudden alteration that we might think of it as "sick." The landscape inhabited by the country doctor, similarly, seems pathologically distressed, plagued as it is by an apparently endless winter and by spatio-temporal discontinuities that on the one hand allow the doctor to move instantly ten miles from his home to the patient's "as if my patient's farmyard had opened up just before my courtyard gate"[29] and on the other prevent him from reaching his fur coat hanging on the end of the wagon in which he is travelling. This landscape stands in dire need of a cure. Unfortunately, this Landarzt is not up to the task.

The *story* (as opposed to the character) named by the expression "Ein Landarzt" succeeds admirably in curing the formal obesity of the "Description" fragments. Here the economy offered by constructing most of the characters from variations on the central narrating self is exploited admirably, and the problematic of textual dissemination receives thorough attention. It is a lean little story but rich in rhetorical complexity. Already in the opening sentence, one of the best in German literature since Kleist's "Michael Kohlhaas," the density of the narrative is evident:

> I was in great perplexity; I had to start on an urgent journey; a seriously ill patient was waiting for me in a village ten miles off; a thick blizzard of snow filled all the wide spaces between him and me; I had a gig with big wheels, exactly right for our country roads; muffled in furs, my bag of instruments in my hand, I was in the courtyard all ready for the journey; but there was no horse to be had, no horse.[30]

The opening phrase gives a hint of the rhetorical compression characteristic of the story as a whole. The expression "Ich war in großer Verlegenheit" points in several directions at once, all of them relevant to the situation as it develops. On the one hand, it suggests that the narrator has a difficult cognitive problem to solve; he is, as the translation puts it, "in great perplexity." On the other, it hints that the narrator's state of mind is tinged by a kind of moral difficulty; *Ver-*

29. *CS* 221; *SE* 125: "Als öffne sich unmittelbar vor meinem Haustor der Hof meines Kranken."

30. *CS* 220; *SE* 124: "Ich war in großer Verlegenheit: eine dringende Reise stand mir bevor; ein Schwerkranker wartete auf mich in einem zehn Meilen entfernten Dorfe; starkes Schneegestöber füllte den weiten Raum, zwischen mir und ihm; einen Wagen hatte ich, leicht, großräderig, ganz wie er für unsere Landstraßen taugt; in den Pelz gepackt, die Instrumententasche in der Hand, stand ich reisefertig schon auf dem Hofe; aber das Pferd fehlte, das Pferd."

legenheit also means "embarrassment." The doctor certainly has a practical problem: how can he call on his needy patient without a horse? But the expression "In großer Verlegenheit" proposes as well that the doctor feels a moral responsibility for the situation that might make him a bit ashamed. The reader does not know as yet what the doctor might be embarrassed about (in the moral sense), and so the phrase functions as a subtle form of prolepsis, anticipating an embarrassment that we will be in a position to understand only later.

In an even more subtle way, the word *Verlegenheit* anticipates the process of textual and personal dissemination that the story will explore. Not only does the word disseminate its multiple meanings over the text it initiates, it even carries within it, in the lexeme *verlegen* ("to publish"), the signifier denoting textual dissemination. Even if we read the opening phrase as decomposed into free signifiers, the text remains readable as appropriate to the fiction in which it participates. The ich, which is here a verbally constructed self, exists only "in" a large-scale process of self-replication (*Verlegen-heit*) that is both this particular document and the text understood as a class of documents reproduced again and again. This textual self is both perplexed and embarrassed by the circumstances in which it finds itself, but it is also proper to say that this ich can be found nowhere save in its perplexity, embarrassment, and replication. In other words, Verlegenheit is not a temporary condition through which the self is passing but the very thing that defines it and conjures it into being.

The environment is already engaged in a powerful act of dissemination in anticipation of what is to follow. Where formerly there had been a great empty space (*Raum*) separating the doctor from his patient, now the space is filling up with a "starkes Schneegestöber," a strong storm full of flying snow. The substantive *Gestöber* is derived from the verb *stieben,* which carries a powerful implication of dispersion, or scattering. The doctor as a narrating subject dwells in the midst of this dispersion and comes into being because of it. The story takes shape as a great empty space becomes filled with scattered stuff, whether we read that space as the open distances of the countryside or the unfilled blank of the (as yet) unwritten page.

The process of addressing the doctor's problem begins with an act of rhetorical dissemination. In his frustration the doctor kicks at the door of an old, unused pigsty. The door opens ("öffnete sich"), perhaps forced open by the doctor's kick but perhaps merely responding to his need. Kafka's paratactic style characteristically leaves unspecified the relation between the two actions. The door's opening seems to release a "warmth and smell as of horses" ("Wärme und Geruch wie von Pferden"), though again Kafka's language merely states that this warmth and smell "came forth" ("kam hervor"). The word "horses" occurs here as part of a figure characterizing the warmth and smell of the pigsty: Kafka is careful not to say "the warmth and smell of horses" but rather inserts an all-important *wie*. The doctor's discourse sets up a rhetorical comparison that the fiction then converts into a proleptic announcement of the facts. In any case, whether as simile or as prolepsis, the horses make their first appearance here as pure language.

One could even argue that the horses are essentially conjured up by the utterance of some magic words, in this case their names. When the doctor looks in the pigsty, the first creature he perceives is the groom. There is no mention of horses until the groom calls them forth:

> "Shall I yoke up?" he asked, crawling on all fours. I did not know what to say and merely stooped down to see what else was in the sty. The servant girl was standing beside me. "You never know what you're going to find in your own house," she said, and we both laughed. "Hey there, Brother, hey there, Sister!" called the groom, and two horses, enormous creatures with powerful flanks, one after the other, their legs tucked close to their bodies, each well-shaped head lowered like a camel's, by sheer strength of buttocking squeezed though the door hole which they filled entirely.[31]

Where were the horses before the groom called them? Is the pigsty so large that two "enormous" creatures could remain hidden in it? Did they just appear out of nowhere? In Kafka's fictional universe, all of these things are possible. At the level of signifying text, however, we can easily trace the genesis of the horses by way of a rhetorical progression: they appear first as part of a figure, then as names in a summons, and finally as the described objects of experience. The

---

31. *CS* 124; *SE* 124: "'Soll ich anspannen?' fragte er, auf allen Vieren hervorkriechend. Ich wußte nichts zu sagen und beugte mich nur, um zu sehen, was es noch in dem Stalle gab. Das Dienstmädchen stand neben mir. 'Man weiß nicht, was für Dinge man im eigenen Hause vorrätig hat,' sagte sie, und wir beide lachten. 'Hollah, Bruder, hollah, Schwester!' rief der Pferdeknecht, und zwei Pferde, mächtige flankenstarke Tiere schoben sich hintereinander, die Beine eng am Leib, die wohlgeformten Köpfe wie Kamele senkend, nur durch die Kraft der Wendungen ihres Rumpfes aus dem Türloch, das sie restlos ausfüllten."

horses, when they finally appear, fit quite comfortably in the structure of the narrative even if horses do not seem to belong in a pigsty.

The presentation of the horses in the pigsty is altogether proper and natural for such a writer as Kafka, who was enamored of the work and persona of the Prussian romantic Heinrich von Kleist. Because of Kleist's "Michael Kohlhaas," the horses in the pigsty exist already as text for readers of modern German literature. One of the most vividly described scenes in Kleist's story shows the two prized horses that Kohlhaas had been trying to transport across the Tronka family lands quartered in a miserable pigsty instead of a stable. Although the conventions and practices of animal care exclude horses from pigsties, the powerful practice of Kleist's story establishes a counter-convention that links horses to pigsties indissolubly and forever. A devoted reader of Kleist, as Kafka was, can no longer think of pigsties without seeing horses in them. One of the first of many doublings in "A Country Doctor" is thus the repetition of this striking element from "Kohlhaas."

Another textual precedent allows for the appearance of a man in this same pigsty. One of the most widely recognized episodes in the *Odyssey* recounts how Circe placed a magic potion in the wine she gave to Ulysses's men:

> Scarce had they drunk when she flew after them
> with her long stick and shut them in a pigsty—
> bodies, voices, heads, and bristles, all
> swinish now, though minds were still unchanged.
> So, squealing, in they went. And Circe tossed them
> acorns, mast, and cornel berries—fodder
> for hogs who rut and slumber on the earth.[32]

Kafka unquestionably knew this passage because he echoes it very closely in that scene in *The Castle* where Frieda drives the peasants in the taproom across the courtyard and into the stalls. He would also have known that, when Ulysses asks for his crew, Circe goes to the pigsty to get them. When Kafka's country doctor looks into the pigsty, then, his mind, furnished with the precedents of the German and antique classics, is prepared to find misplaced horses and swinish men. The reader, furnished with similar reading, is not particularly

32. Homer, *The Odyssey*, trans. Robert Fitzgerald (New York: Doubleday, 1961), 172 (Book 10, vv. 239–245).

surprised to find that the groom remains animallike as he is presented in the text's figures. It seems fitting that he should be found "crawling on all fours," that he bites instead of kisses, and that the doctor addresses him as "you animal" ("du Vieh").

A third textual precedent appears to have played a role in the development of the fictional situation that opens "A Country Doctor," this one no classic but familiar as could be to Kafka. It is a passage from his own diaries:

> Miss F[elice] B[auer]. When I arrived at Brod's on August 13th, she was sitting at the table, though she looked to me like a serving girl. I was not at all curious about who she was, but rather took her for granted at once. Bony, empty face that wore its emptiness openly. Bare throat. A blouse thrown on. Looks very domestic in her dress although, as it later turned out, she by no means was. (I alienate myself from her a little by inspecting her so closely. What a state I'm in now, indeed, alienated in general from the whole of everything good, and don't even believe it yet. . .).[33]

Kafka's discovery in the familiar surroundings of Brod's house of an alien and yet immediately assimilated "serving girl" (*Dienstmädchen*) who from then on occupies his thoughts is too similar to the doctor's discovery of the groom and the (re)discovery of Rosa to be coincidental. Both Rosa and Felice are described as Dienstmädchen, and both are taken for granted at the same time that they are objects of desire. The groom's first act is to display his "open" face, a face which he shortly thereafter pushes up against Rosa's. We should also note that this same diary entry (August 20, 1912) that describes Felice does so only after describing an "empty open wagon and the large, emaciated horse pulling it" and expressing anxiety about the possible publication, or rejection, of some of his fiction by the firm of Rowohlt. Many of the elements of the "Country Doctor" are thus already linked together in the diary.

If the story begins immediately by disseminating the body of Felice

---

33. *DI1* 268; *TB* 285: "Fräulein F.B. Als ich am 13. August zu Brod kam, saß sie bei Tisch und kam mir doch wie ein Dienstmädchen vor. Ich war auch gar nicht neugierig darauf, wer sie war, sondern fand mich sofort mit ihr ab. Knochiges leeres Gesicht, das seine Leere offen trug. Freier Hals. Überworfene Bluse. Sah ganz häuslich angezogen aus, trotzdem sie es, wie sich später zeigte, gar nicht war. (Ich entfremde ihr ein wenig dadurch, daß ich ihr so nahe an den Leib gehe. Allerdings in was für einem Zustand bin ich jetzt, allem Guten in der Gesamtheit entfremdet, und glaube es überdies noch nicht. . .)."

in the figures of the groom and the servant girl, it only repeats a movement of self-dissemination. Kafka evidently associated Felice very closely with part of himself, initially at least with that part in sympathy with "the whole of everything good." A number of Kafka's protagonists show attributes derived from her. The animal-hero of "The Burrow" ("Der Bau") is a "Kafka" by way of his human consciousness in an animal body, but he is also a *Bauer* by calling. Kafka himself took note of the close relation between the name "Georg Bendemann" and "Franz Kafka," but he failed to mention that the given name Georg is derived from a Greek word (*georgos*) that directly translates *Bauer*. A Bauer is both the peasant who improves the land by tilling and the builder who improves it for habitation. Another way of saying Bauer, then, might be to say *Landarzt*.

Felice plays a crucial, if shadowy, role here because in her was focused Kafka's concern about two competing forms of self-dissemination, writing and founding a family. It is significant that Kafka opens his diary entry of August 20, not with Felice herself, nor with the horse and wagon, nor even with Rowohlt. It begins with a little idyll viewed from his window of two little boys in blue shirts carrying hay up a slope. Kafka remarks on the "charm of the whole thing for the eyes."[34] The expression speaks eloquently of Kafka's ambivalence about children, whom he finds charming "for the eyes" and not necessarily otherwise. They are acceptable, even agreeable, when kept at a distance. Up close they might be threatening. They would surely threaten his life as a "nocturnal scribbler" if they were his own children, from whom he could not, would not, distance himself. Kafka was never able to reconcile what he saw as the competing claims of marriage and literature in the management of his life.

In fiction, however, writing itself produces a kind of family of little Kafkas and little Bauers (who are also little Kafkas), textual offspring of the paternal word. The passion of sexual reproduction (which Kafka considered in any case a kind of "punishment") is replaced by the passion of self-reading, and corporeal fertility yields to textual dissemination. But this little family, produced as it is by self-division, is drenched in an incestuous erotic longing. These spectral creatures have come into being just the way Aristophanes, in Plato's *Symposium*, jokingly supposes the two human sexes have come into being: by division of a single entity. The divided self wants nothing more than

---

34. *DI1* 268; *TB* 284: "Annehmlichkeit des Ganzen für die Augen."

to rejoin. If the servant girl and the open-faced groom are rhetorical slices of an originally unified Felice text, it is no wonder that there is an erotic tension between them and that the groom takes the very first opportunity to kiss (or is it bite?) Rosa.[35] The doctor, too, participates in this erotic drama: he represents the initial textual self that is divided into various Kafka/Bauer forms. As we come to realize later in the story, the groom is only acting out the doctor's own sexual desires upon the servant girl.

The only difference between the doctor and the groom (as far as their relationship to Rosa is concerned) would appear to be that the doctor has a minimum of self-control that the groom utterly lacks. The groom acts without restraint, especially when the doctor is safely packed off in his wagon, breaking down the house door in order to rape the undefended Rosa. But at precisely the same moment, the doctor is acting out one of the best-known metaphors of the out-of-control personality in our tradition: like the unskilled charioteer of Plato's *Phaedrus*, the doctor is pulled about in his gig by a pair of horses he is unable to direct. The possibility for loss of self-control is figured forth in Plato's myth, as it will be again in Freud's, by a dialeptic multiplication of entities constituting the self. Part of the self (the horses) may act independently of another part (the charioteer) in the absence of an effective controlling and unifying will. The doctor in his gig drawn by the horses might, all together, make up a complete individual, but the several parts seem to remain alien to each other, like the "Kafka" and "Löwy" sides of Franz as set forth in the "Letter to His Father." The textual dissemination is in a sense all too successful, disastrously so.

The unmanageable horses transport the doctor instantly from the scene of Rosa's suffering to that of the patient, a juxtaposition that suggests the possibility of another doubling. Indeed, the patient participates in a remarkable network of interrelated pairings, not the least of which is his kinship with Rosa. But before the text definitively confirms the patient's connection with Rosa and suggests the nature of that connection, it proposes some other interesting pairings. The patient makes his first appearance in the context of his family—father, mother, and sister—so that the wounded young man belongs to

35. This ambiguity echoes another famous passage from the work of Kleist: Penthesilea excuses her mutilation of the body of Achilles by claiming that kissing and biting, "Küsse" and "Bisse," are equivalent.

a brother-sister pair. But we have already been introduced to such a pair before, when the groom effectively conjured up the horses he calls "Brother" and "Sister." The patient and his sister are thus associated with the horses, as the horses are with the groom-servant pair. In this way all of the doublings are interrelated and are understandable as variations on one and the same paradigmatic doubling, made possible by repeated acts of self-reading.

Even the narrating voice of the doctor is not exempt from this pervasive doubling. There are actually two different narrative perspectives, two widely separated temporal situations, interwoven and presented as one. There is one country doctor who stands apart from his experience and tells about it in the past tense and another who is caught up in the events as they happen and recounts them in the present. The distinction is particularly evident at the beginning and ending of the story: the first paragraph is written entirely in the past tense, whereas the last is composed entirely in the present. In between, however, there is an unpredictable switching back and forth between the two tenses, sometimes even in a single sentence: "'You brute,' I yelled in fury, 'do you want a whipping?' but in the same moment I reflect that the man is a stranger, that I do not know where he comes from, and that of his own free will he is helping me when everyone else fails me."[36]

The vacillation between the use of a narrative past and what may or may not be a "historical" present marks the body of the narrative, and it is so pervasive that it must be read as something more than a stylistic quirk. Although it is true that the conventions of tense usage in German allow for a wider use of the historical present than is customary in English, Kafka engages in what appears to be a conscious effort to make the reader aware of the interpenetration of the two implied temporal perspectives. If so, Kafka would be part of a tradition of "temporal irony" in fantasy fiction that goes back at least to Gérard de Nerval's *Aurélia*.[37] Because "A Country Doctor" is every bit as concerned with the issue of the double as is Nerval's story, it is hardly

36. *CS* 221; *SE* 125: "'Du Vieh,' schrie ich wütend, 'willst du die Peitsche?,' besinne mich aber gleich, daß es ein Fremder ist; daß ich nicht weiß, woher er kommt, und daß er mir freiwillig aushilft, wo alle andern versagen." (I have modified the translation to reflect the tense structure of the original.)

37. Susan Noakes, "Self-reading and Temporal Irony in *Aurélia*," *Studies in Romanticism* 16 (Winter 1977), 101–119.

surprising that Kafka should resort to a similar device.[38] The narrating voice splits apart into a point of view contemporaneous with the events described and one reflecting on those events from a subsequent time. This temporal doubling implies a further dialectic of presence and absence, for the present-tense narrator is on the scene of what he reports, whereas the past-tense narrator is not.

The interplay of presence and absence is necessarily a characteristic feature of texts exploring the issues of doubling, and "A Country Doctor" shows a high level of interest in its exploitation. Just when the doctor despairs over the irremediable loss of Rosa, now at the mercy of the voracious groom ten miles hence, Rosa is restored to him by means of rhetoric:

> Well, this should be the end of my visit, I had once more been called out needlessly, I was used to that, the whole district made my life a torment with my night bell, but that I should have to sacrifice Rose this time as well, the pretty girl who had lived in my house for years almost without my noticing her—that sacrifice was too much to ask, and I had somehow to get it reasoned out in my head with the help of what craft I could muster, in order not to let fly at this family, which with the best will in the world could not restore Rose to me. But as I shut my bag and put an arm out for my fur coat, . . . I was somehow ready to admit conditionally that the boy might be ill after all. . . . In his right side, near the hip, was an open wound as big as the palm of my hand. Rose-red, in many variations of shade, dark in the hollows, lighter at the edges, softly granulated, with irregular clots of blood, open as the surface of a mine to the daylight. That was how it looked from a distance.[39]

38. On the double in Kafka's early fiction, see James Rolleston, "*Betrachtung*: Landschaften der Doppelgänger," *DJK*, 184–199.

39. *CS* 223; *SE* 126–127: "Nun, hier wäre also mein Besuch zu Ende, man hat mich wieder einmal unnötig bemüht, daran bin ich gewöhnt, mit Hilfe meiner Nachtglocke martert mich der ganze Bezirk, aber daß ich diesmal auch noch Rosa hingeben mußte, dieses schöne Mädchen, das jahrelang, von mir kaum beachtet, in meinem Hause lebte—dieses Opfer ist zu groß, und ich muß es mir mit Spitzfindigkeiten aushilfsweise in meinem Kopf irgendwie zurechtlegen, um nicht auf diese Familie loszufahren, die mir ja mit dem besten Willen Rosa nicht zurückgeben kann. Als ich aber meine Handtasche schließe und nach meinem Pelz winke, . . . bin ich irgendwie bereit, unter Umständen zuzugeben, daß der Junge doch vielleicht krank ist. . . . In seiner rechten Seite, in der Hüftengegend hat sich eine handtellergroße Wunde aufgetan. Rosa, in vielen Schattierungen, dunkel in der Tiefe, hellwerdend zu den Rändern, zartkörnig, mit ungleichmäßig sich aufsammelnden Blut, offen wie ein Bergwerk obertags. So aus der Entfernung."

There is the implication buried in the doctor's musings that he could "make arrangements" (*zurechtlegen*) in his head by means of "subtleties" (*Spitzfindigkeiten*) to do what the family could not, that is, restore Rosa to him. The sentences that follow show the doctor doing just that by means of his narration of the patient's wound. The return of the servant girl is even more striking in the German than in the translation, for the sentence that in English begins "Rose-red" in the original opens simply "Rosa." Kafka's sentence is rhetorical in a way the English cannot be, because the adjective *rosa,* thus placed at the beginning of the sentence and capitalized, is graphically indistinguishable from the name that the narrator has been citing so frequently. In its context, and given its syntactic location, the word "Rosa" is more than likely to cause the reader to assume that indeed the topic of the sentence is the girl named Rosa. Only further reading settles the issue firmly in favor of construing the word as an adjective meaning "pink."

The rhetoricity of this "Rosa" is the hinge on which the story turns. The patient, formerly considered only as a hindrance and in no need of the doctor's attentions, is now discovered to need them and, as a version of "Rosa," to deserve them. But of course the doctor, the great disseminator, can only multiply further something that he realizes may already have suffered too much dissemination: "Poor boy, you were past helping."[40] Meanings, however, continue to proliferate, despite the doctor's suspicion that nothing can ameliorate this situation. Even potentially ameliorative rhetoric in the end moves consistently toward the harmful. The boy's wound is implicitly compared to a female genital (the part of Rosa in which the doctor has the greatest interest), but the description turns all the positive values inside out: "But on closer inspection there was another complication. Who could see it without making a low whistle? Worms, as thick and as long as my little finger, themselves rose-red and blood-spotted as well, were wriggling from their fastness in the interior of the wound toward the light, with small white heads and many little legs."[41] How appropriate that

40. *CS* 223; *SE* 127: "Armer Junge, dir ist nicht zu helfen."
41. *CS* 223; *SE* 127: "In der Nähe zeigt sich noch eine Erschwerung. Wer kann das ansehen ohne leise zu pfeifen? Würmer, an Stärke und Länge meinem kleinen Finger gleich, rosig aus eigenem und außerdem blutbespritzt, winden sich, im Innern der Wunde festgehalten, mit weißen Köpfchen, mit vielen Beinchen ans Licht." (I have modified the translation to restore the rhetorical question that *CS* does not reproduce.)

the doctor should introduce this description with a rhetorical question! He may or may not whistle himself, may or may not be asserting the inevitability of such a whistle. He does not indicate whether such a whistle would be one of appreciation or dismay. That there should be *Würmer* emerging from the interior of this very vaginal opening might, under the proper circumstances, call for appreciation, since the word *Wurm* is regularly used in colloquial German as a figure for "little child." As the offspring of "Rosa," they might also be described, properly and happily, as *rosig*. Delighted relatives and friends might well coo over the *Köpfchen* and *Beinchen* of such offspring. But the doctor is right: this wound is past helping, and all of this potentially positive language is put together in such a way as to suggest not only a thoroughly misogynistic reaction to the vagina but a horror of its fertility. The phallic character of the worms suggests both the disseminating power of this wound and its distressing lack of need for the one thing the doctor might be able to provide. Even when the doctor's rhetoric seems to valorize the wound positively, further rhetoric immediately undercuts it: "this blossom in your side was destroying you."[42] By calling the wound a "blossom," the doctor not only suggests its color and form, not only reaffirms its vaginal character, and not only strengthens the tie between the patient and the girl with the name of a flower; he suggests its organic growth—which in this case frightens him—and even its rhetorical character, because *Blume* can be used figuratively to mean "metaphor." The boy is being destroyed by rhetorical dissemination, by a growth in his side (or on his page of text; *Seite* means both) that cannot be arrested.

This rhetorical wound grows to engulf the entire text. When the doctor complains in the final paragraph that his "flourishing practice" ("blühende Praxis") is finished, one has to wonder how true his complaint really is. If the blühende Praxis to which he refers is the kind of medical practice we might imagine a rural doctor to have, then perhaps he is right. But we must confess that we have seen nothing of that practice here. On the other hand, what we have seen, and what is certainly not finished, is the "blossoming practice" of rhetorical dissemination, of taking figurative language at its word. Even the patient's family show themselves to be earnest readers of the country doctor's rhetoric. Although the boy is only metaphorically Rosa and is only figuratively possessed of a female genital, they act as if the sexual

42. *CS* 223; *SE* 127: "An dieser Blume in deiner Seite gehst du zugrunde."

connection between the doctor and this "wound" should be consummated. They undress the doctor and carry him to the boy's bed, putting him "next to the wall, on the side of the wound,"[43] as if to make sure the bridegroom would thus be properly placed to enter the bride.

The doctor's blühende Praxis must be understood rhetorically as his activity with respect to the Blume, the flower that is both the boy's wound and Rosa's maidenhood, both his professional and his sexual aspiration. This blossoming practice may indeed be lost on both counts, and the "successor" who is imagined as "robbing" the doctor might be either a new doctor or a new lover (the groom), either of whom might be said to be taking "Rosa" (wound/girl) as his victim. With respect to the flower of metaphor, however, the doctor's practice continues to flourish. He continues to disseminate himself by reading himself rhetorically, even as he laments his impotence. When he complains that he is in his nakedness "exposed to the frost of this most unhappy of ages,"[44] he turns a pair of apparently literal narrative facts into dizzyingly cosmic metaphors. We know that he is naked and that it is cold, but his text turns the literal *Frost* of the weather into a figurative *Frost* (that is "apathy") belonging to a cultural epoch. With this turn of *Frost* comes a retrospective rereading of *nackt* ("naked") as "unprotected, vulnerable." The doctor's discourse suddenly removes his predicament from the immediate context and places it on a far larger historical scale. The apathy of this unhappy age is illustrated by the indifference of his "limber pack of patients" (suddenly plural), whose mobility does not come to the aid of the "frozen" doctor.

The narrating voice, however, having spun off a startling array of clothed bodies, now remains naked and helpless, pulled along by a mechanism conjured up out of his own discourse. The process of dissemination is still out of hand, just as it was in the "Description of a Struggle," but it reaches its crisis more swiftly and surely than before. In this sense "A Country Doctor" succeeds in curing the textual ground of the earlier story.

43. *CS* 224; *SE* 127: "Zur Mauer, an die Seite der Wunde."
44. *CS* 225; *SE* 128: "Nackt, dem Froste dieses unglückseligsten Zeitalters ausgesetzt."

Chapter 9

LIVED RHETORIC

Early in my inquiry into Kafka's rhetoric, I cited one of the few passages in his writings that could be called autobiographical. The issue I developed out of that quotation involved the reading of the self as text, beginning with the name "Kafka" itself. Much of the discussion so far has centered upon the relation between the self as text and the text as a version of self. In this chapter I want to push further in this direction by examining some of the nonfictional texts Kafka produced—letters and diaries in particular—with an eye to the ways in which the life of the historical person Franz Kafka was caught up in, and to some degree perhaps even determined by, the rhetorical structures he wrote and read. My purpose is to demonstrate that the life of Kafka as it is revealed in the documents he composed was a kind of lived rhetoric, a merging of psychic and textual structures so complete that one can hardly be separated from the other.

I can best begin with an example from a relatively early diary entry (January 19, 1911), which looks back as if from a great distance on Kafka's first beginnings as a writer of fiction. It is, as we have come to expect, a story of pain and failure:

> Once I projected a novel in which two brothers fought each other, one of whom went to America while the other remained in a European prison. I only now and then began to write a few lines, for it tired me at once. So once I wrote down something about my prison on a Sunday afternoon when we were visiting my grandparents. . . . It is of course

possible that I did it mostly out of vanity, and . . . wanted to tempt someone to take what I had written from me, look at it and admire me. . . . An uncle who liked to make fun of people finally took the page that I was holding only weakly, looked at it briefly, handed it back to me, even without laughing, and only said to the others who were following him with their eyes, "The usual stuff," to me he said nothing. To be sure, I remained seated and bent over the now useless page of mine, but with one thrust I had in fact been banished [*vertrieben*] from society, the judgment [*Urteil*] of my uncle repeated itself in me with what amounted to real significance [*mit fast wirklicher Bedeutung*] and even within the feeling of belonging to a family I got an insight into the cold space of our world which I had to warm with a fire that first I wanted to seek out.[1]

As Kafka describes this early scene of writing, two closely connected things take place, one at the level of human relations and the other at the level of rhetoric. On the human level, this is the story of a moment of awakening pain, the discovery of a person's irremediable loneliness even within the circle of the most intimate structure of human relations we know, the family. The young Kafka perceives this discovery as an act of banishment, of being driven out of society by an act of physical violence: "with a push" ("mit einem Stoß"). This language of physical violence is of course a metaphor for the emotional rejection at the hands of his uncle. But the uncle—probably Richard Löwy[2]—has performed another sort of action here, though not a physical one: he has uttered an opinion, passed judgment on the boy's writing. In

---

1. *DI1* 43–44; *TB* 39–41: "Einmal hatte ich einen Roman vor, in dem zwei Brüder gegeneinander kämpften, von denen einer nach Amerika fuhr, während der andere in einem europäischen Gefängnis blieb. Ich fing nur hie und da Zeilen zu schreiben an, denn es ermüdete mich gleich. So schrieb ich einmal auch an einem Sonntagnachmittag, als wir bei den Großeltern zu Besuch waren. . . . Es ist schon möglich, daß ich es zum größten Teil aus Eitelkeit machte und . . . jemanden verlocken wollte, das Geschriebene mir wegzunehmen, es anzuschauen und mich zu bewundern. . . . Ein Onkel, der gern auslachte, nahm mir endlich das Blatt, das ich nur schwach hielt, sah es kurz an, reichte es mir wieder, sogar ohne zu lachen, und sagte zu den andern, die ihn mit den Augen verfolgten, 'das gewöhnliche Zeug,' zu mir sagte er nichts. Ich blieb zwar sitzen und beugte mich wie früher über mein also unbrauchbares Blatt, aber aus der Gesellschaft war ich tatsächlich mit einem Stoß vertrieben, das Urteil des Onkels wiederholte sich in mir mit schon fast wirklicher Bedeutung, und ich bekam selbst innerhalb des Familiengefühls einen Einblick in den kalten Raum unserer Welt, den ich mit einem Feuer erwärmen müßte, das ich erst suchen wollte."

2. He is so identified by Hartmut Binder, *Kafka Kommentar zu den Romanen, Rezensionen, Aphorismen und zum Brief an den Vater* (Munich: Winkler, 1976).

Kafka's mind this judgment (*Urteil*) performs a rhetorical slide into a sentence (Urteil "mit fast wirklicher Bedeutung," "with almost real significance"), so that the uncle's casual and callous dismissal of his nephew's writing as "the usual stuff" is both emotionally and verbally equivalent to a sentence of judgment.

What is most important about this memory text is that one cannot disentangle the rhetorical moment from a moment of personal suffering. The feeling of exile that, the diary entry gives us to believe, this moment initiates neither disappears nor lessens in subsequent years. Kafka remains "as lonely as Franz Kafka"[3] essentially for the rest of his life. The sense of being "banished from society" dominates his fiction from first to last, from "The Judgment" to "Josephine the Singer." At the same time, we must remember that the banishment in question, although genuine in its human context of Kafka's very real pain, is at the same time a linguistic artifact, a figure generated out of the possibility that one sort of Urteil will turn into another. We cannot decide confidently even whether one has temporal or causal precedence over the other; for though it may superficially seem that the pain must have been the origin of the text, only the text's authority allows us to ascribe precedence to the experience of suffering. Rhetoric, after all, controls the (narrated) structure of the event. Although it is certainly true that Kafka's pain could have existed in the utter absence of this rhetoric of Urteile, it is also true that the particular sort of pain he suffered was formed according to the channels of possibility inherent in the German language. Yes, Kafka would have felt the sting of his uncle's rejection no matter what language he used, but he could only have suffered this sort of pain in the medium of this sort of language.

Another special feature of this diary entry that demands attention is its context of poetic production. Although the young Kafka feels the anguish of being banished from society—a rejection, in short, of himself as a human being—Uncle Richard's words are directed not against him personally but against his writing and then not even against the whole of his writing activity but only against its lack of originality. That the boy perceived this as a personal rejection is hardly surprising, but it is nonetheless characteristic enough of Kafka at all stages of his life to deserve note. Kafka cannot separate his concept

3. The phrase is Kafka's, but it has been made famous by Marthe Robert's *Seul, comme Franz Kafka* (Paris: Calmann-Lévy, 1979).

of himself from his discourse. The intensity of the boy's experience of suffering thus depends in no small way upon his own equation of language and self. The experience Kafka reports in the diary is conditioned by a notion of the inseparability of a person and his language, an inseparability that in turn appears in the very language used to frame the report. Precisely that person who is so at one with his language that he can turn one sort of Urteil, the expression of an opinion, into another, a harsh sentence of banishment, is bound to be unable to detect any difference between a rejection of one's discourse and a rejection of one's self.

The intimate complicity of discourse with structures of the self becomes even more marked in the subsequent history of this material. Kafka did not abandon his project of an American novel, in spite of his uncle's magisterial dismissal; he returned to it with great zest in the "ecstatic" period of the autumn of 1912, just days after completing, in one night, the composition of "The Judgment." The story has a substantially different thrust now, however: gone are the two battling brothers, replaced by a single hero who goes to America, not because of fraternal conflict, but because he is banished from his family into the cold space of the world. The central project of this version of the America novel, then, is the narrative figuration of the rejection experience brought about in the context of composing the earlier America novel. An experience of pain initiated by an attempted discourse now forms the mainspring of the new plot and thereby is incorporated into another version of that discourse. Whereas earlier Kafka had felt the judgment on his writing to be a sentence passed upon himself, here the hero Karl Rossmann finds himself banished because his family does not wish to take on the responsibility of supporting his illegitimate child.[4] That there is a figural connection between the family's rejection of Karl's child with the uncle's rejection of Kafka's work seems plausible enough on the face of it; the relation is only underlined by the fact that Karl's child in the novel is given the same name as Karl's uncle, Jakob. Uncle Jakob, too, expressly banishes Karl from the newfound security of the New York branch of his family: "I must, after the incident today, expressly send you away from me.[5]

The symmetry between the insupportable illegitimate text that oc-

---

4. So, at least, Uncle Jacob claims. Cf. *AM* 27, *RO* 26.

5. *AM* 94; *RO* 76: "Ich muß . . . dich nach dem heutigen Vorfall unbedingt von mir fortschicken."

casions Uncle Richard's sentence of banishment and the insupportable illegitimate child that provokes Karl Rossmann's family to pack
him off to America (a banishment approved retroactively by Uncle
Jakob) thickens the texture of connections between human experience and rhetorical structure that characterizes Kafka's entire enterprise. A further thickening of that texture occurs in the story "The
Judgment," written at the same time and under pressure of the same
concerns as *The Missing Person*. Here the rhetorical slide from one sort
of Urteil to another first introduced in the diary entry of 1911 becomes the impetus for a crucial element in the narrative. As Stanley
Corngold has observed, Georg Bendemann goes to his father seeking
his opinion about something but comes away with a sentence.[6] Just as
the young Kafka had, indirectly, solicited the opinion of his uncle
about the document he was writing, so does Georg seek an opinion
about his own piece of writing, in this case a letter written to a friend
in Russia informing him of Georg's engagement to a certain Frieda
Brandenfeld. The father's Urteil, given in a surprising and complex
series of statements, calls into question nearly every conceivable value
the son's writing could have, including its purpose (the friend already
knows about the engagement), its veracity (he calls Georg's letters
"falsche Briefchen" ["lying little letters"]), and even the existence of its
audience ("Do you really have this friend in St. Petersburg?"). That
these criticisms are at least in part contradictory does not decrease
their effect upon Georg. The act of writing for which he hoped to
receive praise and admiration has instead provoked absolute, brutal
rejection. In the story, though, not just Georg perceives this rejection
as a sentence of expulsion. The father conceives it so as well, and he
makes it perfectly explicit by declaring, "I sentence [*verurteile*] you
now to death by drowning."[7] What had otherwise been figured simply
as banishment from the family or community appears here as expulsion from the land of the living (from the land into water, from life
into death). "The Judgment" is in this way (as well as others) a substantially different sort of text from the diary entry of 1911, but the
two share something of considerable importance, a beginning in a
rhetorical moment suffused by personal pain.

6. Stanley Corngold, "Kafka's 'The Judgment' and Modern Rhetorical Theory," *NKSA* 7 (June 1983), 15–21.
7. *CS* 87; *SE* 32: "Ich verurteile dich jetzt zum Tode des Ertrinkens."

The diary entry, the novel fragment, and the story are all part of the same unfinished text with the same implied title: "Der Verurteilte"—"The Condemned/Judged." In all of them we find it impossible to keep separate what we might otherwise suppose would be easily separable elements: the experience of a suffering person and the rhetorical structure of a language of undecidable significance. I am arguing for a conception of Kafka that understands him precisely as opening radically the question of biography, of the relation of "life" to "writing." Kafka will not allow us to ascribe priority to the personal, biographical element in his work or the rhetorical, linguistic one. The one is always already conditioned by the other.

Even when inscribing his own life in diaries meant for no eyes but his own, Kafka writes in the same rhetorically complex way with which we are familiar from the fiction. It seems fair to say that Kafka naturally tended to write in this way, that it was a fundamental part of his character. He was a rhetorical person. Everywhere we look in his writing we find structures of language that are indissolubly linked to the forms of his experience. One cannot help but be struck, for example, by the rhetorical complexity of the travel diary he kept during the summer before he met Felice Bauer and wrote "The Judgment." During his holiday in July of 1912 he visited two places, Weimar and Jungborn, the one a cultural Mecca because of its role in German classicism, the other a somewhat faddish health resort specializing in *Naturheilkunde* (what would today probably be called "holistic medicine"), particularly nudism. It seems a curious combination, with the staid dignity of Goethe and his heritage on the one hand and the rather outrageous behavior of the nudists on the other. But for Kafka both places clearly have equal dignity (or lack of it) and equal claim to a relation to the great cultural tradition. If Weimar has a house named "Goethe" (that is the Goethehaus), Jungborn has one named "Ruth," where Kafka lives while he is in residence. If the Goethehaus functions in the diary principally as a place of assignation where Kafka can meet a young lady with whom he is entranced, the nudist resort serves as the backdrop for discussions of religion and philosophy. Both locations, then, serve as centers for a movement that wants to go in two directions at once.

Kafka's description of his stay at Jungborn shows this double movement especially vividly. The diary entry from July 8, his first full day at the resort, shows a charming candor and a surprising complexity:

My house is called "Ruth." Practically arranged. Four dormers, four windows, one door. Fairly quiet. Only in the distance they are playing football, the birds are loudly singing, several naked people are lying motionless in front of my door. All except me without swimming trunks. Wonderful freedom. In the park, reading room, etc. there are pretty, fat little feet to be seen.[8]

For all its apparent directness and artlessness, this passage tends to conceal in the very language that purports to reveal. Kafka reports, for example, that the house "Ruth" is "fairly quiet" ("ziemlich still"), but the following sentence clarifies this statement less than it undermines it. Is the quiet disturbed by the football game going on "only in the distance"? Is it disturbed or enhanced by the birds with their "robust" ("stark") singing? Is the writer's calm (*Stille*) mirrored or marred by the naked people lying "quietly" ("still") in front of his door? We realize in retrospect that "ziemlich still" could mean either "quiet, with minor exceptions," or "not that quiet." This textual uncertainty undoubtedly expresses the writer's physical condition accurately: he probably did not know himself—and perhaps did not want to know—whether Jungborn was calming or disturbing, or indeed whether he wished to be calmed or excited himself. The textual self, at any rate, does not know and cannot say. The Kafka in the text cannot even say for sure whether he is naked or wearing swimming trunks: the German original translated as "All except me without swimming trunks" ("Alles, bis auf mich, ohne Schwimmhosen") could also be translated as "All, including me, without swimming trunks." That the translator has here made the "correct" choice is supported by evidence from the following entry, but the ambiguity cannot be dismissed. The expression "bis auf" is often used to mean "except" (as in "alle starben bis auf drei," "all died except three") but occasionally also means "including" (as in "alle starben bis auf den letzten Mann," "all died to the last man").

Did Kafka wear his swimming trunks or not? The answer appears to be: sometimes. When he comments parenthetically in the entry of July 9 that "I am called the man in the swimming trunks,"[9] one might

8. *DI*2 302; *TB* 667: "Mein Haus heißt 'Ruth.' Praktisch eingerichtet. Vier Luken, vier Fenster, eine Tür. Ziemlich still. Nur in der Ferne spielen sie Fußball, die Vögel singen stark, einige Nackte liegen still vor meiner Tür. Alles, bis auf mich, ohne Schwimmhosen. Schöne Freiheit. Im Park, Lesezimmer usw. bekommt man hübsche, fette Füßchen zu sehen."

9. *DI*2 303; *TB* 668: "Ich heiße der Mann mit den Schwimmhosen."

suppose that the issue was settled. The confession is startling—though quite in keeping with Kafka's personality—and reeks of embarrassment, hiding as it were behind the protection of parentheses. After all, to go to the trouble of visiting a nudist resort and then to insist on wearing bathing attire reminds one of the White Knight's plan to dye his whiskers green, then "always wear so large a fan / That they might not be seen." But by July 15 he reports that he "posed for Dr. Sch.," and the subsequent observation in the same entry about the "large part the naked body plays in the total impression an individual gives"[10] suggests strongly that he was posing nude. Indeed, Kafka might have doffed his bathing suit in Dr. Sch.'s company earlier. Another rhetorically mystified text explains that on July 12 he was "With Dr. Sch. (forty-three years old) on the meadow in the evening. Going for a walk, stretching, rubbing, slapping and scratching. Stark naked. Shameless."[11] The text refuses to make clear whether only Dr. Sch. or both of them indulged in this "shameless" nudity. By July 16, though, Kafka is ready to let his text be relatively clear on the matter: while talking with another patron of the resort, Guido von Gillshausen, Kafka reports that he "broke out in a sweat (we were naked) and spoke too softly."[12] Once again, Kafka clothes the embarrassing directness of his confession in a pair of modest parentheses.

It is amusing to consider the conflicting embarrassments Kafka put himself through during his sojourn among the nudists, and Kafka himself no doubt shared in the amusement. The comic image of Franz Kafka, doctor of law and supreme poet of twentieth-century angst, and men with names like "Guido von Gillshausen" scampering about nude on the Harz hillsides is hard to suppress, especially after one has seen the photographs of Jungborn and its patrons that were gathered by Klaus Wagenbach.[13] This aspect of Kafka's life and character we would do well to keep in mind, particularly when we are inclined to think of him as the haggard, ascetic face often reproduced from a photo taken not long before his death. Still, it is important to

10. *DI*2 308; *TB* 673: "Die große Beteiligung des nackten Körpers am Gesamteindruck des einzelnen."

11. *DI*2 306; *TB* 671: "Mit Dr. Sch. (dreiundvierzig Jahre) abends auf der Wiese. Spazierengehen, sich strecken, reiben, schlagen und kratzen. Ganz nackt. Schamlos."

12. *DI*2 308; *TB* 673: "Habe Schweißausbruch (wir sind nackt) und rede zu leise."

13. Klaus Wagenbach, *Franz Kafka: Pictures of a Life* (New York: Pantheon, 1984), 136–139.

take note of the way in which Kafka's personal embarrassment becomes embedded in the diary text. The point of this analysis is, after all, not to demonstrate that Kafka, at this or that time, was or was not nude at Jungborn but rather to show that, in his inscribed version of his experience, Kafka was always both nude and clothed, that in his experience of Jungborn, "all" went without bathing trunks "bis auf mich." Although it is clear that Kafka always knew exactly, in a commonsense way, whether he was clothed or naked, it is a knowledge that is extraneous to his affective experience of the place. The situation is directly comparable to the diary entry about the America novel: obviously Kafka "knew" that his uncle had not sentenced him to banishment with his Urteil, but this knowledge was irrelevent to the structure of his pain.

Rhetoric is the solution to, as well as the expression of, the problem of having it both ways at once. The nature of the psychic conflict from which Kafka suffered during his "quiet" holiday is set forth in the dream reproduced in the entry for July 15: "A dream: The sunbathers destroyed one another in a brawl. After the two groups into which they were divided had joked with one another, someone stepped out in front of one group and shouted to the others: 'Lustron and Kastron!' The others: 'What? Lustron and Kastron?' He: 'Right.' Beginning of the brawl."[14] *Lustron* and *Kastron* are nonsense words but evidently not meaningless ones. They appear to be deformations of the ordinary German words *Lust* and *kastrieren* made to conform to a pseudo-Greek paradigm. *Lustron* therefore suggests pleasure, perhaps sexual pleasure, whereas *Kastron* implies the denial of sexuality. Kafka's dream makes explicit the emotional conflict between a desire to participate in an unrestrained "stretching, rubbing, slapping and scratching" of the naked body and an equally powerful feeling that such behavior is "shameless." But that conflict, we discover, is overlaid by another in which the desire to proclaim both Lustron and Kastron at once collides with an incredulous cry ("What? Lustron and Kastron?") suggesting that the two cannot be united. Kafka could not decide for himself whether he was visiting the nudist resort out of "pure" motives (Kafka was, as Klaus Wagenbach has suggested, some-

14. *DI*2 308; *TB* 673: "Ein Traum: Die Luftbadegesellschaft vernichtet sich mittels einer Rauferei. Nachdem die in zwei Gruppen geteilte Gesellschaft miteinander gespaßt hat, tritt aus der einen Gruppe einer vor und ruft der andern zu: 'Lustron und Kastron!' Die andern: 'Wie? Lustron und Kastron?' Der eine: 'Allerdings.' Beginn der Rauferei."

thing of a puritan)¹⁵ or shameless, impure ones. Only the rhetorical text of his experience allows him to preserve both Lustron and Kastron without precipitating an internal brawl that would destroy everything. Only the diary—and not even the dream—allows him to acknowledge both the necessity and the impossibility of Lustron *and* Kastron without mutual annihilation.

The boundary between lived experience and written discourse breaks down, if indeed it had ever existed for Kafka. He is perfectly aware that during his sojourn in Jungborn he is in effect living in a book, not only in the sense that the essential quality of his experience can emerge only in textual form, but also in the sense that the house he lives in carries the name of a book. At the opening of the entry of July 15 he mentions, in connection with the reading he is engaged in, the Book of Ruth ("Buch Ruth"). If he had been reading that section of the Bible, the reason can only have been that it was suggested to him by the name inscribed on his little cabin. The biblical tale of the Moabite woman who "came to a people [she] did not know before" (Ruth 2:11) and yet was at home among them has a certain relevance to Kafka's situation among the sunbathers. Kafka must have realized that his Jungborn diary constituted his version of the Book of Ruth. This book could embody in its language the contradictory structure of his experience by both exposing and covering up his body's nakedness.

Kafka was quite capable of exploiting a similar rhetorical nakedness when it suited him, as it did early in his epistolary relationship with Milena Jesenska. At a point in their friendship when he still addressed her with the formal *Sie*, he made so bold as to open a letter to her in this way: "You see, Milena, I'm lying on the deck-chair in the morning, naked, half in the sun, half in shade, after an almost sleepless night."¹⁶ If Kafka had trouble appearing naked at Jungborn, where it was expected and indeed proper, he has no trouble doing so in this letter, where it is definitely unexpected and not a little impertinent. How can he allow himself this "shameless" behavior? The answer is of course that this nakedness, whether real or feigned, is quite safely

15. Klaus Wagenbach, *Franz Kafka in Selbstzeugnissen und Bilddokumenten* (Hamburg: Rowohlt, 1964), 82.
16. *LM* 45; *BM* 29: "Sehen Sie, Milena, ich liege hier auf dem Liegestuhl, vormittag, nackt, halb in Sonne, halb im Schatten, nach einer fast schlaflosen Nacht."

clothed in epistolary distance. To appear naked before others directly, at Jungborn, was difficult, but to do so indirectly, through the mediation of writing, turns out to be not very difficult at all.

Kafka was perhaps most himself in writing letters: he seems to have tolerated best a situation that both promises intimacy and ensures distance, as letter writing does. Physical intimacy was horrifying— though clearly also necessary—for this man who could declare coitus to be a "punishment for the joy of being together." Letters, however, assume the impossibility of physical closeness but promise instead the hope of a spiritual, intellectual closeness that might surpass physical intimacy. This situation had a powerful attraction for Kafka, and it took a deep hold on his imagination. Perhaps the best evidence of the importance Kafka placed on letter writing comes from a lengthy passage explaining his frustration with it. This text is also from the letters to Milena—one of the last ones—and can serve as a commentary on the problematic of epistolary nakedness:

> All the misfortune of my life . . . derives, one could say, from letters or from the possibility of writing letters. People have hardly ever deceived me, but letters always—and as a matter of fact not only those of other people, but my own. In my case this is a special misfortune of which I won't say more, but at the same time also a general one. The easy possibility of letter writing must—seen merely theoretically—have brought into the world a terrible disintegration of souls. It is, in fact, an intercourse with ghosts, and not only with the ghost of the recipient but also with one's own ghost which develops between the lines of the letter one is writing and even more so in a series of letters where one letter corroborates the other and can refer to it as a witness. How on earth did anyone get the idea that people can communicate with one another by letter! Of a distant person one can think, and of a person who is near one can catch hold—all else goes beyond human strength. Writing letters, however, means to denude oneself before the ghosts, something for which they greedily wait. Written kisses don't reach their destination, rather they are drunk on the way by the ghosts. It is on this ample nourishment that they multiply so enormously.[17]

17. *LM* 229; *BM* 198–199: "Alles Unglück meines Lebens—womit ich nicht klagen, sondern eine allgemein belehrende Feststellung machen will—kommt, wenn man will, von Briefen oder von der Möglichkeit des Briefschreibens her. Menschen haben mich kaum jemals betrogen, aber Briefe immer und zwar auch hier nicht fremde, sondern meine eigenen. Es ist in meinem Fall ein besonderes Unglück, von dem ich nicht weiter reden will, aber gleichzeitig auch ein allgemeines. Die leichte Möglichkeit des Briefschreibens muß—bloß theoretisch angesehen—eine schreckliche Zerrüttung der Seelen in die Welt gebracht haben. Es

To denude oneself before a ghost may have seemed a melancholy act at one moment, but at another it was evidently rather exciting. It is clear that Kafka sometimes believed in the promised intimacy of letters. He had written to Felice in November of 1912 that he treated one of her letters "like some living thing," that is, as evidence of the living bond between them. "Dearest," he goes on, "have you noticed how astonishingly of one mind we are in our letters? If there is a question in one, the following morning brings the answer."[18] Earlier in November he drew an analogy between the intimacy of letters and that of the *du* form of address: "but the *Du* stands firm; it stays here like your letter that doesn't move when I kiss it over and over again. But what a word that is! Nothing unites two people so completely, especially if, like you and me, all they have is words."[19]

The delight in epistolary intimacy is tempered, however, even relatively early in the correspondence with Felice, by an awareness that distance is an integral part of the process. He refers to his letters to her as a "futile striving for an impossibility—i.e., your presence."[20] He reproaches himself with being unable to confront that presence anyway: "But what am I capable of, anyhow? Kissing, yes, kissing from afar!"[21] He is forced to wonder "why I, who force myself upon you

---

ist ja ein Verkehr mit Gespenstern und zwar nicht nur mit dem Gespenst des Adressaten, sondern auch mit dem eigenen Gespenst, das sich einem unter der Hand in dem Brief, den man schreibt, entwickelt oder gar in einer Folge von Briefen, wo ein Brief den andern erhärtet und sich auf ihn als Zeugen berufen kann. Wie kam man nur auf den Gedanken, daß Menschen durch Briefe miteinander verkehren können! Mann kann an einen fernen Menschen denken und man kann einen nahen Menschen fassen, alles andere geht über Menschenkraft. Briefe schreiben aber heißt, sich vor den Gespenstern entblößen, worauf sie gierig warten. Geschriebene Küsse kommen nicht an ihren Ort, sondern werden von den Gespenstern auf dem Wege ausgetrunken. Durch diese reichliche Nährung vermehren sie sich ja so unerhört."

18. *LB* 65; *BF* 126: "Wie etwas lebendiges . . . Liebste, hast Du schon bemerkt, was für unglaubliche Übereinstimmung es zwischen unsern Briefen gibt, wie einer etwas verlangt, was der nächste am andern Morgen schon bringt."

19. *LB* 38; *BF* 90: "Das Du aber, das steht doch, das bleibt wie Dein Brief da, der sich nicht rührt und sich von mir küssen und wieder küssen läßt. Was ist das für ein Wort! So lückenlos schließt nichts zwei Menschen aneinander, gar wenn sie nichts als Worte haben wie wir zwei."

20. *LB* 114; *BF* 194. "Ein nutzloses Andrängen an etwas Unmögliches, d.h. an Deine Gegenwart."

21. *LB* 184; *BF* 287: "Aber was bin denn ich überhaupt imstande! Zu küssen, ja, von der Ferne zu küssen!"

with letters, refrain from doing so in person,"[22] though he presents the question as originating not with him but with a rhetorical Fräulein Lindner and thereby distances himself yet further. He shows himself well aware that "all these letters," no matter how much they reveal of common goals and values, "can't create a presence, only a mixture of presence and absence that becomes unbearable."[23] The kissing from afar, the intercourse with ghosts,[24] is therefore both exhilarating and awful at the same time. And Kafka knows this, too. He knows that this "unbearable" mixture of intimacy and distance is precisely the only kind of intimacy that he can bear. He confesses to Felice in early 1913;

> And what hand, in what dream, made you write that I have won you completely? Dearest, that's what you believe for a brief moment, at a distance. To win you at close quarters, and for good, requires greater strength than the play of muscles that drives my pen. Don't you yourself believe this, when you think about it? It does seem to me sometimes that this communication by letter, beyond which I have an almost constant longing for reality, is the only kind of communication in keeping with my wretchedness (my wretchedness which of course I do not always feel as wretchedness), and that the transgression of this limit imposed on me would lead us both to disaster.[25]

Slipped into the parentheses is the crucially important admission that what he regularly describes negatively, as "wretchedness" and the like, he does not necessarily perceive negatively. If we cancel the double

22. *LB* 188; *BF* 293: "Warum ich, der ich mich mit Briefen so zu Dir dränge, es nicht in Person tue."

23. *LB* 73; *BF* 138: "Mit diesen häufigen Briefen. Gegenwart wird ja dadurch nicht erzeugt, aber ein Zwitter zwischen Gegenwart und Entfernung, der unerträglich ist."

24. The word translated as "intercourse" and "communicate" in the letter to Milena is *Verkehr* (*verkehren*), which has the same sexual connotation as "intercourse."

25. *LB* 197; *BF* 304: "Und mit welcher Hand, in welchem Traum hast Du niedergeschrieben, daß ich Dich ganz erworben habe? Liebste, das glaubst Du, in einem Augenblick, in der Ferne. Aber zum Erwerben in der Nähe, für die Dauer, dazu gehören andere Kräfte, als das Muskelspiel, das meine Feder vorwärtstreibt. Glaubst Du es nicht selbst, wenn Du es überlegst? Scheint mir doch manchmal, daß dieser Verkehr in Briefen, über den hinaus ich mich fast immerfort zur Wirklichkeit sehne, der einzige meinem Elend entsprechende Verkehr ist (meinem Elend, das ich natürlich nicht immer als Elend fühle), und daß die Überschreitung dieser mir gesetzten Grenze in ein uns gemeinsames Unglück führt." (Once again, the word translated as "communication" is *Verkehr*. Kafka implies that their relationship is a kind of "sexual intercourse by means of letters.")

negatives we can hear Kafka confessing that, deep in his heart, he really *likes* communicating by letter, likes even the mixture of intimacy and distance which he has called "unbearable."

When Kafka apparently complains, then, that all he and Felice have is words, the complaint must contain an element of rejoicing. After all, he has chosen that they maintain their relationship in this way, and he has imposed the "limit" of closeness beyond which they dare not go. He feels a need to open himself up, to denude himself before someone, but he can do so comfortably only in the ghostly manner of letters. He can happily declare himself to be naked in front of another only when that other is safely off on the other side of an envelope. What Kafka complains about in his late letter to Milena is the same thing that entrances him earlier on—that is, that epistolary communication involves an address by one fictionalized person to another. The Kafka who opens a letter with a command that she "look" ("Sehen Sie") at his nakedness certainly enjoys the ghostliness of the interchange, revels in the fictionality of his appearing before his female correspondent in the nude. There can be definite advantages to kisses that are received by ghosts and therefore never reach their destination, and Kafka knew how to exploit them.

The pages of Kafka's letters to Milena are full of passion—both joy and suffering—directed toward rhetorical acts of covering and uncovering. Naked ghosts and clothed bodies drift across the scene, sometimes in gay advance, as in the letter about lying naked in the deck chair, sometimes in melancholy retreat, as in the following:

> As for physics, I have never understood it anyhow (at best that about the fiery column, that's physics, after all, isn't it?) and the [scales of the world] I don't understand either, and it surely understands me as little (what could such a vast scales do with my 55 Kg. in the nude, they wouldn't notice it, much less be made to move by it), and I'm here just as I was in Vienna and your hand's in mine as long as you leave it there. ~~Franz~~ wrong, F wrong, ~~Thine~~ wrong, nothing more, silence, deep forest [.][26]

26. *LM* 122; *BM* 100–101: "Und nun bitte, Milena, quäle Dich nicht mehr und Physik habe ich nie verstanden (höchstens das von der Feuersäule, das ist doch Physik, nicht?) und die [Waage der Welt] verstehe ich auch nicht und sie versteht mich gewiß ebensowenig (was finge auch eine so ungeheure Waage mit meinem 55 kg Nacktgewicht an, sie merkt es gar nicht und setzt sich deshalb gewiß nicht in Bewegung) und ich bin hier so, wie ich in Wien war, und Deine Hand ist in meiner, so lange Du sie dort läßt. ~~Franz~~ falsch, F falsch, ~~Dein~~ falsch[,] nichts mehr, Stille, tiefer Wald[.]"

Here Kafka's imagery turns his naked body into a ghost indeed, a tiny thing of such immeasurably small significance that its presence is essentially undetectable by the "scales of the world." Here, Kafka's rhetorical nakedness has nothing of the sly eroticism of the early letter; now it is nothing but vulnerability. But this body, now reduced to virtually nothing, is asserted to be "here just as I was in Vienna" in a seeming attempt to reassure Milena of their continued spiritual intimacy. The gesture is hopelessly undercut by what precedes it; what Kafka insists is "here" is only a ghost. The figure that insists that "your hand's in mine" stands already deconstructed by the foregoing radical devaluation of the body to which his hand belongs.

Kafka closes his letter by parading past his ghostly correspondent a series of ghostly selves decked out in transparent coverings: the self-identifying labels, *Franz, F,* and *Dein* are all presented under erasure, coyly covered over by a mark that leaves them, after all, quite visible underneath. All these labels are not only crossed out, they are also themselves labeled as "wrong" ("falsch"), with the implication that they are insufficient substitutes for—what? For the hand of the fifty-five-kilogram bare body previously described? Or for the nothingness ("nichts mehr"), the "silence" ("Stille") and "deep forest" ("tiefer Wald") that are presented as the final substitute? There would seem to be only a void remaining in the place where the letter writer normally names himself, a void that, because it is "deep," might be understood as more valuable than full presence. Still, the name Franz and the lover's promise "thine" peek out from behind their lines of deletion: the naked body, even if it weighs a mere fifty-five kilograms and makes no mark on the scales of the world, shows itself and has its impact.

Kafka's characterization of letter writing as ghosts denuding themselves in front of other ghosts is an apt description of every act of rhetorical inscription. The interplay of presence and absence that troubles Kafka so much toward the end of his relationship with Milena, which he associates with the "possibility of writing letters," is always visible at the seam between structures of language and structures of experience. Because Kafka's life took place almost entirely at this seam, it is little wonder that he knew the territory so well. No matter where we look in his writing, we find this particular sensitivity displayed. Kafka understood perfectly that rhetoric might at any moment allow the uncanny transformation of the absent into the present, or vice versa. In the following example, we can understand how the transformation can be both amusing and distressing at once:

> What I said about your "lecture" was indeed in earnest [*ernst*] (again and again "Ernest" [*ernst*] squeezes itself [or himself] into the letter. Perhaps I do him an injustice—I can't think about this—terrible injustice, but almost equally strong is the feeling that I'm now bound up with him and more and more closely, I almost said: in Life and Death. If only I could talk to him! But I'm afraid of him, he's very superior to me. You know, Milena, when you went to him you took a large step down from your level, but if you come to me you'll leap into the abyss. Are you aware of this? No, that wasn't my "height" in that letter, but yours)—I was speaking about the "lecture," it was also meant in earnest [*ernst*] by you, I'm sure I'm not wrong about this.[27]

It is important to the structure of this passage that Kafka cites the word *ernst* (in quotation marks, uncapitalized) and the name Ernst as the force pushing its way into the letter. What Kafka does is in effect to "undress" the signifier, previously clothed in its ordinary meaning of "serious," and present it as a bare vocabulary item. Only in the following sentence about doing "him" an injustice does he reclothe the word with the new and distressing meaning of Ernst, the name of Milena's husband. It is because the word *ernst* insinuates itself into Kafka's letter that the topic of the man named Ernst, a topic Kafka and Milena might prefer to avoid, continually reasserts itself. The previous paragraph had begun with Kafka's reproaching Milena for "taking all my silly jokes. . . in earnest,"[28] and this one ends with the assertion that Milena has meant her "lecture" in earnest. The ubiquity of the word in the text acts as an uncanny reminder of the presence of a person whom both correspondents could wish to be absent. No

---

27. *LM* 59–60; *BM* 43: "Was ich über Deine 'Rede' gesagt habe, war allerdings ernst (immer wieder schiebt sich 'ernst' in den Brief. Ich tue ihm vielleicht—ich kann darüber nicht nachdenken—schreckliches Unrecht, aber fast ebenso stark ist das Gefühl, daß ich nun mit ihm verbunden bin und immer fester, fast hätte ich gesagt: auf Leben und Tod. Könnte ich mit ihm sprechen! Aber ich fürchte mich vor ihm, er ist mir sehr überlegen. Weißt Du, Milena, als Du zu ihm gingst, bist Du einen großen Schritt von Deiner Ebene hinabgegangen, kommst Du aber zu mir, so springst Du in die Tiefe. Weißt Du das? Nein, das war nicht meine 'Höhe' in jenem Brief, sondern Deine)—von der 'Rede' sprach ich, sie war von Dir ernst gemeint, darin kann ich doch nicht irren."

28. *LM* 59; *BM* 42: "Du nimmst ja alle meine Späße . . . ernst."

wonder Kafka feels "bound up with him more and more closely": the more serious he becomes, the more he is Ernst.

The man named Kafka could not help but be sensitive to the rhetorical aspect of a man named Ernst. The interconnection of the personal and the linguistic was a fact of life that Kafka acknowledges again and again. Indeed, the opening paragraph of the letter under discussion contains a lengthy parenthetical excursus on Milena's name read as a phonological figure:

> Today something which perhaps explains a number of things, Milena (what a rich heavy name, almost too full to be lifted, and in the beginning I didn't like it much, it seemed to me a Greek or Roman gone astray in Bohemia, violated by Czech, cheated of its accent, and yet in colour and form it is marvellously a woman, a woman whom one carries in one's arms out of the world, out of the fire, I don't know which, and she presses herself willingly and trustingly into your arms, only the strong accent on the "i" is bad, doesn't the name keep leaping away from you? Or is it perhaps only the lucky leap which you yourself make with your burden?)[29]

Kafka the German speaker finds too many syllables after the stress, and the name therefore seems "too full." But this and other phonological features of the name he interprets in relation to the personal qualities of the woman, who "leaps away" on the unaccustomed stress pattern. Even this word that provides Kafka with no opportunity for autonomasia participates in an elaborate play of figuration that makes its phonological structure congruent with his experience of her personality. Language and life merge and blend, and it is no longer possible to determine where one leaves off and the other begins.

One of the most touching and revealing moments in the correspondence with Milena displays especially well this rhetorical merger. The circumstances around which this moment revolves are typically trivial: apparently Milena and Franz had very different tastes in furni-

29. *LM* 58; *BM* 41: "Heute etwas, was vielleicht manches erklärt, Milena (was für ein reicher, schwerer Name, vor Fülle kaum zu heben und gefiel mir anfangs nicht sehr, schien mir ein Grieche oder Römer, nach Böhmen verirrt, tschechisch vergewaltigt, in der Betonung betrogen und ist doch wunderbar in Farbe und Gestalt eine Frau, die man auf den Armen trägt aus der Welt, aus dem Feuer, ich weiß nicht, und sie drückt sich willig und vertrauend dir in die Arme nur der Starke Ton auf dem 'i' ist arg, springt dir der Name nicht wieder fort? Oder ist das vielleicht nur der Glücksprung, den du selbst machst mit deiner Last?)"

ture and had had some disagreement about a certain wardrobe. Milena seems to have brought this issue up in one of her letters, and Kafka takes up the topic with a very light touch and with characteristic rhetorical complexity:

> Yes, the wardrobe. It will probably be the object of our first and last fight. I'll say: "Let's throw it out." You'll say: "It must stay." I'll say: "Choose between it and me." You'll say: "At once. *Frank* and *Schrank*, they rhyme. I choose the wardrobe." "Good," I'll say, and slowly descend the stairs (which?) and—if I haven't found the Danube canal, I'll still be alive today.
> And as a matter of fact I'm all in favour of the wardrobe.[30]

This is at once both an expertly contrived piece of defusing rhetoric and a somewhat disquieting example of self-revelation. Rhetoricians will recognize it as a classic example of prolepsis, that is, of anticipating one's interlocutor's discourse in such a way as to divest it of power. Kafka was particularly fond of this strategy, especially because it was well suited to letters, his favored mode of communication. Prolepsis provides a way of engaging in an intimate dialogue with a person who is in fact not present at all; the writer simply projects the addressee as a fictional voice within his own discourse. Ordinarily in forensic rhetoric, the debater tries to make the fictional voice of his opponent as realistic as possible, to present the opponent's actual arguments if not his actual words. Because the goal is to counter the antagonist's arguments in advance, one does not want to waste time countering points the antagonist would not in fact make. Kafka makes use of this kind of prolepsis—with a twist—at the close of the "Letter to His Father," to be discussed shortly. Here Kafka's goal is not to counter any argument Kafka thinks Milena might make but rather to prevent her from wanting to bring up this topic at all. He disposes of it by making far too much of it, by raising the stakes to a level at which he can feel certain that Milena will not want to play.

The key device in raising the stakes is one typical in jokes—and

---

30. *LM* 141, *BM* 118–119: "Ja, der Schrank. Um den wird wohl unser erster und letzter Streit gehn. Ich werde sagen: 'Wir werfen ihn hinaus,' Du wirst sagen: 'Er bleibt.' Ich werde sagen: 'Wähle zwischen mir und ihm,' Du wirst sagen: 'Gleich, Frank und Schrank, es reimt sich. Ich wähle den Schrank.' 'Gut,' werde ich sagen, und langsam die Treppe (welche?) hinuntergehn und — wenn ich den Donaukanal noch nicht gefunden habe, lebe ich noch heute.' Und im übrigen bin ich ja sehr für den Schrank."

indeed Kafka is presenting this whole paragraph as a sort of joke. The device is "the old switch." The issue is supposed to be the *Schrank*, but Kafka uses another ancient rhetorical device, paronomasia, to transform the issue into Frank, himself. A person is substituted for an object, with the underlying assumption that the two are really in some fundamental way equivalent. It is outrageous and therefore funny, and we can be sure that Kafka expected Milena to smile over the joke. At the same time, however, experienced readers of Kafka's writing, Milena among them, might suspect that the assumption underlying the joke is not so very outrageous, coming from a Czech-speaking person called Kafka. The name itself already suggests the equivalence of the human and the nonhuman that the Frank/Schrank joke assumes. The verbal structure that makes the joke possible therefore conforms to and repeats a structure of experience in which the human and nonhuman become inextricably mixed together somewhere deep inside Kafka's personality. The principle that generates the apparently lighthearted "Frank-Schrank" switch is exactly the same as that which generated the metamorphosis of Gregor Samsa into a monstrous vermin and the transformation of "judgments" into "sentences" in the diary entry of 1911.

Another feature that complicates and deepens the rhetoric of this passage is the melancholy literary echo that Kafka consciously or unconsciously planted in his discourse. When he has Milena say, "*Frank und Schrank, es reimt sich*" ("*Frank* and *Schrank*, they rhyme"), Kakfa alludes to a similar phrase from one of his favorite authors, Heinrich von Kleist. The famous, not to say notorious, excuse given by Penthesilea for her desecration of Achilles' body runs, "Küsse, Bisse, / Das reimt sich, und wer recht von Herzen liebt, / Kann schon das eine für das andre greifen."[31] Kafka thus makes his fictional Milena into a semihumorous version of the Amazon queen: "Frank und Schrank, es reimt sich, und wer recht von Herzen liebt kann schon das eine für das andre greifen." Milena's choice of the wardrobe over the person would thus be a kind of paradoxical proof of her love for the man whom she is rejecting. The allusion is apt in another way: as Kafka spins out this fiction of the Schrank, the consequences of the rhyming substitution are potentially fatal for him, as they were for Achilles. "If I haven't found the Danube canal, I'll still be alive today," he explains.

31. Vv. 2981–2983. Literally translated: "Kissing, biting, they rhyme, and one who loves right from the heart can readily take one for the other."

This is, of course, a parodistic use of the sentimental cliché of the rejected lover, but the comedy is mostly on the surface. Because we know that Kafka more than once thought about ending his life by drowning, the joke tends to stick in the throat.

The sentence about the *Donaukanal* makes an additional contribution to the complexity of the passage by confusing the temporal structure. For the most part, Kafka writes here in the future tense, as is in keeping with a proleptic discourse. But in this sentence, where we would expect Kakfa to say something like, "Wenn ich den Donaukanal nicht finde, werde ich weiterleben," events that had previously been presented as projected in the future are suddenly moved to the past. The whole fiction is suddenly shifted from hypothesis to history, from speculation to accomplished fact. This is no great shock in a text proposing that a Schrank is a suitable substitute for a person, but the thought is still worth noting. Here, as elsewhere in Kafka's works, the act of writing is made to stand in for the event it relates. Although the events may not have actually taken place, the narration has, and the writing on the page can lend its reality to the narrated action by metonymy. Anticipation can become recollection by means of inscription. The written fiction of experience slips quietly into the role of experience itself, and "life" might mean no more or less than "that which is written."

It is not just the capper on the joke, then, when Kafka declares himself in favor of the Schrank. The object has the same sort of advantages over the person that a text has over events: it is more controllable, less threatening, less likely to cause major trouble. Kafka's occasional preference for objects over living things receives candid expression in one of the early letters to Felice, where he notes some of the advantages of the former over the latter:

> There are times when my longing for you overwhelms me. The case [containing a photograph of Felice] is ripped open, and in a friendly and charming manner you at once present yourself to my insatiable scrutiny. . . . And because this little photograph is so inexhaustible, it actually produces as much pleasure as pain. It does not fade away, it does not disintegrate like a living thing; instead it will survive forever, a permanent comfort; it cannot altogether satisfy me, but it won't leave me, either.[32]

---

32. *LB* 127; *BF* 211: "Manchmal geht mir das Verlangen nach Dir an die Kehle. Das Täschchen wird aufgerissen und freundlich und lieb zeigst Du Dich gleich

Although the trace of the person cannot entirely replace the person it represents, it behaves in a more predictable way. It produces no anxiety because it does not threaten loss. Furthermore, it offers the convenience of retiring to its little case when it is no longer needed. It will not come bursting out of its own accord, as the Gregor insect does, to the chagrin of his relatives. Gregor Samsa the bug is somewhat less trouble for his family than Gregor the person had been, but he is even less trouble as a corpse. There is no question that the metamorphosis of Gregor into a dead object is a great boon to the rest of the Samsas. But Kafka knows that he cannot, on this side of the grave, make himself wholly into a harmless and therefore desirable object. He can make himself only into text and that at best partially. Frank can become a Schrank only in discourse. But Kafka can never live a life uncontaminated by rhetoric, either; he can never, that is, experience himself apart from structures of language.

The conversion of intractable persons into more readily manipulable texts is part of Kafka's strategy for dealing with both himself and others. The most dramatic example of such a rhetorization of a human being occurs in the stunning conclusion to the "Letter to His Father," where an apparently standard use of forensic prolepsis suddenly swerves off into something else. The prolepsis begins in an ordinary way: "If you look back at the reasons I offer for the fear I have of you, you might answer: 'You maintain I make things easy for myself by explaining my relation to you simply as being your fault, but I believe that despite your outward effort, you make things not more difficult for yourself but much more profitable.'"[33] The fictional father then goes on to argue that Franz's major effort in the letter has been to make himself appear magnanimous and forgiving, whereas in fact he has behaved more like a vermin (*Ungeziefer*) than an honest antagonist. The paternal voice accuses Franz of being "unfit for life" (*Lebensuntüchtig*) and of making this unfitness comfortable for

---

dem unersättlichen Blick. . . . Und daß dies Bildchen so unerschöpflich ist, das ist freilich ebensoviel Freude wie Leid. Es vergeht nicht, es löst sich nicht auf wie Lebendiges, dafür aber bleibt es wieder für immer erhalten und ein dauernder Trost, es will mich nicht durchdringen, aber es verläßt mich auch nicht."

33. *LF* 120–121: "Du könntest, wenn Du meine Begründung der Furcht, die ich vor Dir habe, überblickst, antworten: 'Du behauptest, ich mache es mir leicht, wenn ich mein Verhältnis zu Dir einfach durch Dein Verschulden erkläre, ich aber glaube, daß Du trotz äußerlicher Anstrengung es Dir zumindest nicht schwerer, aber viel einträglicher machst.'"

himself by making the father responsible for it: "you calmly stretch out and let yourself be hauled through life, physically and mentally, by me."[34] The son in effect lets the father do his dirty work for him, as in the case of the proposed marriage to Julie Wohryzek. Franz, overwhelmed by ambivalence, wanted his father (so the voice argues) to save him the trouble of breaking the engagement by forbidding the marriage. When he did not do so, Franz still blamed the father's antipathy toward Julie for the collapse of the engagement:

> And my consent to your marriage did not prevent your reproaches, for you prove that I am in any case to blame for your not marrying. Basically, however, in this as in everything else you have only proved to me that all my reproaches were justified, and that one especially justified charge was still missing: namely, the charge of insincerity, obsequiousness, and parasitism. If I am not very much mistaken, you are preying on me even with this letter itself.[35]

Thus the recital of the fictional father's objections reaches a conclusion.

The prolepsis is remarkable enough in itself, but the reply that Kafka then makes to it is both typical and unanswerable: "My answer to this is that, after all, this whole rejoinder—which can partly be turned against you—does not come from you, but from me."[36] This turn pulls the rug out from under the prolepsis by drawing attention to its rhetorical nature. Kafka's ultimate assault on the figure of his father—the figure he has created in the text of the letter—is to assert its fictionality. Herrmann may be the father of Franz, but Franz is the "father of the word," as the Greeks called the author of an utterance, and therefore in this case the origin of Herrmann. This assertion effectively inverts the charge made by the father figure in the prolep-

34. *LF* 122–123: "Du aber streckst Dich ruhig aus und läßt Dich, körperlich und geistig, von mir durchs Leben schleifen."

35. *LF* 124–125: "Und meine Erlaubnis zur Heirat hat Deine Vorwürfe nicht verhindert, denn Du beweist ja, daß ich auf jeden Fall an Deinem Nichtheiraten schuld bin. Im Grunde aber hast Du hier und in allem anderen für mich nichts anderes bewiesen, als daß alle meine Vorwürfe berechtigt waren und daß unter ihnen noch ein besonders berechtiger Vorwurf gefehlt hat, nämlich der Vorwurf der Unaufrichtigkeit, der Liebdienerei, des Schmarotzertums. Wenn ich nicht sehr irre, schmarotzest Du an mir noch mit diesem Brief als solchem."

36. *Ibid.*: "Darauf antworte ich, daß zunächst dieser ganze Einwurf, der sich zum Teil auch gegen Dich kehren läßt, nicht von Dir stammt, sondern eben von mir."

sis: although Franz may be "sponging" (*schmarotzen*) off his father both economically and emotionally, the father appears as a textual parasite on the son's bountiful text.

Kafka's strategy is both surprising and effective because it employs prolepsis in its standard forensic form but drives it one step further than the norm. In the "ordinary" use of prolepsis, the orator disarms his opponent by as it were borrowing the opponent's arguments in advance in order to answer them: "You will say X, but in reply I can answer Y." Kafka turns this borrowing into outright appropriation, a tactic that the debater would probably want to avoid. After all, standard prolepsis would be severely undermined by the admission that the arguments ascribed to the adversary were not in fact the adversary's but one's own. It would be a confession that one was engaged in a dialogue with oneself and not with one's antagonist. For Kafka, however, this confession represents an act of aggression against the figure of the father, now unmasked as a textual dummy on which ventriloquist Franz has projected his own voice.

But the act of aggression is also directed against himself and in a number of ways. First of all, as he is careful to note, "not even your mistrust of others is as great as my self-mistrust,"[37] as is demonstrated by the extremely well-aimed thrusts of the proleptic rejoinder. If Franz and not Herrmann is the origin of these barbs, then Franz has dealt himself a number of serious blows. But more important— though unexpressed—is the aggression the unmasking carries out against the entire project of the "Letter." If it is true that the father of the prolepsis is no more or less than Franz's creation, what about the father depicted in the rest of the letter? Is the reader (whether Herrmann, or Franz himself, or we eavesdroppers) not encouraged to nourish some suspicions about the authenticity of the whole presentation of the father, from beginning to end? After all, Franz's creation encompasses not just "this whole rejoinder" but this whole letter as well.

Kafka undermines the project of his letter in the sense that he implies that the father figure is no more than a straw man. At the same time, though, he asserts that, "with the correction made by this rejoinder [that is, the prolepsis] . . . , in my opinion something has

37. Ibid.: "So groß ist ja nicht einmal Dein Mißtrauen gegen andere, wie mein Selbstmißtrauen."

been achieved which so closely approximates the truth that it might reassure us both a little and make our living and our dying easier."[38] The term *Korrektur*, used here in the sense of "revision," is also familiar to authors as the designation for "proofsheets." This latter meaning underscores the textuality of the prolepsis once again but suggests now that this very element contributes to the veracity of the letter. Its truth may lie in its quality as a proofsheet. The "revision" provided by the prolepsis may reside less in its arguments than in its rhetoricity.

At the level of rhetoric, Kafka's letter asserts exactly what its explicit argument seems to deny: that is, a fundamental similarity between father and son. If Franz has reason to fear his father, as he says he does in the opening lines, part of the fear may arise as much from the kinship between them as from the obvious differences. Consider this half-admiring, half-accusatory statement: "Your extremely effective rhetorical methods in bringing me up, which never failed to work with me, were: abuse, threats, irony, spiteful laughter, and—oddly enough—self-pity."[39] Franz gives examples of all these rhetorical forms, demonstrating in detail his father's mastery of them. What he does not mention is that the letter as a whole shows equally well Franz's own great skill with most of these same methods. If Herrmann was an expert practitioner of the art of rhetorical manipulation, Franz was an apt pupil. Although Franz does not directly abuse or threaten his father in the letter, he certainly does attack him with irony, hyperbole, and, oddly enough, self-pity. Just as he makes self-pitying complaint (*Selbstbeklagung*) the father's ultimate rhetorical weapon, so does he employ it himself as the letter's most typical and most effective mode of attack. One could indeed argue that the letter is almost nothing but Selbstbeklagung from beginning to end, with the culminating prolepsis unveiled as the most abjectly self-pitying passage of all.

What Kafka complains most loudly about in his father is a kind of rhetorical exploitation in which the son equaled or exceeded his par-

38. Ibid.: "Mit der Korrektur, die sich durch diesen Einwurf ergibt . . . ist meiner Meinung nach doch etwas der Wahrheit so sehr Angenähertes erreicht, daß es uns beide ein wenig beruhigen und Leben und Sterben leichter machen kann."

39. *LF* 34–35: "Deine äußerst wirkungsvollen, wenigstens mir gegenüber niemals versagenden rednerischen Mittel bei der Erziehung waren: Schimpfen, Drohen, Ironie, böses Lachen und—merkwürdigerweise—Selbstbeklagung."

ent. I am particularly drawn to the paragraph toward the letter's end where Franz analogizes his father's ambivalence to a children's game:

> The fundamental thought behind both attempts at marriage was quite sound: to set up house, to become independent. An idea that does appeal to you, only in reality it always turns out like the children's game in which one holds and even grips the other's hand, calling out: "Oh, go away, go away, why don't you go away?" Which in our case happens to be complicated by the fact that you have always honestly meant this "go away!" and have always unknowingly held me, or rather held me down, only by the strength of your personality.[40]

This analogy is stunningly apt and instantly recognizable as an example typical of Kafkan rhetoricity. It describes perfectly the ambivalence of a man who goes to a nudist resort and wears a bathing suit or of one who gives instructions about the destruction of his manuscripts to the one person in the world least likely to carry them out. As Kafka specifies here, the intention behind the utterance is both genuine and not genuine at the same time and puts the addressee in a rhetorical space exactly like that of Joseph K. in the first chapter of *The Trial*, a space in which Kafka quite clearly felt himself to exist. What he does not specify here, but only suggests later, is that as often as not he puts himself into that space. He throws himself into the rhetorical briar patch, even as in this letter he holds tightly to his father's arm while insisting, "Let me go, let me go, why don't you let me go?"

Franz shows himself to be, in a fundamental and inescapable sense, made of his father's rhetoric, or rather, he makes himself out of it by taking it more seriously than it could possibly have been intended even when he knows that the intention differs from the words. He recalls the power of his father's totally baseless threats: "How terrible for me was, for instance, that 'I'll tear you apart like a fish,' although I knew, of course, that nothing worse was to follow (admittedly, as a little child I didn't know that), but it was almost exactly in accord with my notions of your power, and I saw you as being capable of doing

40. *LF* 108–111: "Der Grundgedanke beider Heiratsversuche war ganz korrekt: einen Hausstand gründen, selbständig werden. Ein Gedanke, der Dir ja sympathisch ist, nur daß es dann in Wirklichkeit so ausfällt wie das Kinderspiel, wo einer die Hand des anderen hält und sogar preßt und dabei ruft: 'Ach geh doch, geh doch, warum gehst Du nicht?' Was sich allerdings in unserem Fall dadurch kompliziert hat, daß Du das 'geh doch!' seit jeher ehrlich gemeint hast, da Du ebenso seit jeher, ohne es zu wissen, nur kraft Deines Wesens mich gehalten oder richtiger niedergehalten hast."

this, too."[41] Life always seemed on the verge of merging with language, even outrageously hyperbolic language. Often enough, if we may judge by the letters and diaries, it seemed to Kafka as if it already had.

41. *LF* 34–37: "Schrecklich war mir zum Beispiel dieses: 'Ich zerrisse Dich wie einen Fisch,' trotzdem ich ja wußte, daß dem nichts Schlimmeres nachfolgte (als kleines Kind wußte ich das allerdings nicht), aber es entsprach fast meinen Vorstellungen von Deiner Macht, daß Du auch das imstande gewesen wärest."

Chapter 10

THE PASSION OF READING

My argument in a nutshell is that Kafka's activity as a writer is based on his reading and specifically on a mode of reading that confronts and exploits the potential of discourse understood as rhetoric. This activity of reading, along with the writing that results from it, is a passion for Kafka in that it is both the object of an obsessive desire and the cause of endless pain. It tortures him, but he cannot live without it. Like the hunger artist's fasting, this passion of reading is an ascesis that, because it is not perceived as the result of free choice, cannot be assigned with certainty to the categories of goodness, truth, and beauty, though that is where the artist devoutly wishes it could belong. It is an art that, because it results from an absolute necessity within the artist, either goes beyond art or falls short of it. Kafka's writing develops from a passion exactly congruent with Schleiermacher's definition of the passion of jealousy (*Eifersucht*): "die Leidenschaft, die mit Eifer sucht, was Leiden schafft" ("the passion that zealously seeks that which brings pain").

Kafka found a particularly suggestive image for his art in the singing or "piping" (*Pfeifen*) practiced by the mouse Josephine. "This piping of hers," asserts the narrator, "is no piping,"[1] in spite of the fact that Josephine's piping is in fact indistinguishable in a crowd from

---

1. *CS* 362; *SE* 174: "Was sie pfeift, ist kein Pfeifen." (The implication is that she may be whistling "Dixie," but she's not "just whistling 'Dixie.'")

THE PASSION OF READING 235

that of any other mouse. Kafka's art, when examined closely, partakes of a similar paradox: although it presents some of the most original fiction in our tradition, it is very often based on clichés and commonplaces. The arrestingly innovative "Metamorphosis" takes its beginning from "gemeine Sprache," from a vulgar trope equating a person with a verminous insect. When Herrmann Kafka called the actor Löwy an Ungeziefer, he was engaged in everyday piping; when Franz Kafka's text calls Gregor Samsa an Ungeziefer, it produces something else, a piping that indeed "is no piping" any more.

Even the term *pfeifen* that Kafka uses to designate Josephine's art is drawn from the commonplace piping of gemeine Sprache, as Josephine herself reminds us when she complains to her audience, "Your protection isn't worth an old song" ("ich pfeife auf euren Schutz").[2] Pfeifen is thus a contemptuous, abusive use of language, a kind of aggressive rhetoric that Kafka knew well and about which he complained in the "Letter to His Father." Calling someone a louse (or Ungeziefer) or an "old crow" ("alter Rabe"), or even complaining that one's coal bucket is so light one can ride on it—all of this piping is transformed by an animal pest (a mouse, a kavka) into an art that is arguably not art at all. It is only fitting that, when Josephine pipes, her audience sits "quiet as a mouse" (*mäuschenstill*) listening to her. They are necessarily made a part of an act of rhetorical reading.

Josephine and the hunger artist are passionate readers in two ways: (1) because what they do both is and is not special; and (2) because the ultimate practice of their art must be a kind of self-effacement. Both the hunger artist and Josephine, we are led to believe, do only what comes naturally, but both still seek recognition and even admiration for what they do. Both figures combine uniqueness and ordinariness in a way that Kafka could well have understood from personal experience. We learn that the hunger artist's unique talent for starvation is quite ordinary in that he would have eaten if he could only have found food he liked, and we discover that Josephine's unique talent is to do what everyone else does all the time and to demand recognition for it. The logical extension of both talents leads to the dissolution of the artistic self, because the hunger artist can starve indefinitely only in death ("in his dimming eyes remained the firm though no longer

2. CS 365; SE 176. See Heinz Politzer, *Franz Kafka: Parable and Paradox* (Ithaca: Cornell University Press, 1962), 310.

proud persuasion that he was still continuing to fast"),[3] and the value of Josephine's song can be recognized only once it has been transformed into a memory ("Was it even in her lifetime more than a simple memory?").[4]

Such an art is both necessary and impossible. Thus Kafka presents it in the fictions of his last years, and thus he presents it in some of the very earliest of his personal writings. A letter from November 1903 addressed to Oskar Pollak describes an ambivalence from which Kafka would suffer his whole life long:

> By the way, no writing's been done for some time. It's this way with me: God doesn't want me to write, but I—I must. So there's an everlasting up and down; after all, God is the stronger, and there's more anguish in it than you can imagine. So many powers within me are tied to a stake, which might possibly grow into a green tree. Released, they could be useful to me and the country. But nobody ever shook a millstone from around his neck by complaining, especially when he was fond of it.[5]

This is Kafka's passion, an irresistible love for something that causes him to suffer "more anguish than you can imagine." It is set here in the immediate context of a description of his writing, but of course that same passion drives the reading from which the writing derives. The relation of this suffering to the reading process is suggested by the larger context in which this discussion of writing appears. The topic of his own writing occurs to Kafka here as an amplificaton on the subject of his reading, a comment on which precedes the material just quoted: "I am reading Fechner, Eckehart. Some books seem like a key to unfamiliar rooms in one's own castle."[6] The metaphor of read-

---

3. *CS* 277; *SE* 171: "Noch in seinen gebrochenen Augen war die feste, wenn auch nicht mehr stolze Überzeugung, daß er weiterhungre."

4. *CS* 376; *SE* 185: "War es denn noch bei ihren Lebzeiten mehr als eine bloße Erinnerung?"

5. *LE* 10; *BR* 21: "Übrigens ist schon eine lange Zeit nichts geschrieben worden. Es geht mir damit so: Gott will nicht, daß ich schreibe, ich aber, ich muß. So ist es ein ewiges Auf und Ab, schließlich ist doch Gott der Stärkere und es ist mehr Unglück dabei, als Du Dir denken kannst. So viele Kräfte sind in mir an einen Pflock gebunden, aus dem vielleicht ein grüner Baum wird, während sie freigemacht mir und dem Staat nützlich sein könnten. Aber durch Klagen schüttelt man keine Mühlsteine vom Halse, besonders wenn man sie lieb hat." On this passage see also Gerhart Kurz, "Schnörkel und Schleier und Warzen: Die Briefe Kafkas an Oskar Pollak und seine literarischen Anfänge," *DJK*, 96.

6. *LE* 10; *BR* 20: "Ich lese Fechner, Eckehart. Manches Buch wirkt wie ein Schlüssel zu fremden Sälen des eigenen Schlosses."

ing that Kafka employs is familiar in the sense that an analogy is often drawn between reading and a process of opening up the doors of richly furnished but hitherto unknown rooms. Perhaps less commonplace is the notion that the "foreign" (*fremd*) rooms that reading makes accessible belong to the structure of the self. This self is figured as a castle (*Schloß*), that is, an independent unit capable of being closed off to the outside world. The castle encloses and protects what belongs to it from everything foreign. It is curious—and potentially very distressing—to discover that within the enclosure the alien and unfamiliar has already established itself. Reading, then, makes familiar some of these unfamiliar places within the self, though at the same time it inevitably reminds the reader of the possibility of additional foreign elements inside the castle keep. Such reading presupposes a divided self, a psyche that is not fully present to itself and therefore inevitably remains unaware of the contents and even the very existence of all the mysterious rooms that make it up. Part of the passion of reading resides in the combination of anxiety and elation that accompanies the discovery of such rooms.

Kafka demonstrates the connection to reading of his writing, and of the divisive mental state that writing requires, in at times the most direct and even abrupt fashion, but at other times he resorts to figuration. The following passage from the second octavo notebook describes an apparently intimate relation between the act of reading and the multiplication of selves we are familiar with from "Description of a Struggle," "A Country Doctor," and other fictions:

> My two hands began a fight. They slammed [shut] the book I was reading and thrust it aside so that it should not be in the way. Me they saluted, and appointed me referee. And an instant later they had locked fingers with each other and were already rushing away over the edge of the table, now to the right, now to the left, according to which of them was bringing most pressure to bear on the other. I never turned my gaze from them. If they are my hands, I must referee fairly, otherwise I shall bring down on myself the agonies of a wrong decision. But my function is not easy, in the darkness between the palms of the hands various holds are brought into play that I must not let pass unnoticed, and so I press my chin on the table and now nothing escapes me.[7]

7. *WP* 67–68; *HO* 67–68: "Meine zwei Hände begannen einen Kampf. Das Buch, in dem ich gelesen hatte, klappten sie zu und schoben es beiseite, damit es nicht störe. Mir salutierten sie und ernannten mich zum Schiedsrichter. Und schon hatten sie die Finger ineinander verschränkt und schon jagten sie am Tischrand hin, bald nach rechts, bald nach links, je nach dem Überdruck der

Although the ostensible battle is waged between the narrator's two hands, the most urgent concern in the narrative centers on the differing roles of the wrestling hands, on the one side, and the refereeing first-person consciousness of the other. The split is presented as beginning with an act of reading (a book), and in fact it does: the possibility of understanding the self as a controlling or mediating force attempting to adjust and at times keep in check various bodily organs is part of the rhetoric of everyday language. The second sentence—which, we need to remember, would be quite ordinary in another context—sets forth a grammatical distinction between the "I" who had been reading the book and the "they" who close it and thrust it aside. Here, as in countless expressions of daily discourse, parts of the body are placed in a separate grammatical category from the person to whom they belong. The "fight" begins when the hands usurp the role of reader, throw away the text the "I" was reading, and instead read the commonplace text that describes their own actions. They insist, that is, on the independence that language ascribes to them.

The independent action of the hands opens up a potential rift in the unity of the self that grammar has already taken for granted. When the narrator expresses concern about being a fair referee lest he should "bring down on myself the agonies of a wrong decision," his logic assumes that the hands are a part of "myself." The opening of the sentence, however, casts doubt on such an assumption, as the narrator openly voices his uncertainty as to whose hands these really are. The form of his expression actually complicates matters by multiplying even further the distinct entities separable from the self. In addition to the narrating "I" and the two third-person hands, there is now a potential object, "myself" (*mir*), hovering somewhere between the observing consciousness and the observed body. The text then proceeds to suggest a further alienation of the hands from the "I" by calling their palms *Handteller* instead of the more usual *Handflächen*. *Teller* ("plates") are after all exactly the sort of objects one would expect to find on a table leading an existence quite independent of

---

einen oder der andern. Ich ließ keinen Blick von ihnen. Sind es meine Hände, muß ich ein gerechter Richter sein, sonst halse ich mir selbst die Leiden eines falschen Schiedsspruchs auf. Aber mein Amt ist nicht leicht, im Dunkel zwischen den Handtellern werden verschiedene Kniffe angewendet, die ich nicht unbeachtet lassen darf, ich drücke deshalb das Kinn an den Tisch und nun ergeht mir nichts."

one's own. Naturally one does not expect either plates or the palms of hands to employ various "tricky holds" (*Kniffe*), but this anthropomorphism is justified logomimetically by a rhetorical slide from the Kniffe ("creases") that all palms really do display.

Kafka's description of the struggle continues, complicating matters further:

> All my life long I have made a favourite of the right, without meaning the left any harm. If the left had ever said anything, indulgent and just as I am, I should at once have put a stop to the abuse. But it never grumbled, it hung down from me, and while, say, the right was raising my hat in the street, the left was timidly fumbling down my thigh. That was a bad way of preparing for the struggle that is now going on. How in the long run, left wrist, will you resist the pressure of this powerful right hand? How maintain your girlish finger's stand in the grip of the five others? This seems to me to be no longer a fight, but the natural end of the left hand. Even now it has been pushed to the extreme left rim of the table, and the right is pounding regularly up and down on it like the piston of an engine.[8]

The reader is likely to accept without protest the extension of the hands' independent existence as separate personalities into the realm of human speech. After all, the narrator does not claim that his hand actually said something: on the contrary, he laments that it never did, that it never *muckste*, that is, never grumbled, sulked, muttered, stirred, or flinched. Because we can understand surprise at its never stirring, we can accept as well the narrator's surprise that it never grumbled.

In the meantime, the narrator has suggested yet another self-division within what is left of the unified psyche. While protesting that, in spite of a lifelong preference for the right hand, he is at heart even-handed, his rhetoric asserts the opposite. The word he uses to say that

8. WP 68; HO 68: "Mein Leben lang habe ich die Rechte, ohne es gegen die Linke böse zu meinen, bevorzugt. Hätte doch die Linke einmal etwas gesagt, ich hätte, nachgiebig und rechtlich wie ich bin, gleich den Mißbrauch eingestellt. Aber sie muckste nicht, hing an mir hinunter und während etwa die Rechte auf der Gasse meinen Hut schwang, tastete die Linke ängstlich meinen Schenkel ab. Das war eine schlechte Vorbereitung zum Kampf, der jetzt vor sich geht. Wie willst du auf die Dauer, linkes Handgelenk, gegen dieses gewaltige Rechte Dich stemmen? Wie Deinen mädchenhaften Finger in der Klemme der fünf andern behaupten? Das scheint mir kein Kampf mehr, sondern natürliches Ende der Linken. Schon ist sie in die äußerste linke Ecke des Tisches gedrängt, und an ihr regelmäßig auf und nieder schwingend wie ein Maschinenkolben die Rechte."

he is just, *rechtlich*, contains a subversive pun. A good translation might be "right-minded," implying that the preference for the right (justice) cannot be separated from a preference for the "right" (right hand). In this case, however, right-mindedness requires that one specifically abstain from any preference for the right. By steadfastly maintaining that preference, the "I" divides itself further into conflicting factions, one evenhanded, the other hopelessly prejudiced.

These troubling contradictions in the mind of the "refereeing" consciousness are as nothing, though, in contrast to the violence of the battle between the two hands. Multiplication is taking place in this arena as well. Additional parties have entered the fray, for now not only the hands but also the wrists are involved, and the hands themselves are resolved into sets of fingers. As the narrative progresses, it creates more and more differences—and thus more sources of conflict—spun from the rhetoric of the description itself. An opposition is set up, for example, between the animate, organic left hand and a right hand figuratively transformed into a senselessly pounding mechanism, a *Maschinenkolben* ("piston"). The text also elaborates logomimetically on the grammatically necessary use of the feminine pronoun *sie* to refer to the left hand ("die Hand"). Its femininity is silently transferred from the grammatical to the organic realm; its fingers, weaker than those of the right hand, receive the adjective "girlish" (*mädchenhaft*). The difference in strength between the two antagonists is suddenly accounted for, ex post facto, by an implied difference of gender.

The outcome of such a one-sided battle would be certain defeat, the "natural end of the left hand," were it not for the intervention of a deus ex machina:

> If, confronted with this misery, I had not got the saving idea that these are my own hands and that with a slight jerk I can pull them away from each other and so put an end to the fight and the misery—if I had not got this idea, the left hand would have been broken out of the wrist, would have been flung from the table, and then the right, in the wild recklessness of knowing itself the victor, might have leapt, like five-headed Cerberus, straight into my attentive face. Instead, the two now lie one on top of the other, the right stroking the back of the left, and I, dishonest referee, nod in approval.[9]

9. *WP* 68; *HO* 68–69: "Bekäme ich angesichts dieser Not nicht den erlösenden Gedanken, daß es meine eigenen Hände sind, die hier im Kampf stehen und daß ich sie mit einem leichten Ruck voneinander wegziehen kann und damit Kampf

This conclusion is on the one hand satisfying in its return to the order we posit as normal, with the hands peacefully obeying the controlling will of the superior consciousness, but on the other it is distressing in its further destruction of the unity of that consciousness. Who, we must wonder, is this "I" who suddenly comes up with the idea that the two warring forces are indeed "my own hands"? How can it be the same "I" who has been narrating until now, an "I" whose very first words acknowledge that the opponents are "my two hands"? It has to be the kind of "I" who can say, with literal intent, "I haven't been myself lately," thereby suggesting the radical breakdown of self-presence. "I" didn't know what "I" was doing. The reader is thus confronted with the disquieting paradox that the moment in which the self allegedly reasserts its full self-presence and complete integration is conditioned by the arrival on the scene of a new fragment of that self not previously present.

The intervention of the new power, moreover, brings the violence to only a temporary halt. At the level of the text's rhetoric, the battle goes on and escalates in horror, though now the verbs are configured in the subjunctive. If the narrator had not produced this saving idea, not only would the left hand have suffered the ultimate defeat of being broken off at the wrist, but the victorious right would have turned its fury on the next available body part, the "attentive face." In another rhetorical slide, the *Zügellosigkeit* ascribed to the right hand is read in two ways at once. In terms of the literal facts, the right hand is indeed now *zügellos* in the sense that the left hand ("die Zügelhand") is now missing. But we may also read *Zügellosigkeit* in the ordinary sense of "impetuosity, recklessness" and ascribe to the hand a psyche capable of becoming intoxicated with victory. Its five fingers become the five heads of the hellhound bent on completing the work of self-destruction begun with the breaking of the left wrist.

Nor is the final sentence entirely reassuring. The description of the two hands does indeed present a peaceful scene of a sort of unity, but there is reason to think the unity is only temporary. The fact that "the two now lie one on top of the other" and that the stronger, more

---

und Not beenden—bekäme ich diesen Gedanken nicht, die Linke wäre aus dem Gelenk gebrochen, vom Tisch geschleudert worden und dann vielleicht die Rechte in der Zügellosigkeit des Siegers wie der fünfköpfige Höllenhund mir selbst ins aufmerksame Gesicht gefahren. Statt dessen liegen die zwei jetzt übereinander, die Rechte streichelt den Rücken der Linken und ich unehrlicher Schiedsrichter nicke dazu."

aggressive partner is shown "stroking the back" of the one earlier characterized as "girlish" makes an uncannily erotic image. These two could certainly be properly described as zügellos in the sense of "licentious," though that term was introduced in the context of extreme violence. The cozy, postcoital atmosphere is calm enough for the present, but it promises nothing for the future. Because the peacefulness of the conclusion is presented explicitly as the result of the intervention of a "dishonest referee" and implicitly as a violent "recklessness" temporarily turned to "licentiousness," there is every reason to believe that the self-division of the psyche, with its concomitant tendency toward self-mutilation and even self-destruction, continues even here. The truce between the hands is supervised, after all, by an "I" who is still apart from it all, who from a distance "gives a nod" to what is happening.

One other important element in this extraordinarily rich and powerful little fiction that deserves discussion is the rhetorical charcter of the narrator's role. The most important thing about him, by his own testimony, is his activity as *Schiedsrichter* ("umpire" or "arbitrator") in the struggle between the hands. It is of some moment, then, to determine exactly how the narrator obtained this office he takes so seriously. Ostensibly, he receives it by virtue of an illocutionary act: the hands, we are told, first "saluted" the narrator—as gladiators did the emperor in the Roman circuses—and then "appointed me referee" ("ernannten mich zum Schiedsrichter"). Because the "I" merely describes this act and does not reproduce the act itself, he can make this assertion in perfectly ordinary language. It would hardly have been ordinary, however, if he had attempted to give us the exact locutionary form of this illocutionary act of appointment. Did they say something like "We hereby appoint you referee"? Did they somehow develop voices for this purpose, or did they signal in some kind of sign language? The narrator does not have to say, and it is a good thing for the story that he does not. The narrator is able to finesse the question of the exact nature of this illocution by simply asserting that it took place.

Still, because we cannot imagine quite how the hands managed their act of appointment, there must be some doubt in our minds about the genuineness of the narrator's office. His position is thus very similar to that of Joseph K. in *The Trial* and Landsurveyor K. in *The Castle*. He occupies a status that both does and does not belong to him because it both has and has not been duly granted to him by a

successful illocutionary act. When at the very end the narrator characterizes himself as *unehrlich* ("dishonest, false"), we might wonder for a
moment just what he means. Although we are most likely to assume
that he is suggesting his intervention in ending the fight to have been
arbitrary and thus dishonorable, we might also catch a hint that he is
confessing to be a "false" referee, an impostor, one not having a
legitimate claim to the title. The peculiar status of the hands in the
story forces the reader to wonder whether the act of appointment
ever really took place. Given evidence offered later that the hands do
not speak, even when highly motivated to do so, not to mention our
own "real-life" knowledge that hands do not ordinarily speak, it might
well be that the narrator's "appointment" never took place. The story
also gives evidence, however, that these hands are not ordinary, and
so we are by no means able to assume that they could not have performed a successful illocution. The appointment is a rhetorical act,
leaving the narrator's status permanently undecidable.

The undecidability calls into question the metaphor from which the
fiction is generated. The figure that presents the psyche as a judicial
entity controlling and directing the forces of the body is a variant on
the classic trope of the charioteer with which we are familiar from
Plato's *Phaedrus*. The story of the battling hands undermines the
trope by raising the embarrassing question of the source of the
charioteer's authority. The narrating "referee" presents himself as
governing by consent of—indeed at the insistence of—the governed,
in that he understands the hands to have given him his office. But the
office may never have been given. In any case the circumstances of
the original act of "appointing" are shown by the conclusion to have
been at best odd: if the narrating "I" has the authority to stop the fight
altogether, to dominate the hands so that they no longer act independently, how did the hands come by the power of independent action
(including the action of appointing a referee) in the first place? They
could do so, one must assume, only by some kind of withholding
abandonment of power on the part of the "I." In short, the "I" has
authority only by giving up authority. The charioteer is shown to have
become charioteer only by letting the horses loose and thereby abandoning his role as charioteer.

Kafka's version of the figure insists on the articulation of the self
into a set of parts, but it projects considerable discomfort with the
hierarchy of authority by which tradition has ordered those parts.
The story of the battling hands has the character of a political chroni-

cle, the description of an incipient revolution nipped in the bud. Like so many of Kafka's fictions, it begins in medias res, never commenting on or seriously questioning the origins of the process it narrates, so that we do not know how the hands managed to acquire the power of independent action. The narrator simply discovers that the hands have already initiated the fight. They are like those "unfamiliar rooms" that are to be found in the castle of the self: they are unquestionably parts of the self, but they remain somehow encapsulated and alien. The narrator might appropriately echo Rosa's reaction at the discovery of the horses in the doctor's pigsty: "You never know what you're going to find in your own house." The doctor, like the narrating "referee," reveals himself to be a master of surprisingly little of his personal castle.

The passion of reading is the discovery of a wonderful/awful alien inside the sanctuary of the self. The letter to Pollak of 1903, with its romantic imagery of keys to mysterious rooms, evokes the excitement and joy of such a discovery and only hints at the Bluebeard-like terrors that might accompany it. In Kafka's last story "Der Bau" ("The Burrow)," however, anxiety clearly predominates.[10] Much of the narrative is given over to the burrow-builder's account of his reaction to the discovery of a previously unheard noise deep within his tunnels. At first he is sure that it is only the whistling of "small fry" (*Kleinzeug*), mice or mouselike creatures who infest the burrower's dwelling. Later on, however, either logic or anxiety compels him to another conclusion:

> But what avail all exhortations to be calm; my imagination will not rest, and I have actually come to believe—it is useless to deny it to myself—that the whistling is made by some beast, and moreover not by a great many small ones, but by a single big one. Many signs contradict this.

10. "The Burrow" has attracted considerable critical attention. See, for example, Mark Boulby, "Kafka's End: A Reassessment of 'The Burrow,'" *German Quarterly* 55:2 (1982), 175–185; Marjorie Gelus, "Notes on Kafka's 'Der Bau': Problems with Reality," *Colloquia Germanica* 15 (1982), 98–110; Winfried Kudszus, "Verschüttungen in Kafkas 'Der Bau,'" in Benjamin Bennet, Anton Kaes, and William J. Lillyman, eds., *Probleme der Moderne* (Tübingen: Niemeyer, 1983), 307–317; Britta Maché, "The Noise in the Burrow: Kafka's Final Dilemma," *German Quarterly* 55 (November 1982), 526–540; Verna P. Snyder, "Kafka's 'Burrow': A Speculative Analysis," *Twentieth Century Literature* 27:2 (1981), 113–126; and Beatrice Wehrli, "Monologische Kunst als Ausdruck moderner Welterfahrung: Zu Kafkas Erzählung 'Der Bau,'" *Jahrbuch der Deutschen Schiller-Gesellschaft* 25 (1981), 435–445.

The noise can be heard everywhere and always at the same strength, and moreover uniformly, both by day and night. At first, therefore, one cannot but incline to the hypothesis of a great number of small animals; but as I must have found some of them during my digging and I have found nothing, it only remains for me to assume the existence of a great beast, especially as the things that seem to contradict the hypothesis are merely things which make the beast, not so much impossible, as merely dangerous beyond one's powers of conception.[11]

The explicit suggestion that the large animal of the burrower's hypothesis may be nothing more than a figment of his imagination (*Einbildungskraft*) accentuates rather than relieves the tension of the situation. If the origin of the "great beast" ("großes Tier") is inside the narrator, his peril may be even more acute. Given the nature of this story and of its narrator, it seems most likely that the alien whistler must be a construction of some kind. The title of the narrative is, after all, "Der Bau," which not only or even primarily means "burrow" but refers more generally to constructions of every kind. The word leaves open the possibility of a rhetorical slide by which the narrator's concern with his burrow merges with an anxiety regarding the constructed enemy. The announced topic of the story is thus both the construction in which the narrator lives and the mysterious creature whose traces infest its interior.

Both these constructions are arguably aspects of the narrator's self. The burrower makes clear his identification with the dwelling in an apostrophe: "It is for your sake, ye passages and rooms, and you, Castle Keep, above all, that I have come back, counting my life as nothing in the balance, after stupidly trembling for it for so long, and postponing my return to you. What do I care for danger now that I am with you? You belong to me, I to you, we are united; what can

11. CS 353; SE 383: "Aber was helfen alle Mahnungen zur Ruhe, die Einbildungskraft will nicht stillstehen und ich halte tatsächlich dabei zu glauben—es ist zwecklos, sich das selbst abzuleugnen—, das Zischen stamme von einem Tier und zwar nicht von vielen und kleinen, sondern von einem einzigen großen. Es spricht manches dagegen. Daß das Geräusch überall zu hören ist und immer in gleicher Stärke, und überdies regelmäßig bei Tag und Nacht. Gewiß, zuerst müßte man eher dazu neigen, viele kleine Tiere anzunehmen, da ich sie aber bei meinen Grabungen hätte finden müssen und nicht gefunden habe, bleibt nur die Annahme der Existenz des großen Tieres, zumal das, was der Annahme zu widersprechen scheint, bloß Dinge sind, welche das Tier nicht unmöglich, sondern nur über alle Vorstellbarkeit hinaus gefährlich machen."

harm us?"[12] That these are rhetorical questions is clear enough, especially in Kafka's original German, where there are no question marks. The narrator intends, we suppose, to perform no genuine act of asking but instead will assert that there is no disturbing danger, nothing to harm the self once it is fully present to itself in a perfect unity. But the rhetoricity of these lines resides precisely in the possibility that the questions may be read as genuine. Their locutionary form, if not their immediate intent, asks us to consider the possible sources of danger and harm to such a self. The story—what we have of it—then moves in the rhetorical space between the assertion and the denial of a dangerous, harmful presence within the unity formed by the builder and the thing he has constructed. As the extant portion of the narrative nears its end, the burrower confesses: "I have reached the stage where I no longer wish to have certainty."[13] He likes living in this rhetorical space; he is only comfortable—in an uncomfortable sort of way—with the passion it provokes in him. It is, after all, his Bau.

The burrower's activity is centrally a matter of rhetorical construction and therefore identifiable with Kafka's writing. "The Burrow" seems to belong to the sequence of artist stories, composed toward the end of his life, that includes "A Hunger Artist" and "Josephine." Like "Josephine," it presents the artist as an animal with a human consciousness engaged in an activity that is natural to its kind. The mouse pipes, the burrower builds, and neither has any choice in the matter. The hunger artist, too, has little choice but to starve, as we discover at the tale's end, when he confesses that he could never find any food he liked. If there is a muse that inspires such artists, it is a malicious one who intends to bestow no blessings. "Ill fortune, constraint and terror generate guileful art; despair inspires," according to the last speaker in John Barth's "Glossolalia."[14] But Kafka and his artists do achieve a kind of success and even joy in their passionate endeavor. The burrower is able to say that his construction "seems to be successful"

12. *CS* 342; *SE* 374: "Euretwegen, ihr Gänge und Plätze und deine Fragen vor allem, Burgplatz, bin ich ja gekommen, habe mein Leben für nichts geachtet, nachdem ich lange Zeit die Dummheit hatte, seinetwegen zu zittern und die Rückkehr zu euch zu verzögern. Was kümmert mich die Gefahr, jetzt, da ich bei euch bin. Ihr gehört zu mir, ich zu euch, verbunden sind wir, was kann uns geschehen."
13. *CS* 358; *SE* 387: "Ich bin so weit, daß ich Gewißheit gar nicht haben will."
14. John Barth, "Glossolalia" in *Lost in the Funhouse* (New York: Bantam, 1969), pp. 111–112.

(*wohlgelungen*), in spite of all the doubts he harbors. The hunger artist dies in the conviction that he is continuing to fast. Josephine disappears, but the memory of her song is as powerful as her song ever was.

This art of rhetorical construction, based on the passion of reading, inevitably and intentionally incites a comparable passion in its audience. That is, in a sense, what it is about. Kafka's writing produces images that we must confront with a combination of discomfort and love that has proven to be extraordinarily powerful. In this way he reproduces in his readers his own most intense experiences of reading, which seemed to combine in a single moment both intimacy and distance, love and contempt, pleasure and suffering. Kafka's experience of Grillparzer's short story "The Poor Fiddler" ("Der arme Spielmann"),[15] as he reports it in a letter to Milena, displays this passion:

> Everything you say about "The Poor Fiddler" is correct. When I said it didn't mean anything to me, I said it only out of caution; for I wasn't sure how you would get along with it, but also because I'm ashamed of the story as though I had written it myself; and actually it starts wrong, it has a number of inaccuracies, ridiculous and even dilettantish features, affectations that make one blush (one notices this especially when reading it out loud, I could show you the passages); and this kind of music practice is really a miserably ridiculous invention, sufficient to provoke the girl to throw—in extreme anger, in which the whole world will share, I above all—everything she has in her shop at the story until the story, which deserves nothing better, perishes thus from its own elements. It must be admitted, though, that there is no more beautiful fate for a story than for it to disappear, and in this way. The narrator, too, that queer psychologist, will heartily agree with it, for probably it is he who is the original Poor Fiddler, who fiddles this story in the most unmusical manner possible, being exaggeratedly thanked for it by tears from your eyes.[16]

15. Heinz Politzer has drawn attention to Kafka's use of Grillparzer's story in "Die Verwandlung des armen Spielmanns: Ein Grillparzer-Motiv bei Franz Kafka," *Jahrbuch der Grillparzer-Gesellschaft* 4 (1965), 55–64.

16. *LM* 96–97; *BM* 77: "Was Du über den 'armen Spielmann' sagst, ist alles richtig. Sagte ich, daß er mir nichts bedeutet, so war es nur aus Vorsicht, weil ich nicht wußte, wie Du damit auskommen würdest, dann auch deshalb, weil ich mich der Geschichte schäme, so wie wenn ich sie selbst geschrieben hätte; und tatsächlich setzt sie falsch ein und hat eine Menge Unrichtigkeiten, Lächerlichkeiten, Dilettantisches, zum Sterben Geziertes (besonders beim Vorlesen merkt man es, ich könnte Dir die Stellen zeigen; und besonders diese Art Musikausübung ist

Kafka had good reason to imagine himself in the role of the story's author. It shows a number of traits typical of Kafka's own fictions, not the least of which is the act of rhetorical reading that sparks the chief narrative invention: the "poor fiddler" ("armer Spielmann") is poor in every sense. He is not only penniless when the narrator discovers him, not only pitiful, but indeed poor at his professed art of fiddling. He is an incompetent musician who cannot play by ear at all, who needs to read written notes before he can play a tune he has heard, and who even then plays excruciatingly badly. But he is (like Josephine) in spite of his technical incompetence a kind of pure artist, and when he dies his beat-up violin is treasured as if it were the relic of a saint.

Clearly what engages Kafka most about Grillparzer's story is its alleged deficiencies, it "inaccuracies," its "dilettantish features," its "affectation," and above all the "miserably ridiculous invention" of its central idea. Kafka understands these deficiencies in a special way: they are not formal matters of presentation but an integral part of the plot structure. The story's shortcomings, in Kafka's reading, belong so much to the heart of the narrative that the characters themselves (such as Barbara, the fiddler's beloved and the "girl" mentioned in the letter) want to pelt them with fruits and vegetables. In fact, no one in the story actually throws anything at the poor fiddler, but his playing is so bad that they might have. Inept performance is both the topic and the method of Grillparzer's tale, as Kafka sees it, so that one's anger at the storyteller's performance is centrally relevant to his enterprise and is in a sense exactly what he wants and expects. Of course, Grillparzer is the "armer Spielmann" at issue. By a further application of rhetorical reading we realize that "Spielmann" ("player") might refer equally well to a man of the theater, a playwright, as well as to a musician. Grillparzer thus invites a negative judgment on his own performance, intending his construction to "perish from its own elements."

---

doch eine kläglich lächerliche Erfindung, geeignet, das Mädchen aufzureizen, alles was sie im Laden hat im höchsten Zorn, an dem die ganze Welt teilnehmen wird, ich vor allem, der Geschichte nachzuwerfen, bis so die Geschichte, die nichts besseres verdient, an ihren eigenen Elementen zugrundegeht. Allerdings gibt es kein schöneres Schicksal für eine Geschichte als zu verschwinden und auf diese Weise. Auch der Erzähler, dieser komische Psychologe, wird damit sehr einverstanden sein, denn wahrscheinlich ist er der eigentliche arme Spielmann, der diese Geschichte auf möglichst unmusikalische Weise vormusiciert, übertrieben herrlich bedankt durch die Tränen aus Deinen Augen."

This is certainly a sophisticated reading of Grillparzer's story, but we might have expected one from Kafka. What is surprising is the generalization that Kafka draws from his reading: "there is no more beautiful fate for a story than for it to disappear, and in this way." The best stories, Kafka implies, not the worst ones, dismantle themselves in this way. "The Poor Fiddler" moves us and makes us angry at its shoddiness at the same time, and this accomplishment is asserted to be the highest attainment of fiction. The story engages in a dramatic act of self-effacement that does not diminish its power but actually constitutes it, so that its disappearance works just like that of Jakob the fiddler to make the tears roll down our cheeks in "exaggerated" thanks. Kafka touchingly—if also somewhat ironically—lets the last sentence of his story of reading "The Poor Fiddler" echo that of "The Poor Fiddler" itself: both offer images of women in tears. Kafka thus sets Milena in an analogy with Grillparzer's Barbara, whose assessment of her lover's art moves between angry rejection and an overblown sentimental attachment. Because Milena, as Kafka's Czech translator, represents his most devoted and careful living reader, there is an implicit instruction in this discussion of Grillparzer's story as to how this man who imagines himself as the "Fiddler's" author wants to be read.

Kafka hopes to incite the passion of reading with his fiction, and he firmly expects that passion to be directed both toward and against his art. The passion to be directed against it comes from the discovery of its faults in a way already described by Stanley Corngold in his discussion of the narrative "breaks" so evident in Kafka's stories. On the evidence of the reading of Grillparzer's story offered to Milena, we have every reason to believe that Kafka would deliberately include elements in his fictions from which they could "perish." That very "perishing" (*zugrundegehen*) is also "getting to the heart of the matter" ("zum Grunde gehen"), to invoke a Nietzschean wordplay. Kafka surely wanted his stories to "disappear" and indeed precisely in this way, in an act of passionate reading. If I have any revision to propose in Corngold's account of the author's paradoxical survival in those very elements that undermine his fictions, it is to suggest that perhaps Kafka's deliberate narrative inconsistencies are less acts of vengeance against a writing that is fundamentally flawed than a way of ensuring for his own writing the "beautiful fate" of self-deconstruction that he finds in Grillparzer. I mean not to deny that self-destructive violence is involved but only to assert that this violence is also full of self-love. Kafka's self-effacement abounds with ambition for self-perpetuation.

Nothing could illustrate this remarkable passion better than Kafka's famous request to Max Brod that Brod burn all Kafka's unpublished manuscripts. Here, if nowhere else, is Kafka's mastery of the rhetorical moment absolutely clear. We must doubt the genuineness of his request (as Brod evidently did), given its addressee. One can make a genuine request only of someone who can be imagined carrying it out: thus, although one might properly ask Babe Ruth to hit a home run in Yankee Stadium, one might not make the same request of T. S. Eliot. Kafka could have enlisted various people for this service, his parents among them. Kafka instead directed his request to the one person least likely to carry it out, thereby putting the greater part of his fiction where he wanted it to be, in rhetorical space, living and dying at once by the same act of reading. He thus assured the ghostly survival of his self-effaced writing and the continuation of the passion of reading.

SELECTED BIBLIOGRAPHY

This list names exclusively works that the author found particularly helpful in preparing the present book. It represents only a small fraction of the material available on Kafka and is heavily weighted toward recent scholarship.

Adorno, Theodor W. "Notes on Kafka." 1967. In Adorno, *Prisms*, translated by Samuel Weber and Shierry Weber. Cambridge, Mass.: MIT Press, 1982, pp. 245–271.

Alt, Peter-André. "Doppelte Schrift, Unterbrechung, und Grenze: Franz Kafkas Poetik des Unsagbaren im Kontext der Sprachskepsis um 1900." *Jahrbuch der Deutschen Schiller-Gesellschaft* 29 (1985), 455–490.

Anders, Günther. *Kafka—Pro und Contra*. Munich: C. H. Beck, 1951.

Austin, J. L. *How to Do Things with Words*. 2d ed. Cambridge, Mass.: Harvard University Press, 1975.

Baumann, Gerhart. "Schreiben: Der endlose Prozeß im Tagebuch von Franz Kafka." *Etudes Germaniques* 39 (Spring 1984), 163–174.

Beck, Evelyn Torton. "Kafka's Traffic in Women: Gender, Power, and Sexuality." *Literary Review* 26:4 (1983), 565–576.

Bedwell, Carol B. "The Force of Destruction in Kafka's 'Ein Altes Blatt.'" *Monatshefte* 58 (1966), 43–48.

Bernheimer, Charles. *Flaubert and Kafka: Studies in Psychopoetic Structure*. New Haven: Yale Univ. Press, 1982.

——. "The Splitting of the 'I' and the Dilemma of Narration: Kafka's *Hochzeitsvorbereitungen auf dem Lande*." *CT*, 7–24. (German version in *DJK*)

Binder, Hartmut. *Motiv und Gestaltung bei Franz Kafka*. Bonn: Bouvier, 1966.

——. *Kafka Kommentar zu sämtlichen Erzählungen*. Munich: Winkler, 1975.

——. *Kafka Kommentar zu den Romanen, Rezensionen, Aphorismen und zum Brief an den Vater*. Munich: Winkler, 1976.

Bloom, Harold. *The Anxiety of Influence*. New York: Oxford University Press, 1973.
Boulby, Mark. "Kafka's End: A Reassessment of 'The Burrow.'" *German Quarterly* 55:2 (1982), 175–185.
Bridgwater, Patrick. "Rotpeters Ahnherren; oder, Der gelehrte Affe in der deutschen Dichtung." *DVLG* 56 (September 1982), 447–462.
Brod, Max. *Franz Kafka: A Biography*. New York: Schocken, 1963.
Canetti, Elias. *Kafka's Other Trial: The Letters to Felice*. 1969. Translated by Christopher Middleton. New York: Schocken, 1974.
Canning, Peter M. "Kafka's Hierogram: The Trauma of the *Landarzt*." *German Quarterly* 57:2 (1984), 197–212.
Caputo-Mayr, Maria Luise, ed. *Franz Kafka: Eine Aufsatzsammlung nach einem Symposium in Philadelphia*. Berlin: Agora, 1978.
Cohn, Dorrit. "Kafka's Eternal Present: Narrative Tense in 'Ein Landarzt' and Other First-Person Stories." *PMLA* 83 (1968), 144–150.
———. "Erleble Rede im Ich-Roman. *Germanisch-Romanische Monatsschrift* 19 (1969), 305–313.
Corngold, Stanley. "Kafka's *Die Verwandlung:* Metamorphosis of the Metaphor." *Mosaic* 3 (Summer 1970), 91–106.
———. *The Commentators' Despair*. Port Washington, NY: Kennikat Press, 1973.
———. "Metaphor and Chiasmus in Kafka." *NKSA* 5 (December 1981), 23–31.
———. "Kafka's Double Helix." *Literary Review* 26 (Summer 1983), 521–536.
———. "Kafka's 'The Judgment' and Modern Rhetorical Theory." *NKSA* 7 (June 1983), 15–21.
———. "The Author Survives on the Margin of His Breaks: Kafka's Narrative Perspective." In Corngold, *The Fate of the Self: German Writers and French Theory*. New York: Columbia University Press, 1986, pp. 161–179.
Davey, E. R. "The Broken Engine: A Study of Franz Kafka's *In der Strafkolonie*." *Journal of European Studies* 14:4 (1984), 271–283.
David, Claude, ed. *Franz Kafka: Themen und Probleme*. Göttingen: Vandenhoeck & Ruprecht, 1980.
Deleuze, Gilles, and Félix Guattari. *Kafka: Toward a Minor Literature*. 1975. Translated by Dana Polan. Minneapolis: University of Minnesota Press, 1986.
De Man, Paul. *Allegories of Reading: Figural Language in Rousseau, Nietzsche, Rilke, and Proust*. New Haven: Yale University Press, 1979.
Derrida, Jacques. "Signature, Event, Context." *Glyph* 1, 172–197.
Dettmering, Peter. "Aspekte der Spaltung in der Dichtung Kafkas." In *Literaturpsychologische Studien und Analysen*. Amsterdam: Rodopi, 1983, pp. 205–220.
Emrich, Wilhelm. *Franz Kafka: A Critical Study of His Writings*. 1958. Translated by Sheema Zeben Buehne. New York: Ungar, 1968.
Frye, Lawrence O. "Reconstructions: Kafka's *Ein Landarzt*." *Colloquia Germanica* 16:4 (1983), 321–336.
Füllerborn, Ulrich. "Zum Verhältnis von Perspektivismus und Parabolik in der Dichtung Franz Kafkas." In Renate von Heydebrand and Klaus G. Just, eds., *Wissenschaft als Dialog*. Stuttgart: Metzler, 1969, pp. 289–313.
———. "Der Einzelne und die 'geistige Welt': Zu Kafkas Romanen." *TP*, 81–100.
Gaier, Ulrich. "Chorus of Lies: On Interpreting Kafka." *German Life and Letters* 22 (1969), 283–296.

Gelus, Marjorie. "Notes on Kafka's 'Der Bau': Problems with Reality." *Colloquia Germanica* 15 (1982), 98–110.

Goffman, Ethan. "Blumfeld's Balls: Notes on a Situation in a Kafka Short Story." *Neue Germanistik* 4 (Fall 1985), 3–6.

Goldstücker, Eduard. "Kafkas Eckermann? Zu Gustav Janouchs 'Gespräche mit Kafka.'" *TP*, 238–255.

Grebenickova, Ruzena. "Kafka und das Thema des Schreibens." *Neue Rundschau* 94:4 (1983), 171–183.

Gross, Ruth V. "Rich Text/Poor Text: A Kafkan Confusion." *PMLA* 95:2 (1980), 168–182.

——. "Fallen Bridge, Fallen Woman, Fallen Text." *Literary Review* 26 (Summer 1981), 577–587.

——. "Questioning the Laws: Reading Kafka in the Light of Literary Theory." *JKSA* 7 (December 1983), 31–37.

——. "Of Mice and Women: Reflections on a Discourse in Kafka's 'Josefine die Sängerin.'" *Germanic Review* 60 (Spring 1985), 59–68. (Reprinted in *CT*).

Harman, Mark. "Life into Art: Kafka's Self-Stylization in the Diaries." *CT*, 101–116.

Hayman, Ronald. *Kafka: A Biography*. New York: Oxford University Press, 1982.

Henel, Ingeborg C. "Die Deutbarkeit von Kafkas Werken." *Zeitschrift für deutsche Philologie* 86 (1967), 250–266.

Hermsdorf, Klaus, ed. *Franz Kafka: Amtliche Schriften*. Berlin: Akademie, 1984.

Hillmann, Heinz. "Fabel und Parabel im zwanzigsten Jahrhundert: Kafka und Brecht." In Peter Hasubek, ed., *Die Fabel: Theorie, Geschichte und Rezeption einer Gattung*. Berlin: Schmidt, 1982, pp. 215–235.

Janouch, Gustav. *Gespräche mit Kafka*. Frankfurt: Fischer, 1951.

——. *Conversations with Kafka*. Translated by Goronwy Rees. New York: New Directions, 1971.

Kaganoff, Benzion C. *A Dictionary of Jewish Names and Their History*. New York: Schocken, 1977.

Karst, Roman. "Kafka und die Metapher." *Literatur und Kritik* 179–180 (1983), 472–480.

——. "Kafkas Prometheussage oder das Ende des Mythos." *Germanic Review* 20 (Spring 1985), 42–47.

Kittler, Wolf. "Brief oder Blick: Die Schreibsituation der frühen Texte von Franz Kafka." *DJK*, 40–67.

Koelb, Clayton. "The Deletions from Kafka's Novels." *Monatshefte*, 68:4 (Winter 1976), 365–372.

——. *The Incredulous Reader: Literature and the Function of Disbelief*. Ithaca: Cornell University Press, 1984.

——. "The Text as Erotic/Auto-Erotic Device." *Midwest Quarterly*, 26:2 (Winter 1985), 212–224.

——. "Kafka and the Sirens: Writing as Lethetic Reading." In Clayton Koelb and Susan Noakes, eds., *The Comparative Perspective on Literature: Approaches to Theory and Practice*. Ithaca: Cornell University Press, 1988, pp. 300–314.

——. *Inventions of Reading: Rhetoric and the Literary Imagination*. Ithaca: Cornell University Press, 1988.

254   SELECTED BIBLIOGRAPHY

————. "The Turn of the Trope: Kafka's 'Die Brücke.'" *Modern Austrian Literature*, forthcoming.

Kramer, Dale. "The Aesthetics of Theme: Kafka's 'In the Penal Colony.'" *Studies in Short Fiction* 5 (1969), 362–367.

Kudszus, Winfried. "Verschüttungen in Kafkas 'Der Bau.'" In Benjamin Bennet, Anton Kaes, and William J. Lillyman, eds., *Probleme der Moderne*. Tübingen: Niemeyer, 1983, pp. 307–317.

Kurz, Gerhard, ed. *Der junge Kafka*. Frankfurt: Suhrkamp, 1984.

————. "Schnörkel und Schleier und Warzen: Die Briefe Kafkas an Oskar Pollak und seine literarischen Anfänge." *DJK*, 68–101.

Kurz, Paul Konrad. "Verhängte Existenz: Franz Kafkas Erzählung 'Ein Landarzt.'" *Stimmen der Zeit* 177 (1966), 432–450.

Lehmann, Heinz-Thies. "Der Buchstäbliche Körper: Zur Selbstinszenierung der Literatur bei Franz Kafka." *DJK*, 213–241.

Loeb, Ernst. "Kafkas 'In der Strafkolonie' im Spiegel 'klassischer' und 'romantischer' Religion." *Seminar* 21:2 (May 1985), 139–141. (English version in *CT*)

Maché, Britta. "The Noise in the Burrow: Kafka's Final Dilemma." *German Quarterly* 55 (November 1982), 526–540.

Miles, David H. "Pleats, Pockets, Buckles, and Buttons: Kafka's New Literalism and the Poetics of Fragment." In Benjamin Bennett, Anton Kaes, and William J. Lillyman, eds., *Probleme der Moderne*. Tübingen: Niemeyer, 1983, pp. 319–330.

Moreau, Kathleen Callahan. "Kafka's *Briefe an Milena*: An Analysis of Epistolary Rhetoric." *Dissertation Abstracts International* 47:7 (1986), 1955A-1956A.

Müller, Joachim. "Erwägungen an dem Kafka-Text: 'Ein Landarzt.'" *Orbis Litterarum* 23 (1968), 35–54.

Nagel, Bert. "Kafka und E. T. A. Hoffmann." *Modern Austrian Literature* 14 (1981), 1–11.

Neumann, Gerhard. "Schreibschrein und Strafapparat: Erwägungen zur Topographie des Schreibens." In Gunter Schnitzler, Gerhard Neumann, and Jürgen Schroder, eds., *Bild und Gedanke*. Munich: Fink, 1980, pp. 385–401.

————. "Werk oder Schrift? Vorüberlegungen zur Edition von Kafkas 'Bericht für eine Akademie.'" *Acta Germanica* 14 (1981), 1–21.

————. "Der Wanderer und der Verschollene: Zum Problem der Identität in Goethes *Wilhelm Meister* und Kafkas Amerika-Roman." In J. P. Stern and J. J. White, eds., *Paths and Labyrinths: Nine Papers Read at the Franz Kafka Symposium Held at the Institute of Germanic Studies on 20 and 21 October 1983*. London: Institute of Germanic Studies, 1985, pp. 43–65.

Nicolai, Ralf R. "Nietzschean Thought in Kafka's 'A Report to an Academy.'" *Literary Review* 26:4 (1983), 551–564.

Noakes, Susan. *Timely Reading: Between Exegesis and Interpretation*. Ithaca: Cornell University Press, 1988.

Norris, Margot. "Kafka's Josephine: The Animal as the Negative Site of Narration." *MLN* 98:3 (1983), 366–383.

Pasley, Malcolm. "Der Schreibakt und das Geschriebene: Zur Frage der Entstehung von Kafkas Texten." *TP*, 9–25.

Pawel, Ernst. *The Nightmare of Reason: A Life of Franz Kafka*. New York: Farrar, Straus, & Giroux, 1984.

Philippi, Klaus-Peter. "Parabolisches Erzählen: Anmerkungen zu Form und möglicher Geschichte." *DVLG* 43 (1969), 297–332.

Politzer, Heinz. *Franz Kafka: Parable and Paradox*. Ithaca: Cornell University Press, 1962.

———. "Die Verwandlung des armen Spielmanns: Ein Grillparzer-Motiv bei Franz Kafka." *Jahrbuch der Grillparzer-Gesellschaft* 4 (1965), 55–64.

Pongs, Hermann. "Ambivalenz in moderner Dichtung." In Adolf Haslinger, ed., *Sprachkunst als Weltgestaltung*. Salzburg: Pustet, 1966, pp. 191–228.

Rakos, Petr. "Über die Vieldeutigkeit in Kafkas Werk." In Paul Reimann, ed., *Franz Kafka aus Prager Sicht 1963*. Prague: Verlag der Tschechoslavakischen Akademie der Wissenschaften, 1965, pp. 81–86.

Ray, Susan. "The Metaphysics of the Doppelgänger Motif in Kafka's 'Ein Landarzt.'" *Seminar* 21 (May 1985), 123–138.

Richards, I. A. *The Philosophy of Rhetoric*. New York: Oxford University Press, 1936.

Robert, Marthe. *Seul, comme Franz Kafka*. Paris: Calmann-Lévy, 1979.

Robertson, Ritchie. "Kafka und Don Quixote." *Neophilologus* 69 (January 1985), 17–24.

Rolleston, James. *Kafka's Narrative Theater*. University Park: Pennsylvania State Univ. Press, 1974.

———. *Betrachtung*: Landschaften der Doppelgänger." *DJK*, 184–199.

———. "Kafka's Time Machines." *CT*, 25–48.

Rubinstein, William C. "Kafka's 'Jackals and Arabs.'" *Monatshefte* 59 (1967), 13–18.

Ryan, Judith. "The Maze of Misreadings: Thoughts on Metaphor in Kafka." *JKSA* 7 (December 1983), 38–43.

Sadock, Jerrold. *Toward a Linguistic Theory of Speech Acts*. New York: Academic, 1974.

Schepers, Gerhard. "The Dissolution of Myth in Kafka's 'Prometheus' and "The Silence of the Sirens.'" *Humanities: Christianity and Culture* 18 (May 1984), 97–119.

Schillemeit, Jost. "Kafkas *Beschreibung eines Kampfes*: Ein Beitrag zum Textverständnis und Geschichte von Kafkas Schreiben." *DJK*, 102–132.

———. "Das unterbrochene Schreiben: Zur Entstehung von Kafkas Roman 'Der Verschollene.'" In Barbara Elling, ed., *Kafka-Studien*. New York: Lang, 1985, pp. 137–152.

Schiller, Dieter. "Kunst als Lebensäusserung: Zum Problem Künstler und Öffentlichkeit in Franz Kafkas letzen Lebensjahren." *Zeitschrift für Germanistik* 5:3 (1984), 284–296.

Schmidt, Ulrich. "Von der 'Peinlichkeit' der Zeit: Kafkas Erzählung *In der Strafkolonie*." *Jahrbuch der Deutschen Schiller-Gesellschaft* 28 (1984), 407–445.

Schwarz, Egon. "Kafka's Animal Tales and the Tradition of the European Fable." *CT*, 75–100.

Sokel, Walter. *Franz Kafka: Tragik und Ironie*. Munich: Langen Müller, 1964.

———. *Franz Kafka*. New York: Columbia University Press, 1966.

———. "Von der Sprachkrise zu Franz Kafkas Poetik." In Wolfgang Paulsen, ed., *Österreichische Gegenwart: Die moderne Literatur und ihr Verhältnis zur Tradition*. Bern: Francke, 1980, pp. 39–58.

——. "Zur Sprachauffassung und Poetik Franz Kafkas." *TP*, 26–47.

——. "Kafka's Poetics of the Inner Self." In Reinhold Grimm, Peter Spycher, and Richard A. Zipser, eds., *From Kafka and Dada to Brecht and Beyond*. Madison: University of Wisconsin Press, 1982, pp. 7–21.

——. "Narzißmus, Magie, und die Funktion des Erzählens in Kafkas *Beschreibung eines Kampfes*: Zur Figurenkonzeption, Geschehenstruktur, und Poetologie in Kafkas Erstlingswerk." *DJK*, 133–153.

Snyder, Verna P. "Kafka's 'Burrow': A Speculative Analysis." *Twentieth Century Literature* 27:2 (1981), 113–126.

Sonnenfeld, Marion. "Eine Deutung der *Strafkolonie*." In Marion Sonnenfeld, ed., *Wert und Wort*. Aurora, N.Y.: Wells College, 1965, pp. 61–68.

Stephens, Anthony. "Er ist aber zweigeteilt: Gericht und Ich-Struktur bei Kafka." *Text & Kontext* 6 (1978), 215–238.

Struc, Roman, and J. C. Yardley, eds. *Franz Kafka (1883–1983): His Craft and Thought*. Waterloo, Ont.: Wilfrid Laurier University Press, 1986.

Stuart, Dabney. "Kafka's 'A Report to an Academy': An Exercise in Method." *Studies in Short Fiction* 6 (1969), 413–420.

Sussman, Henry. *Franz Kafka: Geometrician of Metaphor*. Madison, Wisc.: Coda, 1979.

Thomas, J. D. "The Dark at the End of the Tunnel: Kafka's 'In the Penal Colony.'" *Studies in Short Fiction* 4 (1966), 12–18.

Timms, Edward. "Kafka's Expanded Metaphors: A Freudian Approach to *Ein Landarzt*." In J. P. Stern and J. J. White, eds., *Paths and Labyrinths: Nine Papers Read at the Franz Kafka Symposium Held at the Institute of Germanic Studies on 20 and 21 October 1983*. London: Institute of Germanic Studies, 1985, pp. 66–79.

Triffitt, Gregory B. *Kafka's "Landarzt" Collection: Rhetoric and Interpretation*. New York: Lang, 1985.

Trost, Pavel. "Der Name Kafka." *Beiträge zur Namenforschung* 94 (1983), 184–204.

Wagenbach, Klaus. *Franz Kafka: Eine Biographie seiner Jugend*. Bern: Francke, 1958.

——. *Franz Kafka in Selbstzeugnissen und Bilddokumenten*. Hamburg: Rowohlt, 1964.

——. *Franz Kafka: Pictures of a Life*. New York: Pantheon, 1984.

Wehrli, Beatrice. "Monologische Kunst als Ausdruck moderner Welterfahrung: Zu Kafkas Erzählung 'Der Bau.'" *Jahrbuch der Deutschen Schiller-Gesellschaft* 25 (1981), 435–445.

Weinstein, Arnold. "Kafka's Writing Machine: Metamorphosis in *The Penal Colony*." *Studies in Twentieth Century Literature*, 7:1 (1982), 21–33.

INDEX

Hesse, Hermann, 94, 143
hills, 192, 193
historical present, 203
horses, 198, 199, 202, 203
humanity, 157
humiliation, 185
"Hunger Artist, A," 66, 119, 120, 235, 246
hyperbole, 11, 37–39, 133, 231, 233

ich, 29, 197
identification, 183
illegibility, 180
illocutions, 8, 41–55, 58–65, 194, 242, 243
imagery, 4, 12, 16, 72, 99, 100, 169, 222
imagination, 1–4, 19, 23, 31, 65, 109, 111, 114, 126, 127, 129, 185
"Imperial Message, An," 64, 101, 127
imprisonment, 159
incomprehensibility, 172
indecipherability, 178
influence, 87
inscription, 68, 69, 71, 74, 79, 80, 96, 97, 181, 182, 222, 227
insurance, 40, 41
intention, 15, 16, 43, 46, 47, 49, 50, 54, 58, 64, 95, 110, 111, 127, 129, 133, 157, 232
interpretant, 171
interpretation, 10, 11, 33, 53, 55, 67, 78, 88, 90, 93, 95, 152, 162, 164, 165, 166, 173, 176, 177, 179
intertext, 131, 137, 138, 149
"In the Penal Colony," 12, 17, 66–69, 72, 77, 79, 82, 84, 86, 96, 99, 103, 107, 128
intimacy, 194, 218–21, 247
invention, 1, 4, 11, 15, 110, 135, 160
irony, 167, 168, 172, 184, 231

ja, 43, 44
"Jackals and Arabs," 22–27
jackdaw, 19, 25, 28, 146
"Jacob," 148
jagen, 72
Janouch, Gustav, 88
Jesenska, Milena, 217, 218, 221, 222–27, 249
Jesus, 170–72
"Jesus!", 121
jokes, 136, 137, 225, 226, 227

Joseph, story of, 147, 148
"Josephine the Singer," 66, 147, 210, 234–36, 246
"Judgment, The," 59, 96, 120, 210–13
Jungborn, 213–17

"ka," 19
Kacke, 34, 185
Kafka, Georg, 122
Kafka, Herrmann, 16, 18, 22, 23, 28, 143, 146, 229–31, 235
Kafka, Julie, 18, 22, 28, 146; *see also* Löwy, Julie
Kafka, Ottla, 142, 143, 146
Karl Stauffers Lebensgang, 74, 94
Kastron, 216, 217
kavka, 18, 19, 22, 23, 25, 26, 34, 35, 37, 38, 146
klein, 117
Kleinzeug, 244
Kleist, Heinrich von, 158, 199, 226; "Michael Kohlhaas," 196, 199
Kniffe, 239
Korrketur, 231

La Fontaine, Jean de, 26, 163–66, 170–72
Land, 195
Landarzt, 195, 201
landscape, 191, 195, 196
language, 1–3, 5, 6, 9, 11, 12, 15, 16, 19, 20, 27, 31, 39, 42, 59, 62, 100, 102, 104–9, 111, 113, 114, 117, 233
lauter niemand, 187, 188
law, 40, 41, 63, 64, 76, 78–80, 82, 84, 85, 101, 106, 123, 173–78
Lebensuntüchtig, 228
legend, 132, 133, 134
legibility, 75
leidlich, 151
lethetic reading, 86–88, 100, 101, 103, 106–8, 153, 159
letters, 218, 219, 220, 221
"Letter to His Father," 16, 38, 142, 144, 145, 202, 225, 228, 235
Levenson, J. C., 116
Lévi-Strauss, Claude, 67, 85, 94
liberation, 52, 53, 54, 102, 104
lightness, 39
lion, 23, 146
literalization, 13, 14
"Little Fable, A," 162, 166, 172, 180

pigsty, 198, 199
Plato, 67, 85, 94, 102, 105, 136, 201, 202, 243
playfulness, 97, 98, 106, 107
plenitude, 187
Poe, Edgar A., 90, 93
Politzer, Heinz, 12, 80, 122, 161–63, 165, 166, 169, 174, 177, 178, 180
Pollak, Oskar, 72, 90, 95, 236, 244
Pope, Alexander, 26
"Poseidon," 134, 138
poststructuralism, 11
presence, 219, 220, 222
present tense, 48, 203, 204
preservation, 138
priority, 8, 189, 213
"Problem of Our Laws, The," 62, 78, 80, 97
production, 66
prolepsis, 31–34, 43, 44, 185, 197, 198, 225, 227–30
prologue, 32
"Prometheus," 131, 138
pronouns, 29
proper names, 129
protocol, 125
Prozess, 44, 123
pseudo-story, 103
puns, 36

quibble, 36

rabantern, 21
Rabe, 20–22
Ramses, 148
raven, 20, 21
readability, 7, 56
reading, 1, 10, 16
realism, 109–15, 119, 120
reception, 66, 74
rechnen, 136, 137
rechtlich, 240
recollection, 227
redemption, 6, 84
Red Sea, 87, 92, 93, 152
"referee," 238, 242, 243, 244
rejection, 210, 211, 212
renunciation, 140
report, 8, 9, 105, 152, 153, 155, 159
representation, 84
reproduction, 69, 201
res, 1, 4, 113
restraint, 140

resurrection, 96, 97, 98, 100
revision, 231
revocation, 50
rhetoric, definition of, 5
rhetorical question, 10, 15, 194, 206
rhetoricity, 6, 10, 11, 15, 25, 31, 44, 53, 55, 58, 61, 62, 64, 180, 184, 186, 205, 232, 246
right-mindedness, 240
ritrovarsi, 5
rosa, 205
Roß, 122
"Ruth," 217
Ruth, Babe, 250

sacer, 135
Sadock, Jerrold, 41–42
Sagen, 133
Sallust, 91
scenario, 84, 85, 96, 98
Schakal, 23
Schiedsrichter, 242
Schleiermacher, F. E. D., 234
Schloss, 237
schmarotzen, 230
Schrank, 226, 227
scripture, 2, 3, 75, 101, 128, 174, 177
Searle, John, 40
Seen, 136
sehen, 136
Seite, 76, 206
Selbstbeklagung, 231
self, 19–21, 25, 28–30, 73, 76, 86, 105, 139, 145, 146, 168, 178, 181, 182, 190, 194–96, 208, 214, 235, 238, 244, 245
self-control, 202
self-division, 28, 181, 182, 190, 201, 239, 242
self-effacement, 249
self-inscription, 185, 188, 191
self-love, 250
self-pity, 231
self-reading, 191, 201, 203
self-revelation, 225
sensuality, 140
sentencing, 59–61
seriousness, 98
sermons, 2, 3
sexual imagery, 69, 70, 71
Shakespeare, William, 36
Sie, 30, 217
signified, 14, 134

Library of Congress Cataloging-in-Publication Data

Koelb, Clayton, 1942–
    Kafka's rhetoric.

    Bibliography: p.
    Includes index.
      1. Kafka, Franz, 1883–1924—Style. I. Title.
PT2621.A26Z7644 1989   833'.912   88-43261
ISBN 0-8014-2244-2